DICKENS ON EDUCATION

DICKENS

ON EDUCATION

John Manning

UNIVERSITY OF TORONTO PRESS

TO MY WIFE CONSTANCE

PREFACE

This book is the result of an investigation into what Charles Dickens wrote and said about the education of boys and girls, the schools they attended, and the suggestions he made for improvement.

In 1925, G. R. Gissing asserted in *The Immortal Dickens* that "a review of all the scholastic persons in Dickens's novels would be very interesting and of definite historical value." In 1941, Humphry House remarked in the Preface to his book, *The Dickens World*, that he would omit Dickens's "treatment of schools and education . . . because for various reasons, it has been impossible to collect the necessary materials." As this investigation into Dickens's ideas on education progressed, both statements took on increasing significance. Many critical volumes on Dickens or his writings do not deal with this aspect of his work, or make passing comment only.

Our knowledge of Dickens's own schooling is not very extensive, and minor errors are to be found even in the painstaking Forster's account of the early years. For that reason, Dickens's formal schooling and the other experiences that informed his mind have been analysed in this book.

In his novels and short stories alone, Dickens discussed, at varying length, some fifty schools and more than that number of teachers. These delineations of teachers, schools, and school life have been examined in this book, and the investigation has been extended to Dickens's magazine articles, speeches, and letters. The views that Dickens expressed in his novels and short stories must, however, be judged by standards somewhat different from those that may be applied in assessing his other utterances. Therefore, in an effort not to violate the literary excellence of his fiction and to maintain the maximum validity for whatever educational inferences might be drawn from this study, the discussion of Dickens's novels and short stories has been kept separate from the discussion of his articles, speeches, and letters.

The aim has been to make this study of Dickens's views on education as comprehensive as possible. The Introduction recalls the background against which Dickens was writing, and examines the conditions in education in the light of government documents and the reports of various commissions. Throughout the book, the relevant literary criticism is weighed, and evidence is presented from government documents, inspectors' reports, biographical and autobiographical works, as well as from private diaries, to show the actual conditions that existed in the various types of schools.

Reference lists of the schools and teachers depicted in Dickens have been compiled in an Appendix.

J. M.

ACKNOWLEDGMENTS

I wish to acknowledge my deep appreciation of the generosity of all those persons and institutions whose aid has made this book possible. Over the years of its compilation, I have been indebted to numerous libraries, including the staffs of Queen's University Library, Kingston, Ontario; the University of Toronto Library; the Public Reference Library of the city of Toronto; the Library of the Toronto branch of the Dickens Fellowship; the library of Michigan State University, East Lansing; the library of the University of Michigan, Ann Arbor, for permission to peruse micro-cards of the *Parliamentary Papers* of Great Britain; the New York Public Library; and numerous other libraries which kindly made available many volumes through inter-library loan, including the libraries of Oberlin College, Ohio, the Library of Congress, Washington, the Legislative Library, Toronto, and the Parliamentary Library, Ottawa.

For placing at my disposal their collections of original letters and other manuscripts relating to Charles Dickens, I am especially indebted to the Pierpont Morgan Library, New York; and to the curators of the Berg and Harkness collections in the New York Public Library. In addition, I am grateful to the many institutions which have forwarded photostats or transcripts of unpublished Dickens materials, including the Huntington Library and Art Gallery, San Marino, California, and the Philadelphia Free Library, Philadelphia.

Mr. Leslie C. Staples, editor of *The Dickensian*, and curator of the Dickens House, 48 Doughty Street, London, England, patiently answered my questions and generously forwarded rare Dickens material from his personal collection for my perusal. Various details, from time to time, have been furnished by such scholars as W. J. Carlton of Andover, England, and Edgar Johnson of New York. Mention should also be made of the assistance of Dr. Wilhelmina Gordon who directed my early special studies on Charles Dickens, the encouragement of an award of a Reuben Wells Leonard Fellowship from Queen's University to complete the same, and some later assistance by Dr. Charles Phillips of the College of Education, University of Toronto. More recently, I have been indebted to the All-College Research Committee of Michigan State University who made possible my examination of the Dickens

collections in New York. Moreover, as the book has gone through its
several revisions I have been grateful for the editorial assistance rendered
by my wife and by the Editorial Department of the University of Toronto
Press.

Permission was granted by A. and C. Black, publishers of *A Book
about Schools*, by A. R. H. Moncrieff, to quote from the diary of
Captain J. H. Cooke contained therein, and by the editors of *School and
Society* and the *Journal of the History of Ideas* to include material which
I had previously contributed to those periodicals. Finally, I am especially
indebted to Charles Dickens's grandson, Mr. Henry Charles Dickens of
London, for his blanket permission to quote from any of Dickens's
letters, published or unpublished, the copyright of which he controls.

To all these, and many others, I wish to extend my warmest thanks.

J. M.

CONTENTS

DICKENS ON EDUCATION

INTRODUCTION

Victorian England (as witness the slender girl who ascended the throne in 1837) and Dickensian England (as witness the portly, bespectacled Mr. Pickwick of 1836–7) were ushered in almost simultaneously. Pertinently, however, we are informed within the first dozen lines of *The Posthumous Papers of the Pickwick Club* that Mr. Pickwick's adventures took place ten years earlier, in 1827; and within five pages or so, Dickens has Mr. Pickwick remark: "Travelling was in a troubled state, and the minds of coachmen were unsettled. . . . Stage coaches were upsetting . . . , horses were bolting, boats were overturning, and boilers were bursting." Dickens himself quit the Victorian scene in 1870. About half way between the date of Mr. Pickwick's adventures and the death of his creator, the *Law Magazine*, July 1, 1849, re-echoed Mr. Pickwick: "Society is in a state of transition; strange new doctrines, and stranger revival of old ones, perplex men's minds which are themselves in the infancy of reflection."

History demonstrates that almost every generation is a period of transition; it also demonstrates that some brief periods encompass swifter changes than others. This was essentially true of the period from 1825 to 1875. Old ways of life were giving place to new. Yet old customs not only existed side by side with the new, but also tended to predominate in the entirely new environment that was being evolved out of the rapid change from a rural to an urban economy, from an easy-going domestic to a dynamic industrial system. These social and economic changes gave a jolt to customary modes of thought and, in the vortex of the material struggles, protests arose against the neglect of human dignity and the blatant flouting of individual worth. Charles Dickens gave these protests a distinct utterance, and school life was his forte.

The ideas which guide the schoolroom emerge from the society in which it operates; several generations may elapse, however, before the classroom catches up with changes in society. If, therefore, Dickens's revelations of school life, his interpretation of its purpose, and his contribution to its improvement are to be understood, the changing social situation in Dickensian England needs to be carefully considered. Such matters as communication, living conditions, religious convictions, political unrest, and philosophic ideas are all involved.

Much of this mosaic of which Victorian England was comprised may be gathered from Dickens. From his vivid pages we get unforgettable pictures of his England—flying coaches, galloping horses, quaint old inns, enjoyable dinners, tea-kettles steaming on the hob, jovial imbibings, confusing London fogs, turnpike roads, gloomy marshes, squalid prisons, revolting crimes, suffocating law courts, lively scenes in the pubs or on the street, mysterious boats on the Thames, arrogant masters, brow-beaten boys, droll or impudent servants, and, by no means least, England's Christmas with its savoury turkeys and sparkling ale, its gifts and chimes. But his pictures do not form either a clear or a complete mosaic. Dickens dealt little with the life of the upper classes; he delineated, in the main, the lives of the lower and the lower middle classes. In his treatment of education, for example, the great English public schools are barely mentioned.[1] Moreover, English social conditions were changing too rapidly for him to be able to fix them in a pattern even if his gift of caricature had not tended to depict the changing scene in distorted proportions in the first place.

Dickens began his life in the old stage-coaching days; he closed it in the hey-day of steam. Railways entered his writing as early as *Nicholas Nickleby*; by the time of *Dombey and Son*, they were woven into the narrative. The London-Greenwich Railway had opened in 1834 amid the noise of barrel-organs, sizzling flares, blaring bands, and general fanfare. The advent of steam had both an industrial and a social impact. Well might Lord Mowbray, in the eleventh chapter of Disraeli's *Sybil* (1845) remark on the "levelling" effect of the railways. Excursion trains chugged out of the stations, their coaches jammed with shouting, singing, grimy-faced, tousle-headed youngsters; they pulled into what was formerly an exclusive seaside resort to emit a seething mass of humanity hastening to clamber on the donkeys, pushing among the pink parasols of their betters in a rush to reach the Punch and Judy show, and knocking over little "ladies" daintily gathering little pink and white shells for souvenirs. It is true that Dickens might well give us a partial glimpse of such a scene; still, he would disregard the dandies loitering under the gaslights of the ballading beach minstrels or whistling to the girls who circulated and advertised their wares in the dim shadows.

Meanwhile, the electric telegraph speeded communication for industry, and penny postage gave the poor, at long last, an inexpensive way to

---

[1]There is an occasional reference to the public schools but no full discussion of them. For example, in *Bleak House*, vol. I, towards the close of chap. IV, Richard Carstone recollects having seen Mr. Jarndyce "once, five years ago, at Winchester School"; and again, at the beginning of chap. XIII, in retrospect, Esther questions the educational value of the hours Richard had spent in the composition of Latin verses.

reach distant friends. The Society for the Diffusion of Useful Knowledge and publications such as the *Penny Magazine* or the *Penny Encyclopaedia* aided the spread of information not only among those who had learned to read, but also, because of the Victorian practice of reading aloud to groups in pub or parlour, to the illiterate as well. Margaret Lambert claims there were eighty-five London dailies in 1837, not to mention other papers (smuggled in to escape the stamp duty), the numerous weeklies at a penny, Harriet Martineau's tracts, and children's *Little Guides* to one thing and another, which, along with Chambers's *Journal*, sought "to take advantage of the universal appetite for instruction which now exists."[2]

Rapid industrial advance, the enclosing of more and more of the public commons, the migration of thousands to the factory sites, the large influx of Irish labourers, the drastic surgery of the new poor-laws, the lack of local authoritative bodies and administrative machinery—all these results of the Industrial Revolution accentuated the condition which led Disraeli to say that there were two Englands, the rich becoming richer, and the poor becoming poorer. In the one England were the aristocrats, idle and snobbish, and the wealthy upper middle class, callous and smug; though it is nevertheless true that certain sections of the privileged classes helped the workers in their struggle for a more abundant life. In the other England were the lower middle class, whose ignorance and sentimentality befuddled the development of political acumen; the isolated farm labourers; and the toiling masses in the factories.

Workhouses were ransacked to secure "apprentices" for grinding toil in the mills; strappers were on hand to flog the children to keep them awake, or to exact even more wearisome work from tired bodies.[3] The Report of the Commissioners Concerning the Trades and Manufacturers, 1843, disclosed that "trappers"—children whose job it was to open and close the trap doors in the coal pits—had to stay alone in the dark for twelve hours and had no place to rest but the damp floor. One boy of seven and a half, who according to the report had been down in the pits for about three years, smoked a pipe to keep awake! A girl, Patience Kershaw, whose case was typical, had the job of "hurrying" tubs of coal over a distance of a mile or more for eleven hours at a stretch; a belt round her waist was chained to a tub that held three hundredweight or more of coal, and she crawled through the dark, filthy, damp, underground passages on hands and knees, dragging this "corve" after her; if she was not quick enough, she was beaten by the naked "getters" who

[2]Lambert, "News and Views" in *When Victoria Began to Reign*, pp. 110–30.
[3]Children's Employment Commission, Second Report, 1843, *Parliamentary Papers*, XIII, 1843, pp. 60–87; Second Report, XV, 1842, pp. 27–91.

loosened the coal with their picks.[4] About the same time, another government report revealed the evidence of John Homes as "a very fair sample of the general state of education." John reported to the commissioners as follows: " 'I don't go to Sunday School. . . . I never heard tell of God neither. . . . I am taught to say my prayers, and I say them. I don't know who I pray to.' " Another sixteen-year-old boy thought Jesus Christ " 'was King of London a long time ago.' " In a Yorkshire mine, an eighteen-year-old girl " 'never learned nought.' " Still another thought that " 'Jesus Christ was a shepherd who came on earth to commit sin—yes to commit sin.' "[5]

Conditions in the factories were equally deplorable, as Disraeli shows so vividly and accurately in *Sybil*. The latter, written in the Hungry Forties, gives the picture of little Devilsdust who was placed at threepence a day in the care of the "nurse" at a baby farm, where doses of treacle and laudanum failed to kill him. Shoeless and half-naked, he was placed out in the street to play, where the crush of the horses' feet and carts failed to "get rid" of him. Toddling away from the fever-ridden corpses in the damp cellar where he had been left to sleep "with a dung-hill at his head and a cess-pool at his feet," he was led by chance to a factory at the age of five, where he was put to work. He was more fortunate than most because he eventually learned to read at the factory school.[6]

Disraeli is supported by a closer eyewitness, Mrs. Gaskell, who knew the poor of Lancashire even better than Disraeli or Charles Dickens did. John Barton, let out from the mill through no fault of his own, faces slow starvation for himself and for his small son. His home, where the child is ill with scarlet fever, lies close to the factory smoke, the effluvia of filthy water, and the abominable stench of the privy. As Barton stands before a shop window that displays an array of tempting food, he observes the wife of his former employer emerge and proceed to her carriage, laden with provisions for a party. Bewildered and wrathful, he returns to his home, and finds that his child has died.[7]

[4]Children's Employment Commission, First Report, 1842, *Parliamentary Papers*, XV, 1842, pp. 66, 98, 21, 26, 80.

[5]Children's Employment Commission, Second Report, 1843, *Parliamentary Papers*, XIII, 1843, pp. 155 f.

[6]These pictures in *Sybil* were true to life. They were based on British parliamentary commissions and reports. (See Victor Cohen's Introduction to his edition of *Sybil*.) Echoes of the reports of the employment commissions are quite clear to those who have read the reports of 1842 and 1843.

[7]*Mary Barton*, chap. III. In her introduction Mrs. Gaskell was careful to point out that she had been studying Dr. Kay's sanitation reports. Disraeli entered Parliament in 1837, the same year that Queen Victoria ascended the throne and Mr. Pickwick enjoyed his adventures; Mrs. Gaskell made her first appearance in print in January of the same year.

Only slowly were these conditions relieved by the Factory, Poor Law, and Municipal acts. For example, the act of 1802 stipulated separate bedrooms for the sexes and a limit of twelve hours of work a day for factory children;[8] the 1833 act stated that no child under nine should be employed, and limited children under thirteen to nine hours' work a day.[9] However, neither of these acts meant much because, in the first place, there was no compulsory registration of births; and in the second place, the acts applied only to the textile factories.[10] Not until the factory legislation of 1864 and 1867, which limited the work of children under thirteen to half a day, were the factory laws widely applicable. Children under nine could be employed in the silk mills, which were regarded as a special case, until the Factory Act of 1878.[11] But to emphasize how far legislation had come by the acts of 1864 and 1867, it may be noted that the inspectors could disqualify a factory schoolmaster for incapacity, immoral conduct, or gross ignorance.[12]

The amiable Mr. Pickwick in gaiters and the stately Victoria in her royal robes emerged about the same time as the wide application of machines in industry. The latter development had given rise to the factory or industrial worker, who, as likely as not, was a member of the London Working Men's Association founded by Lovett and Place in 1836, and an ardent supporter of Chartism. Demanding a vote by ballot for every man at annual elections, and paid members of Parliament representing equal electoral districts, Chartism was the political complement of the literary protest. In an endeavour to meet the changing conditions, to cope with the hardness of the manufacturers, and to secure greater participation in the civilization of their day, the industrial workmen tried to band together. Too often, it seemed, the law-courts and the legislators were against them. Attempts to break through the clouds of ignorance were frustrating in the extreme for adult workers, as Dickens points out when he tells of the Chorley brothers, who walked eight miles to classes three times a week after a day in the mines, a sixteen-year-old plasterer from Bury who walked six miles each night, and a moulder in an iron foundry who got up at four in the morning to study.[13] The results of similar attempts to obtain education for the workers' children

[8]42 Geo. III, c. 73. [9]3 & 4 Wm. IV, c. 103.
[10]I.e. cotton, wool, worsted, hemp, flax, tow, or jute.
[11]41 & 42 Vict., c. 16.
[12]"Memorandum Communicated by Alexander Redgrove, Esq., One of His Majesty's Inspectors of Factories" quoted as Appendix no. viii by Kay-Shuttleworth, in his *Memorandum on Popular Education.* Cf. Education Commission, 1861, *Parliamentary Papers,* XXI, 1861, I, 200–4, for review of this legislation; or cf. 42 Geo. III, c. 73; 3 & 4 Wm. IV, c. 103; 27 & 28 Vict., c. 48; 29 & 30 Vict., c. 113; and 30 & 31 Vict., c. 146.
[13]In his speech at Manchester, Dec. 3, 1858. See Shepherd, ed., *Speeches,* p. 216.

were all too meagre; they might have recourse to a little cramming of catechism at the Sunday schools or charity schools, or to the rudiments of learning—at a price—from a dame-school or common day-school.[14]

The Anti-Combination acts which had forbidden the workers to organize were repealed in 1824, and in 1834 the Grand National Consolidated Trades Union came into being; it was said to have over a million members. But this move toward union was staggered by such blows as high taxes on periodicals and the transportation to the colonies of the labourers of Dorset (later known as the Tolpuddle martyrs) for alleged membership in a workers' union. In an attempt to stop employers from taking advantage of the local poor-law subsidies in order to save themselves two-thirds of the current wage, the new Poor Law of 1834 ruthlessly cut off outdoor relief. This drastic action discriminated against temporarily unemployed workers, and presented them with the harsh alternative of starving or accepting the stigma of the workhouse, where, separated from wife and children, deprived of beer and tobacco, and forbidden to play cards, they had the same status as the perennial loafers.[15] Recovering from these blows, industrial workers continued to press for more schools, cheaper newspapers, more humane poor-laws, permission to organize, and a greater voice in government. The Chartist movement, which gave articulation and life to these desires, increased in momentum until the outbursts marked by the petitions of 1839, 1842, and 1848.

In comparison with the violent continental revolutions of 1848, the Chartist fiasco of the same year on Kennington Common seems pathetic if not a little ridiculous. It was the desires back of Chartism, nevertheless, which gave the dynamic to Dickens's campaign for reform of the schools, as well as to the political and sanitary reforms of the Dickensian era.

The growth of the industrial slums during this period was appalling. Thousands of people drifted from the enclosures into the already over-populated factory towns and raised problems of housing, health, and sanitation which are revolting even to discuss. Large families crowded into single rooms, garrets, or cellars in tumbled-down, rat-infested, cholera-ridden houses. Public cesspools, the stench of which was nauseating, oozed under the floors and into the water supply.[16] The workmen's flimsy houses were usually built back to back in double rows around a shabby sort of court, without regard to ventilation or drainage;

[14]See chaps. II and III below.
[15]See Hammond and Hammond, *The Bleak Age*, chap. VII.
[16]See *ibid.*, chap. V; Trevelyan, *English Social History*, pp. 528 ff.; Hayward, *The Days of Dickens*, pp. 93–112; Bryant, *The English Saga*, pp. 65 f.; and Dickens, *Sketches by Boz*.

there would perhaps be a solitary privy at one end and a pump or water-cock at the other. The fact that taxes had to be paid on every window in excess of eight damped any enthusiasm for fresh air, and left privies, cellars, garrets, and closets without ventilation. The fight against cholera and the industrial slums was long and hard, fought by such men as Chadwick through his report of 1842. He was aided by Delane, editor of *The Times*, from May, 1841; by Ashley and others in Parliament; and by men such as Dickens and Disraeli and women such as Mrs. Gaskell through their novels. These were the men and women who made clear to England what the Chartist unrest was about.

After the middle of the century, the sparkling humour of the portly Pickwick in gaiters, or the willowy Winkle on skates, seemed to retreat farther and farther away from Dickens; while the atmosphere of dismal law-courts, smoky factories, monotonous schools, squalid prisons, murky marshes, brooding water, mysterious opium dens, and foreboding cathe-dral crypts, now advancing, now withdrawing, seemed inevitably to draw closer and closer around him. Perhaps the London he knew—and there were few who knew it better than he—*was* changing; perhaps the filthy "rookeries," decomposing rat-ridden burial-grounds, ragged street-urchins, debased schools, vulgar crowds swaying at gruesome public executions, and ill-famed public houses *were* increasing. Yet there were still traces of a brighter life to be found among the sombre. Besides the tramps, thieves, cut-throats, prostitutes, and beggars were winsome, smiling maidens in brightly coloured crinolines, flimsily floating veils, and soft rustling silk; there were still some Pickwicks; there were many bewhiskered gentlemen in brass-buttoned dress coats or navy frock coats, snowy pantaloons, and black top hats; there were always a few six-foot dandies in their immaculate attire.[17] Before Peel's policemen came on the scene, there were Bow-street runners sporting blue, brass-buttoned dress coats over bright red waistcoats;[18] there were hustling white-smocked milkmen and pot-men, advertising their foaming wares.

Just as the bright mingled with the sombre, in like manner the old con-tinued with the new. In contrast to the scarlet-coated postmen, proudly strutting under their glossy top hats with golden bands, could be seen the shabby ticket porters trotting along, like Trotty Veck, carrying their parcels for delivery under their threadbare arms. Anyone who lost his way had best inquire of an officer who could be recognized (as Dickens explained to Macready) "by his being dressed in blue, with very dull

[17]For a description of dandies like Count D'Orsay, and men's clubs, see Lam-bert, *When Victoria Began to Reign*, pp. 184–95; also Shore, *D'Orsay or the Complete Dandy*.

[18]Hogarth and Dickens, eds., *Letters*, p. 544.

silver buttons, and by the top of his hat being made of sticking plaster."
In contrast to this respectable public servant, Dickens warned, "You
may perhaps see in some odd-looking place an intelligent-looking man,
with a curious little wooden table before him and three thimbles on it.
He will want you to bet, but don't do it."[19] Waxworks and graceful
ballets, which had attained some respectability, contrasted with licentious
burlesques and wild-west shows.[20] There were the exclusive clubs, such
as Almack's, where one entered by previously accepted written request
only, and where, at a hundred guineas an evening, Johann Strauss might
be engaged,[21] but Dickens, true to lower-class life, had Miss Evans's
young man escort her to the Grecian Saloon, where to the lilt of the
military band "the waiters were rushing to and fro with glasses of negus,
and glasses of brandy and water; ginger beer was going off in one place,
and practical jokes going on in another. . . . The whole scene was as
Miss J'mima Evans, inspired by the novelty, or the shrub, or both,
observed—'one of dazzling excitement.' "[22]

The cut-throats of the alleys, and the Cyprians or prostitutes of the
fashionable quarter or of the gin-shops, probably belong to both and to
all eras. The supple strawberry girls balancing large baskets on their
heads, the old watchman with his lantern, the dustman's bell, the wily
costermongers,[23] the cries of the lavender girl, the pieman, the organ
grinder, or the ballad singer[24] betokened an age that was passing; trains,
steamships, plumbing, safety matches, photography, telegraphy, and the
great Exhibition of 1851 symbolized the new era that was dawning.

There were contrasts in the country too.[25] The farm labourer became
entangled in the squeeze of the new poor-laws, and could earn only
about ten or eleven shillings a week. This meagre income might be aug-
mented by the few pennies his children could earn—his boys, armed with
clappers of wood, could scare the birds away from the cornfields, or his
girls could open and close gates for travellers.[26] But as a contemporary
American journalist testifies, there was refinement and taste in the social
life of the rural aristocrats of England and Scotland—so pleasant, so
delightful, even if restricted to a select group. Willis found kindness,
courtesy, and luxury, company or solitude, at his easiest disposal.[27]

[19]*Ibid.*, p. 247.
[20]For a good description of Hyde Park Fair, see Lambert, *When Victoria Began
to Reign*, pp. 306–11.
[21]*Ibid.*, pp. 66–70.   [22]"Miss Evans and the Eagle" in *Sketches by Boz.*
[23]Mayhew, *London Labour and the London Poor*, I, 40, 524–31.
[24]See Tuer, *One Thousand Quaint Cuts from Books of Other Days*, pp. 112–20.
[25]Cf. Dickens, *Is She His Wife?*
[26]Lambert, *When Victoria Began to Reign*, p. 147.
[27]Willis, *Famous Persons and Places*, Preface, and pp. 24–5, 69, 197–9.

Liveried grooms escorted prancing horses and were met by powdered footmen. Fitted out with hobnailed boots and a shooting jacket, a gun in the crook of his arm, a hound at heel, a guest would stroll with his host in the woods. At the formal evening meals he would be served fine food on gold plate and enjoy the company of the gentlemen and the ladies; at the informal breakfasts he could relax with exclusively masculine conversation, and without the distraction of servants. The sons of such a country family would be sent to Eton or Harrow, where the system of prefecting and fagging, though tending to "indulgent idleness" and "lack of breadth and flexibility," had "no injurious effect upon the character," exerted "no exorbitant demands upon [the students'] time," and made for friendly relations with the masters.[28]

Generally speaking, the material wealth of Dickensian England was attributed to the philosophy of laissez-faire and utilitarianism. This philosophy provided a policy for both moralist and legislator, and tended to permit matters to run their own course with as little interference as possible. Both conduct and legislation were thought to be motivated and steadied by self-interest, which led men to seek pleasure and avoid pain. Nevertheless, not only were the great minds of the originators of these ideas—Adam Smith and Jeremy Bentham—"unsettled" (to use Mr. Winkle's word) in their theories, since both would have excluded the matter of education from their premises,[29] but other men eventually began to question the philosophy of non-interference, and even to act contrariwise. Men began to question a Parliament, for example, which left the manufacturers alone, but at the same time forbad the workers to combine. Somewhat perplexed, Parliament began to remove restrictions on imports of corn, on the one hand; and, on the other hand, to interfere with families and manufacturers by imposing maximum hours of employment, laws on sanitation, and grants to education. Perplexed public men—Peel and Brougham are examples—felt obliged to reverse their stands on such vital public issues as education, corn laws, and religious toleration.

Side by side with changes in economic and political theories were changes in ethical and cultural ideas. In the midst of an age noted for its hardness toward children and its general belief in their depravity, for example, there were signs of a new philosophy. As early as 1824–6, George Cruikshank gave English children an illustrated edition of Grimm's fairy tales. A little later, Andersen's fairy tales began to arrive from the continent; Thackeray wrote *The Rose and the Ring*; Lewis

[28]Education Commission, 1864, *Parliamentary Papers*, XXI, 1864, I, 42–4.
[29]*Wealth of Nations*, II, Bk. V, 367–70; Bentham, *Works*, I, 570.

Carroll his *Alice's Adventures in Wonderland*; and Kingsley created his world of fantasy in *The Water Babies*.[30] Indeed this changing attitude toward children is one of the chief characteristics of the period, and Dickens contributed not a little to the change.

Similarly, religious ideas were being challenged and modified. When it rose to meet the challenge of Darwin's *Origin of Species*, in 1859, the Established Church, in the minds of some at least, had long been too closely associated with aristocratic government, conservative ideas, and a deference to those who owned land or property. "The truth is," wrote Greville in 1842, "that *The Times* . . . has a corner for High Church and the maximum of bigotry and intolerance . . . and is hostile . . . to every system, in short, which is not under the control of the church, and which does not inculcate its dogmatic theology."[31] As late as 1838, there were as many as four thousand clergymen exploiting non-resident livings, leaving hard-working and underpaid curates to do the work.[32] Small wonder that the clergy of the Established Church were associated with wealth and privilege, for clergymen (like schools), it seemed, were most desirable where they were least available, and tended to concentrate their energies on Sabbath observance, pew-rents, and control of the theatres. In 1856, military bands were silenced in Kensington Park on the Sabbath, and government motions to open the British Museum and the National Gallery on Sundays were lost.[33] The rigid austerity of Methodism joined in the attack on theatres and recreative Sundays, little caring that the necessity of labour debarred the poor from museums or botanical gardens during the week. It is not surprising that Dickens broke out in righteous indignation in his searing pamphlet entitled *Sunday under Three Heads.*

The net result of the hard materialism of the early nineteenth century was a tendency to regard human beings as mere tools, human suffering as an inevitable part of the normal wear and tear of an industrial economy, and human casualties as mere statistical units. To a man like Dickens, this was sheer callousness and outrageous complacency; it was a denial of individual human dignity; it stressed calculated objectivity to the detriment of humanity. Courageously Dickens repudiated the exploiters and took the side of the unprotected workers and helpless children. Thus, inevitably, he found himself arrayed against those manufacturers who exploited the workers; against those within church and

[30]Darton, "Children's Books," pp. 380 ff.
[31]*Letters*, ed. Johnston, p. 70.
[32]Hammond and Hammond, *The Bleak Age*, p. 117.
[33]Greville, *Diary*, ed. Wilson, II, 293–4.

chapel alike who would deny the poor such simple pleasures as the enjoyment of beauty in parks, art galleries, and gardens; and against those legislators who, under a guise of laissez-faire, shamelessly neglected the poor and the unfortunate in such matters as food, housing, sanitation, working conditions, and education. Thus it was that unsettled conditions, perplexed minds, neglect, oppression, and brazen materialism tended to provoke, in other quarters, a re-emphasis on human values. These values, united with the perennial emotions and aspirations of mankind, form the very warp and woof of the stuff from which life and literature are woven. Before the middle of the nineteenth century, novelist and Chartist had joined hands. Dickens, Disraeli, and Mrs. Gaskell sought to lift the veils of the society of their day. They were aided, of course, by other writers such as Blake, Hood, Shelley, Mrs. Browning, Carlyle, and Ruskin. Novels begun with a conscious social purpose may end as tracts. Dickens avoided this danger, however; his novels are full of humanitarian propaganda, but they also contain exciting plots and the warmth of hilarious laughter.

Dickens became the accepted champion and ardent defender of neglected, unfortunate, inarticulate, or exploited groups in society. He was not their sole champion, for others aided him in his attacks on delays in chancery, inadequate divorce laws, slums, lack of sanitation, imprisonment for debt, political oppression, and factory sweat-shops. His forte, however, was childhood and the schools, and in this no other early Victorian writer of fiction and non-fiction exceeded him in wideness of appeal, in persistency, or in sheer volume of work. His achievement is even more significant in view of what one might call the competition Dickens faced in this field of writing, for in the literature of England some of the treatment of school life has achieved high literary merit.

This brief review of the society of Dickensian England, in all its progress, colour, contrasts, and shifting perplexities, serves to illustrate some of the origins of the many problems and controversies that influenced the evolution of England's schools, and the theories that controlled practices within them. The conditions in education which we are to examine in this book bore a close relation to the confused, trial-and-error advances in political, social, economic, and ethical spheres. Such movements as the founding of Sunday schools or Mechanics' Institutes were interwoven with industrial progress; the charity-school movement pre-dated it. It is significant that the first interference of the state in laissez-faire industry, the act of 1802, carried a clause for an hour's schooling a day for each child working in the factories. It was the sectarianism of Mrs. Trimmer that expedited the founding of the National

School Society in 1811, as we shall see in chapter II. The first state grant
to education in England in 1833 was a logical corollary of the political
reforms of 1832. The continued expansion and extension of these grants
coincided with the Chartist agitation and the repeal of the corn laws.
Again, the Forster Education Act of 1870, the year of Dickens's death,
closely followed a further extension of the franchise in 1867.

Perhaps it should have been obvious to the Victorians that, before
much progress could be made in regard to the schools, further municipal
and national machinery was necessary. But the widespread confusion
and contradictory philosophies were carried over into the field of education. The minds of the Victorians were just as unsettled about where
the responsibility for educating their children lay as Pickwick observed
them to be about so many other matters. The Victorians could not make
up their minds whether education was a parental, a communal, or a
national responsibility. As they worked out the answers to this question,
ideas of laissez-faire and government intervention clashed; the contentiousness of church and chapel flared into open flame; the rights of
the individual collided with those of society. "Birthrights" to learning,
or to labour, could no longer be quite so narrowly confined to particular
classes of society; and special privileges to attend exclusive schools
slowly became modified. Gradually, the abstract idea of universal education became a reality in the form of a national system of schools.

An assessment of Dickens's contribution to this enlargement of the
scope of education is greatly clarified by a review of the state's gradual
acceptance of responsibility. As I have already noted, state intervention
in the nineteenth century made its appearance early, in 1802,[34] as part
of a factory act known as "An Act for the Preservation of the Health
and Morals of Apprentices (and Others, Employed in Cotton and Other
Mills, and Cotton and Other Factories)." In addition to requiring mill
owners to ventilate and whitewash the rooms, to separate the sexes for
sleeping, to call in a medical practitioner in the event of infectious disease, and to prohibit work between the hours of 9 P.M. and 6 A.M., the
statute required that the apprentices be instructed for one hour a day
in the rudiments of knowledge and in the principles of Christianity.
"Every such apprentice," ran the statute, "shall be instructed . . . in the
usual hours of work, in reading, writing and arithmetic, or either of them,
according to the age and abilities of such apprentice, by some discreet
and proper person, to be provided and paid by the master or mistress

[34]State intervention in England actually reaches back to the 1662 Poor Law; a
private bill of 1769 secured access to the rates to educate the poor of London. See
Dobbs, *Education and Social Movements*, pp. 95 f.

of such apprentice . . . [and] for the space of one hour at least every Sunday, be instructed in the principles of the Christian religion, by some proper person to be provided and paid by the master or mistress of such an apprentice."[35] But there was little or no enthusiasm for this intervention. The statute was attacked in some quarters as harsh, oppressive, impracticable, and injurious to the manufacturers.[36] This reaction would suggest that the government was ahead of an influential sector of public opinion.

Five years later, in 1807, the idea again asserted itself. Whitbread proposed a bill to establish a school in every parish for poor children who could not afford to pay fees. The bill was very modest, purporting to give poor children two years of schooling sometime between the ages of two and fourteen years; the parish rates were to be used for support. But Whitbread was violently attacked in the House of Commons; Mr. Davies Giddy, for example, who was eventually to become president of the Royal Society, maintained that Whitbread's scheme was injurious to the morals of the labouring poor, that it would make them discontented with their status, "insolent to their superiors," and enable them to read "seditious pamphlets" and "vicious books."[37] It was obvious, moreover, that the Established Church doubted its potential control over such a scheme. Here may be observed not only direct opposition to any extension of education to the poor, but also indirect opposition in the form of anxiety over who would have to pay for such education and who would be in charge of it. Needless to say, perhaps, the bill was defeated.

Whitbread died in 1815, and the next year Lord Brougham took up his work as chairman of a "Select Committee" inquiring into "the education of the Lower Orders." The pertinent questions for us are: What did the state find out? What solutions were suggested? A few examples may be given. John Kelly of St. Patrick's Parish, London, reports that children cannot attend school because they have no clothing.[38] Thomas Leary of Covent Garden examines 215 houses to find that only 97 boys out of 243, and 75 girls out of 187 are receiving any sort of schooling.[39] F. A. Earle, twelve years a vestry clerk, gives an account of three charity schools, a workhouse school, two schools following the Lancaster system, two Bell schools, one Irish free school, and one Dissenters' free school, all of which are located in the parishes of St. Giles and St.

[35] 42 Geo. III, c. 73.
[36] See Montmorency, *State Intervention in English Education*, pp. 209–14.
[37] Hansard, *Parliamentary Debates*, First Series, IX, July 13, 1807, cols. 798 ff.
[38] Education Commission, 1816–18, First Report, 1816, *Parliamentary Papers*, IV, 1816, i, p. 5.
[39] *Ibid.*, p. 7.

George.[40] He reports that the morals of the children, which had been described on the first page of the report as "most depraved" and encompassing every kind of vice, are "in a dreadful state." Of thirty prostitutes arrested during the previous week, several were only thirteen to fourteen years old. He complains further of riotous Sunday afternoons, the frequency with which children enter the workhouse "naked or nearly so," and the necessity to confine the prostitutes in the workhouses.[41] A silk manufacturer, James Honeyman of Spitalfields, reports on parish, Dissenters', and private day-schools, and on five Sunday schools, in addition to a school for adults. He estimates that in a population of 18,000 there are 2,000 children who receive no schooling whatever.[42] Thomas Cooke, a teacher of a charitable foundation, explains that objections would be raised to using school endowments for any purposes other than those prescribed in the charter.[43] In the monitorial schools, it takes one penny to provide each child with the requisite books and two years to educate him, whereas it takes less than two months to educate a master. Fees of fourpence a month are often waived.[44] Robert Owen testifies that because of the insistence on religious catechizing, the National schools of the Church of England are not generally available to Dissenters.[45]

These typical pieces of evidence are presented to give some insight into the problems of the time and to give point to the conclusions of the Select Committee of 1816–18. Small wonder it reported that "a very great deficiency exists in the means of educating the Poor." It noted, moreover, that "the anxiety of the Poor for education continues not only unabated but is daily increasing."[46] It pointed out that schools for Anglicans and schools for all comers were "two opposite principles" and that both types presented difficulties for Roman Catholics as being contrary to both doctrine and discipline. It also revealed abuses in charitable foundations: funds at Eton and Winchester had been misused through carelessness, ignorance, and even misappropriation; there was "equal negligence and malversion in all charities"; and "many great neglects and abuses exist in charities which have special visitors."[47]

It is amazing that the recommendations of this committee proved essentially those which were ultimately adopted: the local parish was to control taxation; the most impoverished districts were to receive greater

[40]See chap. II below for descriptions of Bell and Lancaster schools.
[41]Education Commission, 1816–18, First Report, 1816, *Parliamentary Papers*, IV, 1816, pp. 8–11.
[42]*Ibid.*, pp. 11–12.   [43]*Ibid.*, pp. 21–39.
[44]*Ibid.*, pp. 31–3.   [45]*Ibid.*, pp. 238–41.
[46]Education Commission, 1816–18, Second Report, 1818, *Parliamentary Papers*, IV, 1818, iii, p. 56.
[47]*Ibid.*, pp. 58–60.

state support as a means of assisting "those parishes where no school-houses are erected"; the less impoverished districts were to get state assistance for buildings, but they were to retain "the burthen of paying the schoolmaster" who was to be chosen by the vestry and the clergyman, paid a grant of 24 pounds sterling a year, and permitted to augment his stipend from other employment; and although there was to be diocesan inspection, religious freedom was to be recognized.[48] Clearly, the filling of the educational gaps and the conscience clause of the 1870 act (which sought to provide escape from denominational religious instruction for those who wished to avoid it) were portended, and the 1833 government aid to buildings was envisioned.[49]

If the Select Committee went no further, it at least put Brougham, its chairman, in possession of the pertinent facts. He reported to Parliament on June 28, 1820. He had sent questionnaires to 11,400 clergymen, and all but 200 of the forms were completed and returned. In general, one child in sixteen received some schooling, but in counties such as Middlesex, the proportion was only one in forty-six. Some thirty-five hundred parishes (about one-quarter of the total) had no school of any description. Brougham suggested a bill to provide schools, where needed and asked for, from the consolidated fund, and to let the parish rates foot the master's salary. The master, who would have to be between twenty-four and forty years of age and a member of the Church of England, was to be certificated by the local clergyman and three householders and might be removed by the school visitors. The local clergyman was to set the course of study. No provisions for clothing, boarding, or lodging the pupils were to be made.[50] "Whether they learned less or more was of little consequence, the moral discipline was the great consideration."[51] But Dissenter and Catholic alike forced the withdrawal of the bill.[52] The view that Dickens later came to was that nothing but religious contentiousness had barred the way.

Thirteen years later, Brougham was aided in the fight by Roebuck, who, on July 30, 1833, introduced a bill for the education of the poor which would serve to minimize the numbers of "stack-burning peasants and sturdy paupers." The parents of the poor were to have some control over what was to be taught (with some guidance from the upper class) through annually elected local committees. Roebuck's aims were an infant school in every parish, compulsory attendance, normal schools for training teachers, and a senior officer who was to be a member of

[48]*Ibid.*, pp. 56 f.
[49]Cf. Montmorency, *State Intervention in English Education*, p. 227.
[50]Hansard, *Parliamentary Debates*, Second Series, II, cols. 48–9.
[51]*Ibid.*, col. 89.   [52]Brougham, *Life and Times*, II, 291.

the cabinet. But a plan that involved state inroads on parental authority was too much for the legislators, and Roebuck was forced to withdraw the bill. Nevertheless, a positive outcome of all the discussion was a government grant of 20,000 pounds sterling for the erection of school buildings. This money went, of course, to the support of the voluntary schools, and was distributed through the two major school societies, the British and the National,[53] whose origins are described in chapter II of this book.

Charles Dickens was engaged as a parliamentary reporter during the late summer of 1832 to the late autumn of 1836. It is, therefore, more than likely that he heard Roebuck's speech in 1833 which we have just discussed, and also the address of Brougham in the House of Lords on May 21, 1835. By this time Brougham had had a change of heart. The number paying tuition had actually doubled in ten years, and now constituted half the total enrolment. Brougham was ready to admit that a quarter of a million children between the ages of seven and eleven had no schools which they could attend; that the state should make initial grants, on a fifty-fifty basis with local groups, toward new buildings; that the establishment of schools for infants might well reduce crime; that training schools for teachers should be established; and that the misappropriation of the funds of endowed schools could be checked by competent supervision so as to increase their effectiveness by 1,200 per cent.[54] Nevertheless, he considered that it was inexpedient to attempt to establish parish schools at public expense and that voluntary effort would do; moreover, it appeared to offer individual choice and religious freedom. It is fairly apparent that to a man such as Charles Dickens, who lacked a sense of history and of political expediency, Brougham's desertion of Roebuck seemed a betrayal.[55] Dickens, apparently, made up his mind that when the opportunity arose he would strike a blow for the education of the poor.

In 1839, however, further state intervention occurred as an inevitable consequence of the grant of 20,000 pounds made in 1833. A committee of the Privy Council was appointed to control the distribution of the funds and Dr. Kay-Shuttleworth of Manchester was made its permanent secretary. Since the admittance of state inspectors was a condition

---

[53]Hansard, *Parliamentary Debates*, Third Series, XX, cols. 139–74.

[54]*Ibid.*, XXVII, cols. 1293–333. (The speech is also quoted in full in Montmorency, *State Intervention in English Education*, Appendix III.)

[55]Political expediency, combined with the vested interests, prevented the state from auditing the endowments of the charitable schools, so that while this censure of the charity schools in 1816 led, in 1835, to a recommendation for a permanent board, such a board was not actually established until 1853.

demanded with the payment of each government grant, this financial support inevitably led to some measure of state control. Some such control was sadly needed: Kay-Shuttleworth's biographer quotes Inspector Tremenheere's anecdote of a youngster in Glamorgan, who, boldly inattentive to his lessons, surreptitiously consumed his schoolmaster's mug of beer during school hours, his eager eyes meanwhile furtively watching the pedagogue's back over the mug's rim.[56]

Kay-Shuttleworth's next concern was with the training of teachers. As a former Poor Law Commissioner for East Anglia, he had introduced a system of training older pupils as teachers in Norwood Workhouse, and had watched how it worked. He had visited David Stow's training school in Glasgow, Scotland (of which Dickens thought highly), and had been sufficiently impressed to bring Alexander Wilson down from Scotland to teach at Norwood and men like Dunlop and Horne to teach in other workhouses.[57] Since he did not like the system followed in the monitorial schools,[58] Kay-Shuttleworth sought to establish a scheme whereby prospective teachers would spend two years at a training college after having served an apprenticeship of five years (from the ages of eight to thirteen) under a schoolmaster. But whereas Stow's training school was already well established,[59] Kay-Shuttleworth's was destined to failure. In the first place, he failed to secure sufficient government support. Then, nothing daunted, he promoted a private training school at an old manor house in Battersea, and placed his mother and sister in charge. But the two years ostensibly being devoted to practice in teaching were rugged ones for the students. Up at five-thirty, gardening until eight, tending the cows, goats, and pigs, scrubbing their own floors, preparing their own meals, they were kept busily engaged until nine at night. No moments were free from either occupation or supervision. The students were thus kept continually cognizant of their lowly status in society, and their uniforms of "rifle green" and "fustian cord" were calculated to implant lessons of duty and self-denial.[60] Later in this book we shall see how Dickens scorned this particular aspect in any type of

[56]Smith, *The Life and Work of Sir James Kay-Shuttleworth*, pp. 95, 103.

[57]For Stow's methods, see chap. v below; and for the abuse of them, see chap. ii below.

[58]The monitorial system is described in chap. ii below.

[59]By 1854, Stow had been in the business over twenty years. He boasted at that time of 2,000 graduates, 2,000 written parental testimonials, 442 Wesleyan students, and of the fact that since 1837 he had sent more than 200 "trainers" to the Poor Law Union of England.

[60]Smith, *The Life and Work of Sir James Kay-Shuttleworth*, pp. 115–16; or for a first-hand report, see "First and Second Reports of the Training School at Battersea, 1841," pp. 170–99. In a letter dated Feb. 19, 1843, Greville praised this training school highly.

training school. In spite of Kay-Shuttleworth's efforts, the Committee of Council decided against extending state support to his normal school. Reluctantly, rather than abandon the venture entirely, he permitted it to pass into the hands of the Established Church, which had founded a similar institution at Chelsea in 1841. Gallantly carrying on his work, Kay-Shuttleworth persuaded the Committee, in 1846, to institute a system whereby pupils of thirteen years of age were apprenticed to a headmaster for five years, during which time the state awarded grants to both master and pupil. Any just appraisal of Dickens's criticism of teachers and their training, for example his criticism of Bradley Head-stone in *Our Mutual Friend*, necessitates a knowledge of these facts.

The state was not quite as unmindful of education as Dickens would have us believe. Grants were extended to other voluntary societies besides the two major ones—the British and the National. From this it was but a step to the establishment of a "Department" of Education in 1856.[61] Frustrated in its aims by denominational rivalry, the irregular attendance of children at school, and their early withdrawal to more immediately lucrative work in factories, the state began to investigate the conditions in the schools by appointing a commission. The Newcastle Commission reported in 1861 that, roughly speaking, only two-thirds of the children who ought to have been in school were nominally there. Of those who *were* there, approximately two-thirds attended the voluntary schools; the other third, presumably, attended private schools.[62] It is evident, therefore, that when Dickens pleads for neglected children who do not attend any school, he pleads for one child in three. Further, when he is concerned about private schools, he is concerned with no small portion of the children who *were* within the educational system (again one child in three). Close to ten thousand schools were inspected by the Newcastle Commission, but one-fifth of these did not receive any state grant;[63] and of the approximately one million pupils attending them, only one-quarter remained long enough to acquire even the mere rudiments of learning, and one-sixth attended less than fifty days. Eighty-five per cent of these schools were under the control of the Established Church,[64] which emphasized the value of religious instruction and jealously guarded its right to religious control.

The expressed aims of the Newcastle Commission had been to see "what measures, if any, are required for the extension of sound and

[61]Smith, *The Life and Work of Sir James Kay-Shuttleworth*, p. 249.
[62]Education Commission, 1861, *Parliamentary Papers*, XXI, 1861, I, vi, pp. 572–4, 591.
[63]*Ibid.*, p. 574.
[64]*Ibid.*, p. 656.

cheap elementary instruction to all classes of the people." But it did not recommend a national educational system, believing that it was neither desirable nor attainable.[65] The Commission was even divided on the question of whether the obligations of the state went beyond the care of the destitute and the criminal. It did recommend, however, a new set of regulations which became known as "payment by results." When incorporated into the Revised Code, this vicious system reduced the annual government grant by a definite amount for each child who failed to pass each of the subjects at an annual examination.

In order to ensure a grant for the school, the pupils had to be drilled incessantly for the day of inspection; and, in order to earn his eight shillings for the school, each pupil had to be in attendance on the day of inspection to be examined individually. The Revised Code led to a narrowing of the curricula to the three R's, to brutal coercion, and to sheer memorization of facts.[66] Dickens did not discuss grants *per se*, but in *Hard Times* he attacked the emphasis on facts in Mr. Gradgrind's school, and in his speeches and articles he pleaded for the ragged schools. The latter were schools for the very poor, which were attended by children from the slums, and usually conducted by voluntary or poorly paid teachers. The Commissioners of 1861, however, considered 189 out of the 192 schools of the London Ragged School Union ineligible for a government grant.[67] According to the Commission, a teacher did not require "a very inquisitive mind or very brilliant talents," was not regarded very highly socially, nor did he feel the vicissitudes of trade.[68] Such views Dickens scorned—as we shall see.

Dickens sometimes failed to appreciate administrative difficulties, but educationists such as Kay-Shuttleworth sided with him against the Commission's stand on factual knowledge. Kay-Shuttleworth agreed that country children who had migrated into the towns could not be expected to assimilate factual knowledge straight off: they had never seen a book before; they sat, crouched over, like sheep dogs; they were agitated by the crowds in the streets; and at high tension in the classroom. He agreed also that city children from East London, sharp-witted, reared, like as not, in a brothel, picking up both good and evil ways from the streets where they earned their living as crossroad sweepers or costermongers or beggars, did not need drill in the three R's as much as they needed instruction in the decencies of life.[69] Reporting in 1868, two years before

65*Ibid.*, pp. 297–300.
66Arnold, *Reports of Elementary Schools*, p. 124.
67Education Commission, 1861, *Parliamentary Papers*, XXI, 1861, I, p. 395.
68*Ibid.*, p. 163.
69Kay-Shuttleworth, *Four Periods of Public Education*, pp. 583–5.

Dickens's death, Kay-Shuttleworth stressed that education turned on the skill and character of the teacher, that schools were often fewest where they were most needed, that the poor were discriminated against, and that religious contention barred progress. Yet he saw beyond Dickens that "all efforts to promote a secular, or purely civil system, supported by rates, and governed solely by ratepayers outside the pale of religious groups had failed."[70] When local contributions and initiative did not respond as the central grants fell off (owing to the Revised Code), Kay-Shuttleworth saw that the government was still far ahead of public opinion.[71]

Today, even as then, in surveying weighty official records there is always the danger of forgetting that these were the conditions observed in the inspection of those schools which received government grants.[72] The private schools carried on very much as they pleased, and thousands of children did not attend any school at all before the Education Act of 1870. The Statistical Society, founded in 1833, reported that fewer than five thousand out of twelve thousand children received any kind of schooling in a working-class area of Manchester;[73] in Liverpool there were some "thirty thousand children between the ages of five and fifteen receiving no education either real or nominal" in 1838;[74] in another district where there were about eleven thousand children of school age, "eight thousand attended no school, and . . . a great many of those who did, might as well have stayed away for anything useful that they were taught."[75] Church, charity, parental initiative, private enterprise, meagre state subsidies for voluntary efforts—all were not enough. Dickens, as we shall see, tried to bring these facts home to the public.

[70]Kay-Shuttleworth, *Memorandum on Popular Education*, pp. 2–9.
[71]*Ibid.*, pp. 31–4.
[72]For actual conditions in specific church, charity, and private schools, see below, chaps. II, III, and IV.
[73]Woodward, *The Age of Reform*, p. 459.
[74]The Bishop of Durham, May 7, 1838, Hansard, *Parliamentary Debates*, Third Series, XLII, p. 940.
[75]Macaulay, April 19, 1847, Hansard, *Parliamentary Debates*, Third Series, XCI, p. 1009.

CHAPTER I

Charles Dickens Receives an Education

Dickens remarked in a letter to Wilkie Collins that he was born at Portsmouth on February 7, 1812, and that his father, John Dickens, was at that time a clerk in the Navy Pay Office at Portsmouth.[1] The register at the church of St. Mary-le-Strand, London, reveals that John Dickens married Elizabeth Barrow on June 13, 1809. The actual birthplace of their first son, Charles, the second child of eight children, was 387 Commercial Road, Landport (a division of Portsea, Hampshire), formerly known as Mile End Terrace. Before the end of June, 1812, John Dickens moved his family to Hawke Street, where he probably remained until Midsummer Day, 1814.[2] Little is known, definitely, of Charles's infancy at Portsea, and some minor claims about his memories of those days, made by himself and by his biographer, Forster, are open to question.

In a letter to Dr. Künzel, July, 1838, Dickens remarked that he was in London at two years of age,[3] and it is known that in 1814 John Dickens and his family accepted lodgings for a short time on Norfolk Street, Fitzroy Square, on the east side of Middlesex Hospital.[4] In the same letter Dickens added that when he was six he left London for Chatham, where he remained half a dozen years or so.[5] Forster leans to the view that the date of this moving to Chatham was 1816.[6] If this date is correct, the place where the Dickens family lived for the first few months of their residence in Chatham at that time has not been established. However, in spite of the fact that Forster makes no mention of any house, the rate-books show clearly that the family lived at what was then 2 (now 11) Ordnance Terrace from June, 1817, until Lady Day, 1821.[7] Since John Dickens was, at that time, favourably situated in the Navy Pay Office, it has reasonably been inferred that Charles spent many happy days at Ordnance Terrace. His playmates included his

[1]Dexter, ed., *Letters*, II, 778 f.   [2]Kitton, *The Dickens Country*, pp. 3–5.
[3]Dexter, ed., *Letters*, I, 168 f.   [4]Kitton, *The Dickens Country*, p. 7.
[5]Dexter, ed., *Letters*, I, 168 f.
[6]Forster, *The Life of Charles Dickens*, I, 24, where Charles is said to have been "between four and five years old" when he left Chatham.
[7]Langton, *The Childhood and Youth of Charles Dickens*, p. 21.

sister, Fanny, and a boy and girl who lived next door—George Stroughill and his sister Lucy. George, apparently an open and rather daring character, suggests young Steerforth in *David Copperfield*. Lucy, with her beautiful golden hair, appears to have been a special favourite of Charles.[8] It is interesting to recall, in this respect, that Lucie Manette in *A Tale of Two Cities* had golden hair, as did Lucy in "The Wreck of the Golden Mary."

It would appear that as a boy Dickens was an observer rather than a participant. Since he was somewhat frail, he chose to watch such games as marbles, cricket, pegtop, and prisoners' base rather than play them himself; and he was often reading while other children were playing. His love for reading, certainly acquired without formal schooling, seems to contradict Forster when he says that Dickens owed little to his parents. Indeed, Forster himself goes on to say that Dickens had frequently remarked that "his first desire for knowledge, and his earliest passion for reading, were awakened by his mother, who taught him the first rudiments not only of English, but also, a little later, of Latin."[9]

In 1881, Langton was greatly interested in a fragmentary letter of Dickens which appeared in a footnote in Forster's biography. The letter read, in part: ". . . I feel much as I used to do when I was a small child . . . and Somebody . . . hummed the evening hymn to me."[10] Langton eventually made the acquaintance of an old lady, Mrs. Thomas Gibson, who proved to be this "Somebody." Her maiden name was Mary Weller, and she had been with the Dickens family both when they lived at Ordnance Terrace and later, when they moved to the house on the Brook, 18 St. Mary's Place.[11] "Sometimes," observed Mary Weller to Langton, "Charles would come downstairs and say to me, 'Now Mary, clear the kitchen, we are going to have such a game.'" Then, with Fanny at the piano, brother and sister sang duets; or, with the assistance of George Stroughill, acted parts of various plays; or Charles recited with great enthusiasm the recitation that was then his favourite: "The Voice of the Sluggard." Mary Weller also added that at that time (about 1819) Dickens "was a terrible boy to read," and "had certainly not been to school, but had been thoroughly well taught by his aunt and mother."[12]

John Dickens was a welcome guest at the near-by Mitre Inn, run by an old friend, J. Tribe. Here Charles recited or sang for the company gathered in the parlour of the inn.[13] One pictures him, his face flushed,

[8]*Ibid.*, p. 23.

[9]Forster, *Life*, I, 26 f.; cf. Johnson, *Charles Dickens*, I, 13.

[10]Forster, *Life*, I, 24.

[11]Langton, *Childhood and Youth*, p. 29.

[12]*Ibid.*, p. 26.   [13]Kitton, *The Dickens Country*, p. 13.

standing on the table for a better view of his listeners; and one wonders
whether any member of those great crowds which he held spellbound on
those gigantic lecture tours of his later life caught a fleeting glimpse of
the little boy of long ago eagerly reciting to his first audience. The
Theatre Royal stood at the foot of Star Hill, in neighbouring Rochester,
and John Dickens once took his wide-eyed son there (Charles was then
only eight years old), to see Grimaldi, the famous clown. A critical
interpreter of school life, or an appraiser of such scenes as Dotheboys
Hall, Salem House, or Doctor Blimber's Academy should not be unmindful of these glimpses of Dickens's early flair for the theatrical.

Attention has been drawn to Forster's minimization of the education
which Dickens received from his mother at home, and also to his failure
to make any mention of Dickens's four years of happy boyhood at
Ordnance Terrace. Since Charles was nine years old (not four or five
as given by Forster) when the family left Ordnance Terrace in 1821
and moved to the much smaller house at 18 St. Mary's Place, otherwise
known as the house on the Brook, and since the family remained there
for nearly a year and a half, he must have been close to the age of eleven
when he eventually left Chatham, late in 1822 or early in 1823, for
London.

Because of such inaccuracies, as Langton revealed in 1891,[14] Forster's
assertion that Dickens went to some sort of preparatory school in Rome
Lane[15] should not be accepted with confidence. In support of Forster, of
course, there is Dickens's reference in his article entitled "Our School"
to a "preparatory" school, some of his references to Mrs. Pipchin of
Dombey and Son (see below, and chapter III), and some rather am-
biguous remarks in his extant letters. The extent to which the article
"Our School" is fact or fiction is an open question. After his few remarks
about a preparatory school over a dyer's shop, Dickens hastens to add
that the actual school which he purports to be describing was a different
school altogether. Is it not peculiar that, exclusive of the location in
Rome Lane (which Dickens does not mention in "Our School") the few
details which Forster gives about such a school, as well as the extract
which he quotes, were all taken from this very article? In the light of
Langton's thorough investigations of the 1880's, and of the several
inaccuracies already indicated in Forster's account, I hazard the suspi-
cion that this rather weak piece of evidence—"Our School," which may
have been a fusion of fact and fiction by the time Dickens wrote it in

[14]Langton, *Childhood and Youth*, chap. VI.
[15]Forster, *Life*, I, 28; also Johnson, *Charles Dickens*, I, 13; but see Langton,
Childhood and Youth, pp. 54 and 92.

1851—was probably the only source for Forster's statement. Moreover, since Mary Weller testified that by about 1819 young Charles had not been to any school, and yet, having been taught by his mother and aunt, was by that time a very fluent reader, there would be no need for Charles to attend a dame school at all. Furthermore, since his aunt continued to live with the Dickens family until her marriage to Dr. Lamert in December, 1821, she would have been on hand to take care of Charles well up to the time when he began to attend Giles's school. It has also been asserted, erroneously, that Charles Dickens attended a school kept by a Mr. Dawson in Hunter Street, Brunswick Square—probably an assumption from the knowledge that Dickens's brothers went to school there. Dickens may have attended a preparatory or dame school as Forster claims for a very short time, but no really decisive evidence has come to light.

It has been fairly well established, in spite of the above, that about Lady Day, March 25, 1821, when the Dickens family lived in the house on the Brook, Charles began to attend a school conducted by a Mr. Giles of Chatham, who was a son of Rev. William Giles, said to have been a Baptist minister of Providence Chapel situated next door to the Dickens's house.[16] When Mrs. Godfrey, young Giles's eldest sister, was residing at Liverpool, she gave Langton her recollections of Dickens and of her brother's school. It appears that Giles was known locally as a reader and elocutionist. In his school were gathered the children of the officers in the garrison, his own younger brothers and sisters, and the children of a few of the neighbours. The school was first held in a house in Clover Lane, later at the corner of Rhode and Best streets, and finally at Gibralter Place, Chatham. Mrs. Godfrey reported that the theatricals continued, and that the curly-headed Charles enjoyed parties, birthdays, and Guy Fawkes festivities around bright bonfires.[17] It was during this time also that he had access at home to that "little room upstairs" where he read over and over again the books mentioned in *David Copperfield*[18] as well as the *Tatler*, the *Spectator*, the *Idler*, Goldsmith's *Citizen of the World*, and a book by Mrs. Inchbald.[19] He watched the parades of the scarlet-coated regiments, or listened, wide-eyed and open-mouthed, to

[16]Humphreys, *Charles Dickens and His First Schoolmaster*, pp. 2–4; Kitton, *The Dickens Country*, p. 14; but cf. Johnson, *Charles Dickens*, I, 19. There is some confusion in Forster. As a Nonconformist the schoolmaster could hardly have been *in residence* at Oxford.

[17]In addition, see a letter to Dr. Künzel in Dexter, ed., *Letters*, I, 169.

[18]*Roderick Random, Humphry Clinker, Tom Jones, The Vicar of Wakefield, Don Quixote, Gil Blas, Robinson Crusoe, Arabian Nights*, and *Tales of the Genii*.

[19]Forster, *Life*, I, 38.

the musketry of their sham battles. When not singing, reciting, or play-acting, he amused himself by writing a play entitled *Misnar: The Sultan of India*. At night, as he lay awake in bed, he speculated on the frightening principles of "the radicals" who were reputed to insist that the army and navy must be "put down," that the Prince Regent "wore stays," and that nobody should receive a salary.[20]

Since Dickens was accustomed to satirize uniformity in children's dress, one wonders what he thought of the wearing of white hats by the pupils of Giles's school.[21] White hat or no, Dickens was apparently happy—at any rate, there is no evidence to suggest that he was not—and his experiences at the school probably furnished some of the material for Doctor Strong's school in *David Copperfield*, which was founded on "the faith and honour of the boys."

Since Dickens spoke so highly in later life of his education at Giles's school, it would be interesting to know exactly what was taught there. Unfortunately, we do not know exactly. It is known, however, that Giles conducted, at varying times, no less than five schools. Before conducting his little school at Chatham, he had apparently been a master at St. Aldgate's School, Oxford. The *Manchester Guardian*, January 22, 1831, carried an advertisement of Barton Hall, a boarding-school kept at Patricroft, a few miles out of Manchester, by William Giles, formerly of Chatham. On January 5, 1839, the same newspaper carried an advertisement of another school conducted by Giles known as a "Gentlemen's Academy," at 38 Ardwick Green, in Manchester. The *Liverpool Mercury*, January 7, 1843, advertised that Giles, late of Barton Hall, had opened yet another school for boys at Seacombe House, Cheshire, opposite Liverpool. The same newspaper, June 27, 1848, published an account of the removal of Seacombe House School to Netherleigh House, Chester, where Giles carried on a school for some ten years.[22] The prospectus of the Barton Hall school referred to the earlier school at Chatham as a "classical, mathematical, and commercial" institution. The curricula at Barton Hall included English, commercial studies, modern languages, science, mathematics, and classical studies. The last of these included reading Greek and Latin, parsing, and writing prose and verse as part of the daily routine. Annual prizes were awarded; a laboratory, a gymnasium, an archery range, and playing-fields were provided.[23] It would appear reasonable to assume that, except for its less extensive grounds, Giles's school at Chatham did not differ radically from the other

[20]*Ibid.*, p. 37.   [21]*Ibid.*, p. 74.
[22]Humphreys, *Charles Dickens and His First Schoolmaster, passim.*
[23]*Ibid.*, from a photostat copy of the prospectus, opposite p. 9.

schools which he conducted elsewhere. There was a telling sentence in
the announcement for Seacombe House which any modern parent or
teacher would be proud to associate with the education of his charges:
"The domestic treatment will be paternal and liberal, the Management
firm and kind; the Instruction in accordance with the Pupils' prospects
in life; and the Masters will be men of tried talent, experience and
character. . . ."[24]

It is not known whether all the masters were of such high calibre, but
when Giles himself reached his fiftieth birthday, a number of his former
pupils honoured him with a silver tea-service; and a testimonial paid
tribute to his "tact, energy, and facility . . . in developing the moral and
intellectual faculties" of his pupils;[25] at this time, too, many individual
commendations were tendered to Giles for his "care and fidelity as a
tutor," his "uniform kindness and parental care," and his "sterling"
beneficial instruction.[26] A letter from Dickens, who had never forgotten
that Giles had once pronounced him "a boy of capacity,"[27] explained
that while he regretted his early loss of Giles's instruction, he was "not
the less sensible of its value."[28] Sam Giles, a brother of the schoolmaster
and a former schoolfellow of Dickens, mentioned Charles's manly and
generous qualities, and his diffusion of "sound and truthful views of
[the] evils in society."[29] Perhaps it was his recognition of William Giles's
sound qualities that led Dickens to place so much emphasis on the
intrinsic qualities possessed by teachers, rating personal qualities higher,
perhaps, than training in the techniques of teaching. In any event, Mr.
Giles was no Squeers or Creakle, for it was said that he often visited
Charles in the evenings, and that when the boy was about to leave
Chatham, Giles came "flitting in among the packing cases" to present
him with a copy of Goldsmith's *Bee* as a keepsake.[30] Many years later,
shortly after the publication of *Pickwick Papers*, Dickens received the
gift of a silver snuff-box from his former schoolmaster.[31]

By the spring of 1823 at the latest, however, these happy days came
to an end, for Dickens's father, during the winter of 1822–3, had been
transferred from Chatham back to London. Mrs. Godfrey, Giles's sister,
recalled that young Charles was left behind in Chatham for a short period
at the schoolmaster's home (probably to the end of the winter term)
while the rest of the family moved to London to settle on Bayham

24*Ibid.*, p. 12.   25*Ibid.*, p. 21.
26*Ibid.*, pp. 18–19.   27Forster, *Life*, I, 36.
28Dexter, ed., *Letters*, II, 142.
29Humphreys, *Charles Dickens and His First Schoolmaster*, p. 20.
30Forster, *Life*, I, 39.
31*Ibid.*, p. 36.

Street.[32] Charles followed later, travelling alone. This brief sojourn and its aftermath probably formed the basis for that wonderful account of David Copperfield's first journey alone. It is also more than likely, as Forster and others have noted, that the sense of utter loneliness and dreariness which Dickens experienced at this time found expression years later in "Dullborough Town," of *The Uncommercial Traveller*.[33] Upon his arrival in London, the boy found no relief from this sense of desolation. Poverty was stalking the family, and, for the time being, Dickens's schooldays came to an end. There was sorrow, too, for one of the younger children had died. Perhaps we are given a glimpse of this time in *The Haunted House* where Dickens wrote: "I was taken home, and there was Debt at home, as well as Death, and we had a sale there."[34] Charles longed to go back to some sort of schooling. Neglected, he paid visits to his uncle, Thomas Barrow, who lent him books to read; he wrote sketches of the barber, and of an old deaf woman; and he amused himself with a small model of a theatre which James Lamert, a "cousin" acquired by his aunt's second marriage, had made and painted for him.[35] Eventually, his father's resources became so low that the family concocted a scheme calculated to retrieve the family fortunes by moving to Gower Street, where his mother proposed to set up a school of her own. Once more Charles began to have hopes that he would leave off such menial tasks as cleaning his father's boots or looking after the four younger children, and go to school instead.

Mrs. Dickens's business venture was announced to the general public by means of a great brass plate, affixed to the door of the house, which bore the inscription: MRS. DICKENS'S ESTABLISHMENT. (Number 4 Gower Street, later numbered 147, was held in Mrs. Dickens's name from Michaelmas, 1823, to Lady Day, 1824.) Charles was then called upon to distribute around the district numerous circulars advertising the location and the advantages of his mother's school. But evidently nobody came, and Dickens did not remember any preparations having been made to accommodate pupils if any had come. Forster pointed out that Christopher Huffam was to have used his influence to entice a nucleus

[32]Langton, *Childhood and Youth*, p. 63; Kitton, *The Dickens Country*, pp. 20, 23, 25; but cf. Johnson, *Charles Dickens*, I, 24–6; and note that the rate-books show Oct. 8, 1823, for John Dickens's occupancy of 16 Bayham Street. Then cf. Dexter, *Letters*, II, 777 f.

[33]Cf. "I call my boyhood's home Dullborough. . . . I left it in a stage coach. . . . There was no other inside passenger, and I consumed my sandwiches in solitude and dreariness, and it rained hard all the way, and I thought life sloppier than I had expected to find it."

[34]Christmas story for 1859.

[35]Forster, *Life, passim*.

of pupils, but at this point he became bankrupt.[36] Dickens remembered that often there was "not too much for dinner," and that finally his "father was arrested."[37] The blow had fallen. It was followed by the many miserable struggles of the family and the endless pawning of their possessions, even of the precious books which Charles carried to the drunken bookseller. Once again we are given evidence of the boy's rudimentary learning,[38] for the pawnbroker always liked to hear him conjugate a Latin verb while the clerk was making out the duplicate pawn ticket.

The account of the confinement of Dickens's father in the Marshalsea is well known. Following the fortunes of the boy, now twelve years old, we find him maintaining himself at daily work in a blacking-factory which was under the management of James Lamert. The boy's wages were 6 or 7 shillings a week. His work, when one considers the revelations of the Children's Employment Commission, was not very strenuous, if somewhat monotonous. Many years later, Dickens himself described it in the following words: "My work was to cover the pots of paste-blacking; first with a piece of oil-paper, and then with a piece of blue paper; to tie them round with a string; and then to clip the paper close and neat, all round, until it looked as smart as a pot of ointment from an apothecary's shop. When a certain number of grosses of pots had attained this pitch of perfection, I was to paste on each a printed label; and then go on again with more pots."[39] That his parents were not as unmindful of the boy's education as both Forster and Dickens would have us believe is shown by the arrangements which were made with Lamert to give him some instruction every day from twelve to one o'clock, as Dickens noted in the fragment of autobiography which he gave Forster. Apparently, however, this agreement was not carried out for any great length of time.

The vital point to be noted concerning this experience of Dickens in the blacking-warehouse is the serious mental suffering which he endured. The monotony of the task was oppressive to a sensitive and imaginative boy. The feeling of utter neglect, the crushed hopes for further schooling, the miserable Sundays spent at the Marshalsea, the lonely meals of bread, cheese, and beer, his gnawing hunger as he looked at the pineapples on Covent market on the days when he had no money for dinner, and the secret shame he felt over his menial position seemed to squeeze the joy of life from his heart. Alphonse Daudet, who is often called the French Dickens, and who, similarly, began to earn his daily bread very early in

[36]Lindsay, *Charles Dickens*, p. 49.
[37]Forster, *Life*, I, 50.
[38]*Ibid.*, p. 54.   [39]*Ibid.*, p. 61.

life, said of his boyhood: "I felt in my heart the love which Dickens felt for the unfortunate and the poor, and for childhoods spent in the wretchedness of large cities."[40] There is little doubt that, looking back, in later life, to the days of the blacking-warehouse, Dickens pitied every unfortunate child.

Having said all this, however, one feels that Dickens indulged a little too much in self-pity. Many an apprentice in the textile mills of Manchester or down in the pits of Staffordshire began work at a much earlier age, had no schooling whatever, and certainly endured much more abuse.[41] The reason the blow fell so heavily on Charles was that until then he had not experienced very much hardship. It is scarcely surprising that he suffered spells of depression and physical weakness. As André Maurois has remarked, no one "can suffer as a child suffers."[42] But though Charles was a bookish, imaginative, and extremely sensitive child, he cannot be accused of lacking grit. He determined to go on doing his work well. Probably Chesterton came near the truth when he described him as a boy of the type whom "anybody can hurt, but nobody can kill."[43] So well did he learn his task and so dexterous did he become that he and another boy, Bob Fagin, were a sort of window advertisement; they worked near the light, and the passers-by would stop to watch their nimble fingers tying up the blacking-pots.[44]

Mrs. Dickens and the younger children were eventually forced to live in the Marshalsea with Mr. Dickens, and Charles went to live with "a reduced old lady" named Mrs. Roylance. She is of interest here because she has generally been accepted as the original Mrs. Pipchin, that "child queller" of *Dombey and Son*. She "took children into board, and had once done so at Brighton. . . . She had a little brother and sister under her care, . . . and a widow's little son."[45]

Exactly how long Dickens worked at the blacking-factory is not clear. He entered it, close to his twelfth birthday, shortly before his father was committed to the Marshalsea in February, 1824. His father was discharged from the prison on May 28 of the same year, and very shortly after, following a quarrel between the boy's master and his father, young Charles was removed from the factory. The period therefore could hardly have been much longer than five months or so.[46]

[40]Kitton, *Charles Dickens*, p. 16.
[41]Midland Mining Commission, 1843, First Report, *Parliamentary Papers*, XIII, 1843.
[42]*Dickens*, p. 12.
[43]*Charles Dickens*, p. 59.
[44]Forster, *Life*, I, 82.   [45]*Ibid.*, p. 65.
[46]Dexter, "Charles Dickens One Hundred Years Ago," pp. 12–17.

Although Charles's mother was anxious that he should return to the warehouse—something for which he never forgave her—his father determined that he should go back to school. And go he did. This second period of schooling lasted over two years, perhaps into the first quarter of 1827. Charles was probably about twelve and a half years old when he began to attend Wellington House Academy, a school kept by a Mr. Jones on the corner of Granby Street and Hampstead Road. There is little doubt that reminiscences of this school are to be found in Salem House of *David Copperfield,* in Dotheboys Hall of *Nicholas Nickleby,* and in the establishment of Doctor Blimber in *Dombey and Son.* In his autobiographical notes, Dickens gives a glimpse of his entrance upon his studies at Mr. Jones's academy.[47] His father had sent him to the school to inquire for a "card of terms," and when Charles arrived he discovered Mr. Jones in the act of carving the roast for dinner. Mr. Jones promptly placed a card in the boy's hand and piously remarked that he hoped Dickens "would become a pupil." Dickens in his account briefly remarks: "I did. At seven o'clock one morning, very soon afterwards, I went as a day scholar to Mr. Jones's establishment. . . ."[48]

According to Dr. Henry Danson, who was one of Dickens's schoolmates at Mr. Jones's Wellington House Academy, the school "was most shamefully mismanaged, and the boys made very little progress. The proprietor, Mr. Jones, was a Welshman; a most ignorant fellow, and a mere tyrant, whose chief employment was to scourge the boys."[49] Another schoolmate, Mr. Owen Thomas, agreed with Dr. Danson that the principal, like the headmaster whom Dickens later described in "Our School," was "always ruling ciphering-books with a bloated mahogany ruler, smiting the palms of offenders with the same diabolical instrument," or caning the boys unmercifully.[50] It may be remarked that day-scholars such as Dickens were likely to have received more lenient treatment in this regard than the boarders, and indeed, one of his schoolmates gave evidence to that effect: "I do not think that he [Dickens] came in for any of Mr. Jones's scourging propensity; in fact, together with myself, he was only a day pupil, and with these there was the wholesome fear of tales being carried home to the parents."[51]

Music appears to have formed part of the curriculum, for Mr. John Bowden, another schoolfellow, recalled that Charles took violin lessons in the front room of Jones's school, and further, that the English master, Mr. Taylor, was "a constant flute player."[52] Some of the pupils, at least,

[47]Forster, *Life,* I, 91.
[48]*Ibid.*
[49]*Ibid.,* p. 100.
[50]*Ibid.,* pp. 91–5.
[51]*Ibid.,* p. 100.
[52]Langton, *Childhood and Youth,* p. 89.

were taught foreign languages. Owen Thomas remembered a French master, and also a Latin master named Mr. Manville. Dickens's schoolmates, however, did not agree as to whether he studied Latin or not. Thomas affirmed that Dickens did study Latin.[53] Dr. Danson insisted that Dickens did not.[54] Later evidence, however, supports Thomas. In a letter to the Camden and Kentish Town *Gazette*, January, 1872, a certain "R.S." of Kentish Town, whose father was said to have been a junior master at Jones's academy, testified that Dickens certainly won a prize for Latin, and that this was all the more remarkable because it was usually the boy with three or more brothers as prospective pupils who took the prizes.[55] Further, there is another extant letter, dated July 18, 1904, written to Mr. T. Wright by Mr. R. Shiers, son of *the* Shiers who, as tutor, apparently coached Dickens in Latin. According to this letter, Dickens certainly won a prize in Latin, and in appreciation tendered his tutor a small gift in the form of a copy of the works of Horace. According to Wright, this volume was exhibited at the Dickens Exhibition in 1904.[56]

It is obvious then, that in spite of that "bloated mahogany ruler," there was another side to the picture. Dickens regained his enthusiasm and youthful spirits. He is depicted in a jaunty pepper-and-salt jacket, writing and telling stories, editing his class paper, and participating in productions of plays with the aid of elaborate scenery painted by a schoolmate named Beverley, who later became a well-known artist. Charles played pranks on elderly ladies in the streets, frolicked during the church service, and enjoyed keeping white mice at school.[57] His broken heart and the blacking-warehouse appeared to have vanished as if waved airily aside by a fairy wand.

Because of these brighter glimpses, there is something to be said for the comment of Matchett: "Let us be fair to Jones!" And there is the inscription on Jones's tombstone in the old St. Pancras churchyard which makes reference to his many years as "master of a respectable school in this parish," to "the inflexible integrity of his character," and to his "social and domestic virtues."[58] To this rather pious testimony, one might add that the discipline, if severe on occasion, was tempered with sufficient laxity to permit the keeping of white mice, clandestinely, in the pupils' desks. Even from a modern pedagogical view, the school had

[53]*Ibid.*, p. 88. [54]Forster, *Life*, I, 100.
[55]Matchett, "Dickens at Wellington House Academy," pp. 76–86.
[56]Wright, *The Life of Charles Dickens*, pp. 44 f. See also Dexter, ed., *Letters*, I, 169.
[57]Forster, *Life*, I, 95–100.
[58]Matchett, "Dickens at Wellington House Academy," pp. 76–86.

many fine features, such as the class paper, the writing and presentation of plays, the building of model coaches, and the making of miniature boats.[59]

Speculation naturally arises as to whether Dickens meant his article entitled "Our School" (which originally appeared in *Household Words* on October 11, 1851),[60] to be a faithful description of Giles's school in Chatham, of Jones's school in London, or of some other school, real or imaginary. Information concerning the location, which might narrow our speculation, is not conclusive. As if to tantalize the investigator, a vague reference is made in the article to the progress of transportation, in the course of which the school building was demolished to provide a right of way for the railroad. The article opens as follows: "We went to look at it only this past summer, and found that the railroad had cut it up root and branch. A great trunk line had swallowed the playground, sliced away the schoolroom, and pared off the corner of the house." In Forster's description of Giles's school we read: "It was in the boys' playing ground near Clover Lane in which the school stood. . . . Nor was it the least of the disappointments of his [Dickens's] visit in after life to the scenes of his boyhood that he found this playfield had been swallowed up by a railway station."[61] A hasty investigator might well conclude that "our school" was Giles's school. However, when this description is placed beside the words of Dickens in which he described Wellington House Academy—"I went as a day scholar to Mr. Jones's establishment, which was in Mornington Place, and had its schoolroom sliced away by the Birmingham railway, when that change came about"[62] —it is readily seen that "our school" could be either Giles's or Jones's.

The trenchant criticism to which Dickens subjected the headmaster in "Our School" carries the mind back to his days at Wellington House Academy, and also to the teachers portrayed in his novels. Mr. Owen Thomas testified that Jones was not only the original of this sketch,[63] but was also the prototype of Mr. Creakle of Salem House.[64] It should be pointed out, however, that there is no similarity between Mr. Jones and Creakle in respect of personal appearance—Mr. Jones was rather handsome, whereas Creakle was notably plain; but there is a link between Creakle and the master of "Our School"—Creakle is described

[59]Forster, *Life*, I, 102; Langton, *Childhood and Youth*, p. 90.

[60]All quotations (unless otherwise stated) are from "Our School" in *Reprinted Pieces*.

[61]Forster, *Life*, I, 37. [62]*Ibid.*, p. 91.

[63]*Ibid.*, p. 94.

[64]*David Copperfield*, chaps. v–vii. See chap. iii below, for a discussion of Salem House.

as having been a hop-dealer before he took up schoolmastering, and the master of "Our School" as having been in the leather trade. In "Our School," the principal was pilloried as follows:

The master was supposed among us to know nothing, and one of the ushers was supposed to know everything. We are still inclined to think the first-named supposition perfectly correct. . . . The only branches of education with which he showed the least acquaintance were ruling and corporally punishing. He was always ruling ciphering-books with a bloated mahogany ruler, or smiting the palms of offenders with the same diabolical instrument, or viciously drawing a pair of pantaloons tight with one of his large hands, and caning the wearer with the other. We have no doubt whatever that this occupation was the principal solace of his existence.

The viciousness of the headmaster is also revealed in another little incident, as we shall see in a moment.

In addition to the headmaster, "our school" had two ushers: a Latin master and an English master. Actually, the English master was also writing master, mathematics master, and general assistant. He was paid the generous tribute of having "a good knowledge of boys." Because of his gentlemanly manners he was always chosen to visit the homes of the sick boys. "A bony, gentle-faced, clerical-looking young man in rusty black," he was supposed to know everything, and gave vent to his musical propensities by blowing, in the evenings, an old trombone, part of which was apparently missing. It may be remembered that the English master at Jones's school "was a constant flute player."[65]

Striking as it is, this sketch of the English master is not so vivid as that of the Latin master, who was a short-sighted, feeble hunchback, carrying a crutch. Dickens described this man as being "always cold, and always putting onions in his ears for deafness, and always disclosing ends of flannel under all his garments, and almost always applying a ball of pocket handkerchief to some part of his face with a screwing action round and round." But there was no complaint against his scholarship, since he "took great pains where he saw intelligence and desire to learn: otherwise, perhaps not." The following incident possibly refers to the "otherwise" type of schoolboy, and reveals the character of both usher and principal in contrast. Dickens tells of remembering

. . . with terror how he [the usher] fell asleep one sultry afternoon with the little smuggled class before him, and awoke not when the footsteps of the Chief fell heavy on the floor; how the Chief aroused him, in the midst of a dread silence, and said, "Mr. Blinkins, are you ill sir?" how he blushingly replied, "Sir, rather so," how the Chief retorted with severity, "Mr. Blinkins,

[65]Langton, *Childhood and Youth*, p. 89.

this is no place to be ill in" (which was very, very true), and walked back solemn as the ghost in Hamlet, until catching a wandering eye, he caned that boy for inattention, and happily expressed his feelings towards the Latin master through the medium of a substitute.

Mr. Owen Thomas not only assured Langton that "the Chief" was a portrait of Mr. Jones, but also that the usher depicted as "the clerical-looking young man" was Mr. Taylor, the English master there; and that the second usher (portrayed with the "ends of flannel") represented, with some heightened colour, Mr. Manville, the Latin master of the same school.⁶⁶ This evidence concerning the teachers, therefore, appears conclusive.

In regard to the studies which were carried on, Dickens mentions in the article the subjects taught by those masters just discussed, and asserts, in addition, that he was old enough to enter the class which was studying Virgil, and also that he won prizes for his scholarship. "Our School" also mentions a fat little dancing-master who taught hornpipes, and a dapper little French master, owner of the "handleless umbrella," who, when provoked, would, like Becky Sharp in Thackeray's *Vanity Fair*, confound his superiors with the volubility of his French, to which their ignorance of the language rendered any reply impossible. One of the ushers is also represented as having a knowledge of Italian. This evidence in regard to the studies is not as conclusive as the evidence in regard to the masters, but it at least suggests that this part of the description was also based on Jones's school.

From the boys who were ostensibly intent upon these studies, five were selected as being worthy of special mention in the article "Our School." There was the boy at first designated "Mr." and later named Dumbledon, who enjoyed steaks and currant wine in the parlour, and always insisted on coffee and rolls for breakfast. This special treatment extended to his studies, which were conducted according to his inclinations—and his inclinations were very slight. The home of his fabulously wealthy parents was situated in some far-off corner of the world, vaguely associated with the sea, storms, sharks, and coral reefs. Dickens's description of this pupil, who vanished as suddenly as he appeared, catches a child-like enthusiasm as he recalls "an idiotic goggle-eyed boy, with a big head and half-crowns without end, who suddenly appeared as a parlour boarder, and was rumoured to have come by sea from some mysterious part of the earth where his parents rolled in gold." In his letter to Langton about Wellington House Academy, Thomas said, "Amongst the boarders were three Keys, and their sisters, mulattos, the latter, of course, under Mrs.

⁶⁶*Ibid.*, p. 86.

Jones's care. They were children, it was understood, of parents who resided in India."[67] To Langton's suggestion that the brother and sister Landless in *Edwin Drood* are modelled after the Keys,[68] the guess is added here that Dumbledon, described above, has some connection with the Keys; and it is interesting to note that Toots of the famous Doctor Blimber's Establishment in *Dombey and Son* also has some similarities to Dumbledon. Some other pupils mentioned in "Our School," such as the mulatto, and the boys known as "Holiday-stoppers" whose parents lived in India, also appear to be faint echoes of the Keys. No further light has been shed on three other pupils whom Dickens recalled in the article—the curly-haired son of a viscount, the young man with a silver watch and a wonderful knife, and the boy who was born on the twenty-ninth of February.

It may be recalled that the pupils at Wellington House wrote and performed tragedies, and kept various pets in their desks; it may also be remembered that Dickens wrote plays and the boy Beverley painted the required scenery. There is therefore little doubt about the school Dickens had in mind when he wrote:

Our School was remarkable for white mice. Redpolls, linnets, and even canaries were kept in desks, drawers, hat boxes, and other strange refuges for birds; but white mice were the favourite stock. The boys trained the mice much better than the masters trained the boys. We recall one white mouse, who ran up ladders, drew Roman chariots, shouldered muskets, turned wheels, and even made a very creditable appearance on the stage as the Dog of Montargis. He might have achieved even greater things but for having the misfortune to mistake his way in a triumphal procession to the Capitol, where he fell into a deep inkstand, and was dyed black and drowned.

Dickens closed his article with the picture of an old serving-man called Phil, who had a genuine contempt for learning, was a sort of mechanical genius, and had a heart of gold. Reputed never to smile except when he was toasted at the holiday break, when he "would slowly carve a grin out of his wooden face," he is recorded to have "nursed all the sick boys of his own accord, and was like a mother to them." (Phil Squod of *Bleak House*, who so tenderly nursed Jo, the crossing-sweeper, comes to mind.) Since it has been ascertained that such a person actually lived at Chatham during Dickens's residence at Ordnance Terrace,[69] Dickens may have had Giles's school in mind in this instance.

This detailed analysis of "Our School" reveals that the description does contain authentic reminiscences of Dickens's own schooldays, at

[67]*Ibid.*, p. 87. [68]*Ibid.*
[69]*Ibid.*, p. 91.

both Giles's and Jones's school. The brief references to a dame school and to one or two other pupils, such as the boy with the wonderful knife, are matters for speculation. The disagreement among former school-fellows over minor details shows elusive memory playing around the facts. Did Dickens believe that he was drawing a faithful picture of his own schooldays? Did his memory, so greatly intensified by the power of his imagination, bewitch minor details, and simply heighten and colour the picture? His account appears a curious mixture of fact and fancy, but judging from accounts of the schools of nineteenth-century England, it cannot be said to have been much overdrawn. It is, rather, a fairly accurate picture of conditions likely to have been found in some of the best schools.

Furthermore, there is in this article none of that fierce indignation and bitter satire, so prevalent elsewhere in Dickens's novels, on the subject of schools and school life. On the contrary, a lightness of touch and a playful humour pervade the whole article. One recalls such touches as that of Miss Frost, the proprietor of the "preparatory school" over the dyer's shop, holding her pinafore over the heads of the impressionable Dickens and the unmannerly Mawls while she whispers to them about somebody being "screwed down" in a coffin; and, at the other school, the triumphal procession of the mouse to the Capitol, the confusion of the headmaster in his inability to speak French, and Mr. Blinkins's ill-timed nap. Even that diabolical ruler causes a wry smile. Humour always entered the schools of Dickens, even if it had to go around by the back door; but it has a twilight softness here, especially in the wistful memory of Phil slowly carving a grin from his "wooden face," Phil who was a "mother to them." There is more optimism than pessimism in Dickens's closing sentence, that the world "had little reason to be proud of Our School, and has done much better since in that way, and will do far better yet." It suggests that Dickens has related in retrospect as authentic an account of his own schooldays as a person of his imaginative character could do.

We may profitably follow the experiences of Dickens a little beyond his actual attendance at school, for those factors which mould a man's character, which develop his talents, inspire his ideals, and best fit him for life, obviously extend far beyond mere rudimentary instruction in the three R's. Moreover, in the past, far too much has been made of Dickens's experience in the blacking-warehouse, and not nearly enough of the insecurity which he experienced within his boyhood home, and of the fickleness and snobbery to which he was subjected as soon as he moved out into the workaday world in his early teens.

The precise date on which Dickens left Wellington House Academy to enter employment is not definitely known. We do know, however, that he was employed as an office boy in the law firm of Ellis and Blackmore from May, 1827, to November, 1828.[70] It may be noted in this connection that there is extant, in the Widener Library at Harvard University, a petty cash book which Dickens kept during his tenure at the law firm, the first entry of which is dated January 5, 1828. About that time Dickens purchased a copy of Gurney's *Brachygraphy*, and apparently under the direction of his uncle, John Barrow,[71] a reporter on the staff of *The Times* and of the *Morning Chronicle*, he began to study shorthand with great vigour. In mastering this accomplishment, as he had done by the time he left Ellis and Blackmore, Dickens appears to have been following in his father's footsteps.[72]

Dickens then joined a distant cousin, Tom Charlton, in the sharing of a reporters' box, and shared with one of the proctors, Charles Fenton, the expenses of renting a room in the Consistory Court as a transcribing office. There, as a free-lance reporter, among the bewigged doctors who held a cosy and exclusive control over wills, ships, and vestries, Dickens waited for business in Doctors' Commons.[73] He spent two years or so in that sort of work prior to joining the staff of the *True Sun*, as a reporter, in March, 1832. Then, about this time, possibly on August 7, 1832, he became a parliamentary reporter for the *Mirror of Parliament*, edited by John Barrow.[74] A little later, probably in August, 1834, he was appointed reporter to the *Morning Chronicle*[75] through the recommendation of Thomas Beard, and stayed in that position until the end of 1836.[76]

[70]Forster recorded as well that Dickens was employed for a short period of time in the law office of Charles Molloy of 6 Symonds Inn. It would appear logical to assume that the boy left school at Easter, went to work for Molloy, and then a few weeks later entered the office of Ellis and Blackmore. Carlton insists, however, that Dickens went to Molloy *after* he worked for Ellis and Blackmore rather than before. Cf. Langton, *Childhood and Youth*, p. 94; Dexter, ed., *Letters*, I, 29–31; and Carlton, "Charles Dickens," p. 58.

[71]Dexter, ed., *Letters*, II, 42–4.

[72]Langton, *Childhood and Youth*, p. 97.

[73]Dexter, "Charles Dickens: Journalist," pp. 705 f.; see further, Carlton, *Charles Dickens: Shorthand Writer*.

[74]Dexter, "Charles Dickens: Journalist," p. 706; but cf. Johnson, *Life*, I, 61.

[75]Dickens, in a letter to Collins, mentions the *Mirror* and *Chronicle* only (Dexter, ed., *Letters*, II, 777); Dexter thought that Forster confused the *True Sun* with the *Morning Chronicle* (Dexter, "Dickens and the 'Morning Chronicle,'" pp. 591–8); whereas G. G. Grubb makes out a case for Dickens's having worked on the staff of the *Mirror*, then concurrently on both the *Mirror* and the *True Sun*, then on the *Mirror* exclusively, and finally on the staff of the *Morning Chronicle* (Grubb, "Charles Dickens: Journalist," pp. 138 ff.).

[76]Dexter, "Dickens and the 'Morning Chronicle,'" p. 593. The resignation is dated Nov. 5, 1836; cf. Johnson, *Life*, I, 95.

There are scattered accounts of these reporting days in Dickens's letters to his friends (Wilkie Collins for instance), in which he says that, after a couple of years in the law office where "he didn't much like it," he gave himself over to studying to be "a first-rate parliamentary reporter," and that when he gave up reporting, after the publication of *Pickwick*, he left behind a reputation "of being the best and the most rapid reporter ever known."[77] In a speech at New York, he paid tribute to the value of his newspaper training, and his pride in having reached this first rung on the ladder of success. In another address to the Newspaper Press, he gave some reminiscences of his reporting days, telling how he had "often transcribed for the printer, from my shorthand notes, important public speeches in which the strictest accuracy was required . . . writing on the palm of my hand, by the light of a dark-lantern in a post-chaise and four, galloping through a wild country, and through the dead of the night. . . ."[78] He was referring, of course, to those occasions when his paper sent him from London to all parts of the country to cover the speeches of various parliamentary leaders; the speeches had to be fully taken down in shorthand, transcribed later, and since there was no telegraph, then taken by coach to London. In the same address, Dickens humorously described the manner in which two fellow reporters held a handkerchief as a sort of canopy over his notebook to protect it from the rain, as he took down an important speech by Lord John Russell. He complained, moreover, of wearing out his knees with his notebook in the old House of Lords.[79] A letter to Forster, in 1845, described how he had to charge for a new overcoat destroyed "from the drippings of a wax candle, in writing through the smallest hours of the night in a swift-flying carriage and pair."[80]

Dickens clearly spent something like five years in legal offices and courts of the law, and something like another four years as a reporter in the parliamentary gallery or on election circuits. What an education that must have been! Even a casual glance at Hansard for those years, or a brief examination of one of those ponderous three-volumed Victorian biographies, say the biography of Henry Brougham, would reveal a gallaxy of powerful personalities and a solid amount of epoch-making legislation. Consider some of the personalities whom Dickens watched at that time: such men as Brougham, Cobbett, Lord John Russell, Sir Robert Peel, Nassau Senior, Lord Grey, Stanley, Gladstone, O'Connell, the Duke of Wellington, Macaulay, Bulwer-Lytton, Palmerston, Lord

[77]Dexter, ed., *Letters*, II, 777 f.; I, 168 f.

[78]Shepherd, ed., *Speeches*, p. 247.

[79]*Ibid.*, p. 248.   [80]Cf. Forster, *Life*, I, 23.

Melbourne, Lord Althorp, and many another. And then reflect on some of the debates to which he presumably listened—debates on the Reform Bill, the New Poor Law, the abolition of slavery, factory reform, the India Act, the Municipal Reform Act, grants-in-aid to education, taxes on newspapers, disturbances in Ireland, and conditions in the Canadas. Where is the college graduate who would not envy such an opportunity?

The books which Dickens read as a boy in that "little room upstairs" and the list in *David Copperfield* have already been mentioned. His love of Shakespeare, Addison, and Goldsmith took him, as soon as he had reached the regulation age of eighteen, to the British Museum where his name appears on the books for February 8, 1830.[81] T. W. Hill has compiled another lengthy list of books which Dickens is known to have read in the course of his life. Among them one would find Goldsmith's *History of England*; the works of Addison; those of Monboddo, *Lights and Shadows of Scottish Life*; Goldsmith's *Bee*; Berges's *The Roman Senate, The Dance of Death*; Moore's *Lalla Rookh*; Byron's *Don Juan* and his *Childe Harold*; Sterne's *Sentimental Journey*; Belzoni's *Explorations*; Ross's *Voyages*; *The Newgate Calendar*; *State Trials*; and Scott's *Demonology*;[82] and to this list may be added Tennyson's *Idylls of the King*, mentioned by Miss Boyle.[83] We are told, moreover, that in his youth, with his friend Wiffin, a silversmith apprentice, Dickens carried home armfuls of sensational novels from a little circulating library in Fetter Lane.[84]

Dickens also had a consuming interest in the drama as witness his make-believe at home, his recitations at the Mitre Inn, and his writing and acting of plays at school. His many biographers have noted his haunting of the theatres of Covent Garden and of Surrey, his amateur corps of dramatists, his "knocking up a chaunt or two" with friend Kolle, Beard, or Longhurst,[85] not to mention his very extensive and successful dramatic performances in later life.

Simultaneously with his newspaper reporting, Dickens had at least two other experiences in the school of hard knocks which deeply affected him. His friend Kolle was engaged to Anne Beadnell, the second daughter of a bank manager, and through Kolle, Dickens met the Beadnell

[81]C. W. Charlton, one of the guarantors for this venture, was married to an aunt of Dickens's mother, and kept a boarding-house at 16 Berners Street, where Mr. Blackmore of Ellis and Blackmore had once been a resident. Langton, *Childhood and Youth*, pp. 61, 102; Wright, *Life*, pp. 46 f., 51, 61.

[82]Hill, "Books That Dickens Read," pp. 81–90.

[83]Boyle, *Mary Boyle: Her Book*, p. 240.

[84]Lindsay, *Charles Dickens*, pp. 98 f.

[85]Dexter, ed., *Letters*, I, 7–11; II, 17 f. See also Pemberton, *Charles Dickens and the Stage*; Fawcett, *Dickens the Dramatist*.

family. All three Beadnell girls were musical, and Kolle and Dickens were frequent visitors at their home in Lombard Street, singing to the girls' instrumental accompaniment. Charles fell in love with the youngest daughter, Maria. The Beadnells, however, considered that Dickens had no prospects, and may even have been shrewd enough to discover his family background. Maria, for her part, appears to have been indulging in flirtation, and, aided by her family's astuteness in putting the English Channel between her and an unwanted suitor, she provoked Dickens into withdrawing his attentions.[86] As is well known, Maria appears in *David Copperfield* as Dora and in *Little Dorrit* as Flora Finching; in the interval between the two portrayals she had married and grown stout— changed from a fragile slender lily into a plump peony. Dickens's father was having trouble with bankers, too, but it was trouble of a far different nature. When his creditors pressed him too sharply, John Dickens would disappear for a time, leaving Charles to deal with the creditors as best he could. Charles had to resort to borrowing money from his friend Mitton to settle their claims. On other occasions when Shaw and Maxwell, "the quondam wine people," reached into the pockets of the father through the son, Dickens resorted to his friend Beard for money. The family home was broken up again, and Charles took his brother Fred into his own lodgings.[87] The experience of seeing his love affair ended by snobbery and his advancement in life continually hindered by his family's pecuniary difficulties made a profound impression on Dickens.

There were, obviously, other moulding influences. Who can estimate, for instance, the influence of his many friendships? One recalls such friends as Talfourd, Macready, Mark Lemon, Hullah, Stanfield, Delane, Forster, Hans Andersen, Carlyle, Lady Blessington, Lady Holland, Count D'Orsay, Angela Coutts, Sydney Smith, John Black, Thomas Beard, Harrison Ainsworth, Landor, and Bulwer-Lytton—to name only a few. There were, also, the broadening effects of two visits to America, and the cultural enrichments derived from lengthy periods of residence in France, Italy, and Switzerland. Reluctantly, these later influences are dismissed, and we turn to an appraisal of Dickens's education.

What were the effects on Dickens of his education, both formal and informal? From his mother and aunt, as we have seen, he acquired an early love of reading; from his father and others, a delight in elocution and dramatics. During his schooldays at Chatham he caught the possibilities for good in the qualities of a good schoolmaster such as Giles, as well as the stimulus of good books and amateur theatricals. From his experiences, between that rainy day when he left Chatham in the damp

---

[86]Dexter, ed., *Letters*, I, 16–24.   [87]*Ibid.*, I, 33, 35 f.

straw in the stage-coach until the day that he was sent to Mr. Jones's academy to get a card of terms, he acquired a consciousness of insecurity.[88] There was a sense of being cast off by his sister, Fanny, who had won a place in an academy of music, and of being rejected by his family-ridden mother and debt-harassed father. An all-pervading sense of loneliness seemed to oppress him. It was never thrown off. Out of this poverty-stricken period developed his sympathy for the poor, and for neglected children. Moreover, at Jones's school he had observed, in sharp contrast to the kindness and sound scholarship of Mr. Giles, the wretchedness inflicted on schoolboys by harsh schoolmasters. It is important to remember that Dickens had experienced these things and made all these observations while he was a young boy. It is important to remember also that his recourse to reading and theatricals as a refuge from unhappiness taught him to appreciate their value.

Dickens, then, had already learned much, at home, at school, in the warehouse, and on the streets, before he entered the law offices as a clerk. There he learned the delays and the confusions of the law, the insolence of office, and the petty tyranny of authority. It was probably from his Uncle John Barrow's tutorship in shorthand and his own experience in Doctors' Commons that Dickens learned to work hard and, unlike his ne'er-do-well father, to husband his earnings. From his experiences with the Beadnell family, he learned to recognize the snobbishness too often associated with mere money, as well as something of feminine fickleness. To this bitter lesson of humiliation was added the pressure of his father's debts. Still later, from his journalism and his work in the parliamentary gallery, Dickens learned resourcefulness, self-reliance, and responsibility. And although in all his writings there are very few words in favour of parliamentary government as he saw it, Dickens learned that reform is more easily achieved by appealing to men's emotions, humour, and imagination rather than by appealing exclusively to their intellects.

Shall we contend, in conclusion, that Dickens was well educated? Andrew Lang considered him neither a scholarly nor a well-read man.[89] Mowbray Morris, while admitting that a more scholarly background would have added little to Dickens's genius, thought that it would have saved him from some of his faults.[90] An anonymous critic opines that

[88]Wilson, "Dickens: The Two Scrooges" in his *Eight Essays*, p. 15, considered that the warehouse experiences produced a trauma from which Dickens suffered all his life; Symons, *Charles Dickens*, pp. 26 f., thought that Dickens showed manic-depressive traits.

[89]"Andrew Lang on Dickens," pp. 59–63.

[90]See his "Charles Dickens," pp. 762–79.

it was Dickens's lack of knowledge which led him to deal unfairly with government and the upper classes.[91] George Bernard Shaw snapped: "Compared to Goethe, he is almost a savage."[92] It is true that Dickens did not have the educational advantages of a cultured Victorian home. He had some knowledge of the classics, but certainly he was not steeped in the literature of Greece and Rome. He had neither the advantages of a grammar school nor of a college education. His views of government, in spite of his opportunity to watch its workings at close range, showed, as we shall see, a lack of historical perspective.

We should remember, however, that Dickens did not engage in literary pursuits solely for leisure, he did not write expressly for scholars, or even exclusively for cultured circles. His heroes were not aristocratic gentlemen, but people of the lower orders; indeed, more often than not, his heroes were bastard children. It may even be said that the disciplined thought of the philosopher, the nuances of the trained mind, the more subtle complexities of administration, the careful weighing of historical evidence—all appeared to be beyond his horizon. Yet his education had been such that it peculiarly fitted him for his life's work. He had learned, as we have seen, self-reliance, determination, the necessity of hard work, the acceptance of responsibility, the value of security, and the isolating effects of sharp social contrasts. He had taught himself order, method, and punctuality. He had developed secret springs which gave him a flowing well of sympathy for children and the poor, a powerful river of imagination, and an ocean of humour. Even Shaw was forced to add, grudgingly, that Dickens was "by the pure force of his genius one of the greatest writers in the world."

These advantages and disadvantages of Dickens's own education affected his views on schools and education, his writings related thereto, and his contributions to the advancement of education. Aided by this knowledge of his schooling and background, we now turn to the delineations of school life in his novels and short stories.

[91]"The License of Modern Novelists," pp. 124–56.
[92]"Charles Dickens," p. 103.

CHAPTER II

Education through Church and Charity

The wide variety and frequent overlapping of recognized types of schools in Dickens's day make it difficult to decide where elementary education leaves off and secondary education begins, and whether a particular school should be identified as a grammar school, a charity school, or a monitorial school. The same problem arises in deciding on a method of reviewing and identifying the kinds of schools described by Dickens in his novels and short stories. The least arbitrary method seemed to be to group the nineteenth-century schools and Dickens's numerous and scattered depictions of them according to the agencies responsible for their administration and according to the purpose envisaged for them.

Charity schools, which provided meagre education for the very poor, included a wide variety of institutions variously known as parochial, ward, industrial, workhouse, hospital, free, catechetical, Sunday, and evening schools. In the sixteenth and seventeenth centuries, the founders of the grammar schools had hoped that even the poorest boy, who had the necessary leisure and ability, might participate in classical studies; yet these same founders did not dream of educating the mass of the people. By the time of Queen Anne, however, zealous churchmen were beginning to devise ways and means of increasing the membership of the church; and, since the imparting of religious knowledge to the poorer classes seemed to be an effective way of drawing them into the church, there sprang up all over England a group of schools known as charity schools, supported by both endowment and subscription, that drew boys and girls from the ranks of the labouring poor. These charity schools were also regarded as a means of social control, as garrisons of the Hanoverian régime, and as Protestant outposts against Roman Catholicism. After 1698, the charity schools of the Church of England were given both a great impetus and a loose organization by the Society for the Promotion of Christian Knowledge, usually known as the S.P.C.K.

Generally speaking, intellectual activity was not stressed, lest the poor should become discontented with their status. The teachers were instructed, instead, to inculcate principles of industry and frugality; and there were attempts, linked with practice in church ritual, to educate the poor into an acceptance of subordination and to lull them into lowly gratitude, obedience, and passivity when they were young and impressionable. The charity-school pupils were dressed in conspicuous uniforms which were a reminder, not only to themselves but also to the public, of the inferior station in life which they occupied. Dressed in this manner, they were paraded in the streets, two by two, as symbolic brands plucked from the fires of debauchery and ignorance. On Sunday mornings they were forced to sit in a body in the church gallery. On Sunday evenings, some of the crowds who flocked to church remained after the regular service to hear the charity children examined and catechized.

Throughout the week, reading and a little writing were taught; a smattering of arithmetic was meted out to the boys and a little needlework to the girls. In a few schools near the sea, potential marine apprentices were taught a little navigation. Singing, started in the earlier days, was soon snuffed out—it might lead to the sin of pride. The cost of the schools was small: a few benches, slates, and pencils served for equipment, and an old unoccupied home for a building; a teacher could be obtained at twenty pounds a year, and uniforms at sixteen shillings each, or less. Once a year, a "charity sermon" was preached, during which the charity children, branded by their picturesque uniform and the distinctive badge of their benefactor, were seared with admonitions of their duty to their betters. The offertory for the day was given to the support of these conspicuous examples of public charity, who were, as usual, arrayed in the gallery of the church for all to see.[1]

Beginning early in the eighteenth century and continuing infrequently into the nineteenth, alternate days were given over to manual training in some of these schools, which thus became known as schools of industry. Such attempts to fit the yoke of labour to the necks of the poor were not entirely new. Locke had suggested industrial schools of this type for the children of paupers. Later, the devout Mrs. Trimmer wished to extend the labour and to limit the already meagre academic instruction to the Sabbath. The idea was to make the school self-supporting through the sale of the products of the children's labour. Inevitably, the pressure to produce salable goods tended to reduce instruction in the three R's. The girls were usually taught knitting, sewing, spinning, and straw-plaiting; a few were taught to make artificial flowers. The boys were usually taught cobbling, printing, carpentry, and gardening; a few were taught to put heads on pins, and to set up machinery for carding wool. It was customary to deduct a few pence per week from each child's earnings to

[1]Jones, *The Charity School Movement*, pp. 1–60.

pay for his instruction. A child's total earnings seldom exceeded two shillings per week.[2]

Some workhouse administrators made similar attempts to use the proceeds of the labour of child inmates to cover at least part of the cost of maintenance and whatever modicum of instruction was meted out. As early as the close of the seventeenth century, as noted before, John Locke had suggested teaching the pauper children spinning, knitting, or cobbling, on an allowance of bread to which a little gruel was added in the winter. Such a "school" was conducted in the London workhouse as early as 1698, in the double hope of instilling the scriptural discipline of work and reducing the maintenance costs. Other workhouses made similar attempts to carry on a "school" but with indifferent success.

Generally speaking, the workhouse schools and schools of industry were dismal failures. It was difficult to find work suitable to the children's feeble strength or mental capacity, to find cheap materials, to eliminate the wastage resulting from their lack of skill, to secure competent instructors or to retain promising pupils, and to find a market for the inferior products of defective workmanship. As a solution to such problems, workhouse officials promoted the system of "farming out" or "apprenticing" pauper children to farmers, chimney-sweeps, undertakers, or almost anyone who would take them off the hands of the parish for a small premium. With the rise of the factory system, the workhouses were ransacked to find such "apprentices" to work in the factories and mines, as shown by the evidence of the Children's Employment Commission discussed in the Introduction to this book. Nevertheless, the Newcastle Commission found, as late as 1861, that 84 per cent of the 44,608 pauper children receiving instruction were still being taught in workhouse schools, although inmates were no longer used as teachers.[3]

The rapid industrialization gave an even greater impetus to two other recognized types of schools—apprenticeship schools and Sunday schools. A lengthy period of apprenticeship had previously been required in England to learn a trade, and indentures binding both apprentice and master customarily contained clauses requiring the master to give assurances that the apprentice would be instructed in the three R's, and that some attention would be given to his health and morals. After the rise of the factory system, such a lengthy period of apprenticeship seemed unnecessary for the unskilled tending of machines, and as a result

[2]*Ibid.*, pp. 154–62; Birchenough, *History of Elementary Education in England and Wales*, pp. 34–6, 222 f.

[3]Jones, *The Charity School Movement*, pp. 31, 34, 91–4; Adamson, *English Education*, pp. 19, 216.

apprentices no longer received personal care and supervision in a master's household.[4] As a further result, factory apprentices were ignorant, unlettered, diseased, overworked, and abused almost beyond belief, and finally these wretched conditions led to state intervention. Schools known as apprenticeship schools, in which the factory children received an hour or two of instruction each day, were then rather indifferently set up in some of the factories to conform to the legislation.[5] But the factories that acknowledged any such responsibility were few, and not until the appointment of state inspectors in 1834 to visit the factories were the regulations generally followed.

Because instruction on Sundays occasioned little interference with work in factory or mine, Sunday had come to be accepted as the day on which the poor should be given instruction in reading and in church catechism. Thus, although Sunday schools did not begin with Robert Raikes or the Industrial Revolution, it would be true to say that they were given an impetus by both. In opening his Sunday classes in 1780, Raikes of Gloucester helped to spread abroad ideas of group instruction and mass education. It was Raikes's hope that society, relieved of ignorance and Sunday idleness, would be reformed. The Bible continued to be the main text for reading, and the core of all instruction. Moreover, the theory began to be spread abroad that Sunday classes filled the total need of schooling for the poor, and, further, that such education should be very cheap and very meagre. The movement was expanded by such workers as Hannah More, Mrs. Trimmer, and William Wilberforce. Some of the Sunday schools widened the instruction to include the three R's, but Hannah More allowed no writing for the poor, and most schools confined their efforts to reading. Others began to open two or three times a week, or even daily. In this manner, the idea of a daily school for the poor was adopted and put into practice, and when the number of such schools increased so greatly that the people who had advocated them could no longer support them, the tutorial methods of Lancaster and Bell found ready acceptance, as we shall see. By the 1830's it was usually conceded that, of the six out of ten children who attended any sort of school, three attended these Protestant undenominational Sunday classes.[6]

The major voluntary effort to provide education for the poor during the nineteenth century in England, however, was made by a number of school societies which were formed through humanitarian motives, re-

[4]Brubacher, *A History of the Problems of Education*, pp. 278 f., 388 f.
[5]Health and Morals of Apprentices Act, 1802. See Introduction above.
[6]Gregory, *Robert Raikes*, pp. 50, 140 f.

ligious zeal, or denominational rivalry.[7] Our purposes here may be served by an account of two societies, the British and the National, which came into existence just shortly before Dickens was born in 1812 and were by far the largest of the group.

In the year 1798, Joseph Lancaster, then only twenty years old, opened a school for poor children at his home in Southwark. He was a Quaker, but he welcomed all the poor children of the district, no matter what their creed. In 1803, or perhaps even earlier, he published a treatise entitled *Improvements in Education*. Within the next five years, aided by three men—William Corston, Dr. Fox, and an influential scientist named William Allen—Lancaster was able to found the British and Foreign School Society, but he became involved in financial difficulties, and in 1811 a new committee had to be organized. This group of able and public-spirited men—Wilberforce, Romilly, Brougham, Whitbread, James Mill, and the Duke of Bedford, for example—began to promote non-sectarian schools, both in England and abroad, and to train some of the pupils to be teachers. Lancaster and the British Society may therefore be said to have promoted Protestant non-sectarian education in England and in this sense to have begun popular instruction. By 1851, the British Society had fifteen hundred schools and a quarter of a million pupils.[8]

The National Society for the Education of the Poor in the Principles of the Established Church had its birth in 1791 on the sands at Malabar, India, when Dr. Andrew Bell, an Anglican clergyman in charge of the Military Orphan Asylum at Madras, observed an eleven-year-old native boy named Johnnie Friskin writing in the sand with a pointed stick. Dr. Bell, struck with the possibilities of this method in teaching children to write, decided to use it in the military school, and immediately appointed some of the older pupils as monitors to use sand-writing as a method of instruction. The monitorial method, as it soon came to be described, proved so successful that it rapidly spread throughout the Madras school and was extended to subjects other than writing. Gradually, one by one, the teachers in Dr. Bell's school were dismissed, and only monitors were used as instructors.

[7]The following societies may be cited: the British and Foreign School Society, the National Society for the Education of the Poor in the Principles of the Established Church, the Wesleyan Educational Committee, the Congregational Board of Education, the Roman Catholic Poor School Society, the London School Society, the Ragged School Union, the Infant School Society, and the Home and Colonial Infant School Society.

[8]Binns, *A Century of English Education*; the statistics given are quoted in Curtis, *History of Education in Great Britain*, p. 118; reprints of three articles on the founding of the societies and the monitorial system may be found in *American Journal of Education* (Dec., 1862), 355 ff.

After Dr. Bell returned to England, he published, between the years 1797 and 1800, a treatise entitled *An Experiment in Education*. It happened that just at that time, Mrs. Trimmer became exceedingly alarmed at the inroads of the "godless schools" then becoming popular under the Lancaster system, and, in great trepidation lest the poor should be lost forever from the Anglican fold, she proceeded to fan the latent flame of denominational rivalry in a monograph entitled *A Comparative View*. Aided by the organizing ability of a Dr. Herbert Marsh of Cambridge, the services of Dr. Andrew Bell, and the writings of Mrs. Trimmer, the faithful were able by 1811 to found the National Society for the Education of the Poor in the Principles of the Established Church. The first school was opened in Baldwin Gardens, near Gray's Inn, for 600 boys and 400 girls; Rev. W. Johnson, who afterwards taught Wordsworth's children at Grasmere, was headmaster. The Church of England, no matter what its motives, had embarked on a necessary, a worthy, and a national task. By 1851, there were some seventeen thousand schools with close to a million pupils.[9] The pupils in the National schools not only received instruction in the Bible (as did those in the Lancaster schools) but also practice in the Anglican liturgy. Often church attendance was demanded as well. It should be added, however, that the Select Committee of 1816 noted that many National schools taught the catechism only, and that they demanded church attendance solely of their Anglican charges.[10]

Both societies, the British and National, administered their schools on the monitorial plan. Before their time, most instruction had been given individually, to each pupil in turn. This method was satisfactory in private schools, and with small numbers; but in large classes it was an obvious waste of time, and very expensive. Both Bell and Lancaster arranged a minute grading of rudimentary subject-matter, and then attempted to place pupils of equal attainments in groups, each group under the direction of a monitor. All the pupils of the school, sometimes as many as a thousand, were gathered together in a large building of one room, something like a barn, measuring at least one hundred feet by sixty. The arrangement of the benches in this large room varied; some schools followed the Bell system, some the Lancaster.

Under the Bell system, the benches were placed all the way around the room facing the walls, and the centre of the floor was marked off into a series of chalked squares. In each square stood a monitor and often an assistant. At the word of command, the pupils, who stood for all lessons

[9]Curtis, *History of Education in Great Britain*, p. 118, gives the statistics.
[10]Education Commission, 1816–18, *Parliamentary Papers*, IV, iii, 1818, p. 56.

except lessons in writing, would leave their benches and take their places in their respective groups in the chalked-out squares. Six, eight, or more such classes were conducted, all at the same time, under the direction of their respective monitors. The latter, equipped with a manual outlining each minute step in the lesson, mechanically guided their groups through a purely mechanical recitation, the pupils learning by rote.[11]

Under the Lancaster system the lessons were conducted on the same principle but the arrangement was different. The forms or benches were arranged in the centre of the room so as to leave a wide clear border around the walls. A series of chalked semi-circles in this border served the same purpose as the squares in the centre of the floor under the Bell system. Lancaster's groups were smaller, often numbering only eight to ten pupils, and thus more monitors were needed and there was a great deal more noise.

Everything in the monitorial schools was reduced to a system. The classes revolved like clockwork. A series of charts was hung on the walls; each chart represented a single step in the process of learning and was mastered in turn. Definite rules and signals were formulated for marching and for moving from group to group; and standard punishments were imposed for any failure to comply with the regulations. Even matters of dress were strictly regulated: the pupils' hats had to be slung on cords down their backs. And, of course, there were monitors everywhere: monitors to record attendance, to note the absentees, to accept their excuses, to dictate assignments, to record mistakes, to allot marks or grades, to dictate spelling, and so on; and there was a head monitor to supervise all the other monitors.

The monitorial schools were free at first, but they gradually began, whenever it was feasible, to charge a small fee to help defray expenses, so that eventually the charity schools again became the only free schools.

It is significant of the temper of the times, and something to be borne in mind when examining the school life depicted by Dickens, that the monitorial schools, in theory at least, were regarded as humane institutions. An examination of actual practices as revealed by Lancaster in his *Improvements in Education* shows an elaborate system of rewards and punishments which arouses mixed reactions today. The attainment of a higher position in a class, or promotion to the next class, was an inducement to work hard, but there were more particular incentives also: prize-winners were paraded from time to time with a crier at the head of the procession; medals were presented, and worn, as proof of merit; and it was the practice to decorate individual pupils with large placards,

[11]*Ibid.*, IV, i, 1816, pp. 26–34; 158, 238.

sometimes complimentary, sometimes derogatory.[12] Classroom offenders might be awarded the dunce's cap, have wooden logs tied to their necks or legs, be shackled, be yoked together and be forced to walk backwards, or be hoisted to the ceiling and suspended in a bag or basket. A dirty-faced boy might be forced to have his face washed before the whole school by a girl, who was instructed to administer a few judicious slaps across the culprit's cheeks in the process. Lancaster even tells of one incorrigible idler whose father used to chain a log to his son's foot and beat him to school every day.[13]

I repeat that we must not lose sight of the fact that these schools were administered in a spirit of charity by men who were full of sympathy for the poor and conscious of their needs, men who followed Lancaster's ideal of training pupils in moral habits conducive to the welfare of society, or Bell's ideal of training them in habits that would produce good Anglicans, good subjects, and good Christians. It is evident, nevertheless, that these schools debased the meaning of education: instruction was reduced to rule of thumb and slavish memory work; the standards were necessarily exceedingly low, for boy monitors ten years of age could provide little inspiration, and at best could possess only crude techniques.[14] There were, as I have said, various societies besides the British and the National, but the description of these two monitorial schools, and of the workhouse and charity schools already given, will suffice for an understanding of the schools of those three types that were described by Dickens in his novels and short stories.

It is a peculiar and interesting fact that the very first description of a school and its master penned by Charles Dickens was tolerant and kindly. There is not even a touch of satire in the picture of the schoolmaster in "Our Parish."[15] The old pauper schoolmaster is rather a pathetic figure who, having suffered at the hands of fortune, still dutifully carries on his work in the twilight of life, literally within the walls of the poorhouse. Unfortunate in his speculations, disappointed in public office, left destitute by a revoked will, deserted by his children, and weighed down by the death of a broken-hearted wife, he has secured this position through the influence of an old friend. He is described as "an old man now":

Meek, uncomplaining, and zealous in the discharge of his duties, he has been allowed to hold his situation long beyond the usual period; he will no doubt

[12]E.g.: "Take care of him, he bites," Copperfield's placard at Salem House.
[13]*Improvements in Education*, p. 100.
[14]Cf. Stow, *The Training System*, pp. 10–12.
[15]Written before 1836. In *Sketches by Boz*, chap. I.

continue to hold it, until infirmity renders him incapable, or death releases him. As the grey-headed old man feebly paces up and down the sunny side of the little courtyard between school hours, it would be difficult, indeed, for the most intimate of his former friends to recognize their once gay and happy associate, in the person of the pauper schoolmaster.

Judging from the historical records of most workhouse schools, the old man's charges were certainly more fortunate than most. This little-known sketch comes as a surprise to many readers of Dickens, who find in its tone of forbearance and compassion a strange contrast to the tone of satire that marks his more widely known pictures of schoolmasters. "Our Parish" calls to mind the lightness of touch and the playful humour revealed in "Our School," and it is interesting that the one, written before 1836, should have come before Dickens's severe portrayals, and the other, written in 1851, afterwards.

The complement of "Our Parish," however, is found elsewhere, in the story of *Oliver Twist*, which was begun shortly afterwards, in 1837. Dickens's description of the pauper schoolmaster in "Our Parish" shows that he knew it was a fairly common procedure to give some sort of instruction to children who were confined to the workhouse, and also to give them some work to do which would help defray the cost of their maintenance. In *Oliver Twist*, however, he makes scant reference to the fact:

"Well! You have come here to be educated, and taught a useful trade," said the red-faced gentleman in the high chair.
"So you'll begin to pick oakum to-morrow morning at six o'clock," added the surly one in the white waistcoat.

Instruction, the learning of a trade, and the provision of food, shelter, and clothing were, of course, all part of the system, and doubtless Dickens meant his readers to take them for granted.

We may profitably follow the fortunes of Oliver a little further. We see him eagerly polishing his little bowl with his huge spoon to catch "any stray splashes" of gruel that chanced to adhere to it. Dickens's sympathy with Oliver's pangs of hunger and ravenous eyes is as catching as his drollery over the "thinning" of the inmates and the size of the spoons is unexpected. The irony in this picture of slow starvation is pungent; as in the picture that follows, its asperity is relieved only by the humour which is as delightful as it is surprising. In desperation, lots were cast to see who should have the temerity to ask the master for more, and the lot fell to puny little Oliver.

The evening arrived; the boys took their places. The master, in his cook's uniform, stationed himself at the copper; his pauper assistants ranged themselves behind him; the gruel was served out; and a long grace was said over the short commons. The gruel disappeared; the boys whispered to each other, and winked at Oliver; while his next neighbors nudged him. Child as he was, he was desperate with hunger, and reckless with misery. He rose from the table; and advancing to the master, basin and spoon in hand, said: somewhat alarmed at his own temerity:

"Please, sir, I want some more."

The master was a fat, healthy man; but he turned very pale. He gazed in stupified astonishment on the small rebel for some seconds; and then clung for support to the copper. The assistants were paralyzed with wonder; the boys with fear.

"What!" said the master at length, in a faint voice.

"Please, sir," replied Oliver, "I want some more." The master aimed a blow at Oliver's head with the ladle; pinioned him in his arms; and shrieked aloud for the beadle.[16]

This is a justly famous scene; it is one of the best in Dickens. The imposing setting of the copper, the master in his apron, the group of hungry urchins, and puny little Oliver advancing, spoon and porringer in hand, make a masterly picture. The conversation has an inevitable ring: the boy's question is naked in its simplicity, like the cry of a hungry animal; the master's reply is the ejaculation of a single word of astonishment. The winks of the boys at the beginning and the shriek of the master at the close, supplied from the boundless fertility of Dickens's imagination, relieve the tension in a burst of laughter.

The upshot of this episode is that Oliver is hustled into immediate confinement, and offered as an apprentice to anyone who will take him off the hands of the beadle for five pounds. Before we are permitted to leave Oliver's educational experiences, however, we are given another glimpse of him as he is in a fair way to be apprenticed to a villainous master as a chimney-sweep. The satire on the inadequacy of the law, which stated as the only safeguard that the consent of the apprentice had first to be secured, is vulpine in its ridicule:

"Well," said the old gentleman, "I suppose he's fond of chimney-sweeping?"

"He dotes on it, your worship," replied Bumble: giving Oliver a sly pinch, to intimate that he had better not say he didn't.

"And he *will* be a sweep, will he?" inquired the old gentleman.

"If we was to bind him to any other trade to-morrow, he'd run away simultaneous, your worship," replied Bumble.[17]

[16]*Oliver Twist*, chap. II, pp. 13, 14, 15.
[17]*Ibid.*, chap. III, pp. 23–4.

This peculiar hilarious tone gives *Oliver Twist* an appeal all its own. Not only literary but educational historians have responded to it.[18] The ludicrous "He dotes on it, your worship," is certainly an example of the style that Leacock termed "comic-relief."[19] These little touches of comedy, and the undertone of satire, ensure that genuine sympathy will not deteriorate into mere sentimentality, and that the descriptive passage will not break down under the weight of emotion. Indeed, were it not for the comic relief, the book might now be forgotten; it is Dickens's selection of hilarious detail that lifts the pathetic figure of puny Oliver out of the nineteenth century and makes him timeless.

Although Mr. Dombey of *Dombey and Son* did not believe in general education, he approved of charity schools in so far as "the inferior classes should be taught to know their position and to conduct themselves properly." So, since he had the power to nominate a child to a school known as the "Charitable Grinders," he condescended to bestow that favour on young "Biler," the son of Mrs. Toodle, otherwise known as Richards. It is to be assumed that the white hat worn by Dickens and the other pupils of Mr. Giles's school at Chatham was an honourable distinction, but the practice in the charity schools of wearing a distinctive uniform branded the wearer as a pauper. Young Biler was even given a number—one hundred and forty-seven—as an added insult to his outlandish uniform. " 'The dress, Richards, is a nice, warm, blue baize tailed coat and cap, turned up with orange-coloured binding; red worsted stockings; and very strong leather small-clothes. One might wear the articles one's self,' said Mrs. Chick with enthusiasm, 'and be grateful.' "[20]

It was small wonder that Richards's eyes swam with tears when she pictured the spindly legs of her offspring encased in such a preposterous outfit, or when she considered that his legs were not only the subject of "verbal criticisms and revilings, but had been handled and pinched." Nor is it hard to understand that Biler was forced to slink along unfrequented paths to avoid being tripped into the gutter, splashed with mud, or robbed of his colourful cap by the young vagabonds who lay in wait for him; or that he lived an existence comparable to the denizens of

[18]Cf. Smith, *The Life and Work of Sir James Kay-Shuttleworth*, p. 44: "We can still feel the depth of this emotion in the pages of *Oliver Twist* . . . and the passion then aroused seems likely to outlive the workhouse itself." From the standpoint of the educational historian, however, it may be noted that by this date (1837–9, when *Oliver Twist* was published), the earlier legal right of Poor Law authorities to bind out apprentices without compulsory instruction had been modified by such statutes as those of 1802 and 1834 (42 Geo. III, c. 46; and 4 & 5 Wm. IV, c. 76).

[19]Leacock, *Charles Dickens*, pp. 39–40.

[20]*Dombey and Son*, I, chap. v, p. 72.

Dante's *Inferno*. "That very morning he had received a perfectly un-
solicited black eye on his way to the Grinders' establishment, and had
been punished for it by the master—a superannuated old Grinder of a
savage disposition, who had been appointed schoolmaster because he
didn't know anything and wasn't fit for anything, and for whose cruel
cane all chubby little boys had a perfect fascination."[21] Later, in one
devastating paragraph, Dickens ridiculed the practice of stuffing charity
pupils with Scripture verses, and parading them humiliatingly at church
in order to indoctrinate them with a sense of inferiority and passivity:

> Rob the Grinder, whose reverence for the inspired writings, under the
> admirable existence of the Grinders' School, had been developed by a per-
> petual bruising of his intellectual shins against all the proper names of all
> the tribes of Judah, and by the monotonous repetition of hard verses, espe-
> cially by way of punishment, and by the parading of him at six years old in
> leather breeches, three times a Sunday, very high up, in a very hot church,
> with a great organ buzzing against his drowsy head, like an exceedingly busy
> bee—Rob the Grinder made a mighty show of being edified when the Captain
> ceased to read, and generally yawned and nodded while the reading was in
> progress.[22]

Forced to suffer such indignity, and immersed in such a deluge of
piety, young Biler eventually fell, or was driven, into bad ways. His
father, Mr. Toodle, is depicted breaking the news, deferentially, and
rather wistfully, to Mr. Dombey and the Major, Dombey's friend, both
of whom are unmoved by the mute appeal of the father's obvious anxiety
and dejected appearance. But there is no doubt about where Dickens
places the blame for the sequel: "The simple father was beginning to
submit that he hoped his son, the quondam Grinder, huffed and cuffed,
and flogged and badged, and taught, as parrots are, by a brute jobbed
into his place as schoolmaster with as much fitness for it as a hound,
might not have been educated on quite a right plan in some undiscovered
respect, when Mr. Dombey angrily repeating, 'The usual return!' led the
Major away."[23] In a public address ten years later (1857), Dickens gave
an account of the "schools he didn't like," in which he specifically stated
that he did not like schools whose pupils "in leather breeches and with
mortified straw hats for bonnets were forced to file along the streets in
long melancholy rows under the escort of that surprising British monster
—a beadle."[24]

The foundation school is another type of charity school mentioned by

[21]*Ibid.*, I, chap. VI, p. 82.   [22]*Ibid.*, II, chap. IX, p. 130.
[23]*Ibid.*, I, chap. XX, p. 336 f.
[24]*Speeches by Charles Dickens*, pp. 290–6. See also chap. VI below, on Dickens's
speeches.

Dickens; it differed from the common day-school in emphasizing moral and religious training and in regarding secular instruction as a secondary consideration. There are at least three characters in Dickens's works who were the products of such a school: George Silverman, Uriah Heep, and Grandfather Smallweed's father.[25] Little account is given of George Silverman's life at the foundation school. The hypocritical sermons delivered to the pupils by Brother Hawkyard are scathingly condemned, but Silverman testifies that the school was a good one, and, as the story shows, he became a good university scholar. Dickens must have regarded Silverman as an exception to the general rule, for he cited Grandfather Smallweed's father—a skinny, money-grabbing spider who had lived, married, and died for the "God of Compound Interest"—as an example of the type of pupil whom these institutions sent out into the world: "As his character was not good, and he had been bred at a Charity School, in a complete course, according to question and answer, of those ancient people the Amorites and the Hittites, he was frequently quoted as an example of the failure of education."[26]

Perhaps the best-known graduate of a foundation school is Uriah Heep. With the same vitality with which Dickens arouses our moral indignation and our sympathy on behalf of Oliver Twist, he arouses a feeling of repulsion and disgust against the snivelling, close-cropped hypocrite, Uriah Heep, dressed in his black suit and white neckerchief. Pecksniff was deceitful, Chadband was smooth and oily, but neither was quite so slimy as Uriah Heep, stealthily wiping the palms of his clammy hands. Dickens does not describe the actual teaching-procedure in these schools, but he makes us see the system as he saw it, and see the deceitful, fawning characters it produced:

Father and me was both brought up at a foundation school for boys; and mother, she was likewise brought up at a public, sort of charitable, establishment. They taught us all a great deal of umbleness—not much else that I know of, from morning to night. We was to be umble to this person, and umble to that; and to pull off our caps here, and to make bows there; and always to know our place, and abase ourselves before our betters. And we had such a lot of betters! Father got the monitor-medal by being umble. So did I. Father got made a sexton by being umble. He had the character, among the gentle folks, of being such a well-behaved man, that they were determined to bring him in. "Be umble, Uriah," says father to me, "and you'll get on." It was what was always being dinned into you and me at school; it's what goes down best. "Be umble," says father, "and you'll do." And really it ain't done bad!

[25]In "George Silverman's Explanation," *David Copperfield*, and *Bleak House*, respectively.
[26]*Bleak House*, chap. XXI, p. 344.

Dickens has selected the word "umble," a sort of catchword, to describe the cumulative effect of the system. He obviously does not regard "this detestable cant of false humility" simply as a family trait of the Heeps, for he has David Copperfield reflect that there were other possible origins for it: the charitable schools.[27] His corrosive invective against them is a terrible indictment, especially if one compares it with the closing sentence in *Sybil*, where, after Disraeli has described the evils of the baby farms where children were dosed with laudanum and treacle for threepence a week, he affirms: "The youth of a nation are the trustees of posterity." One prefers the neglected Devilsdust of *Sybil* to the obsequious Uriah of *David Copperfield*.

Nevertheless, false humility was definitely taught in the charity schools, as the wording of this typical prayer shows: "Make me dutiful and obedient to my Benefactors, and charitable to my Enemies. Make me temperate and chaste, meek and patient, just and true in all my dealings, content and industrious in my station."[28] Dickens's picture is also substantiated by the typical charity sermons,[29] and by other novelists of the period. Kingsley, for example, has John Crossthwaite remark that the church retained a monopoly over education in order to serve out "a miserable smattering of education—just enough to serve as sauce for their great first and last lesson of 'Obey the powers that be—whatever they may be; leave us alone in our comforts, and starve patiently; do, like good boys, for it's God's will.' "[30] Dickens has Lady Bowley express the typical attitude of the administrators of the charity schools:

"Last winter, when I introduced pinking and eyelet-holing among the men and boys in the village, as a nice evening employment, and had the lines,

> Oh, let us love our occupations,
> Bless the Squire and his relations,
> Live upon our daily rations,
> And always know our proper stations,

set to music . . . this very Fern . . . said, 'I humbly ask your pardon, my lady, but *an't* I something different from a great girl?' "[31]

It is refreshing to turn from these pictures of suffocating piety to Old Betty Higden's Minding-School. A woman of indomitable courage, Betty Higden is, nevertheless, haunted by a perpetual fear of dying in the work-

---

[27]*David Copperfield*, II, chap. XXXIX, pp. 164–5.
[28]From *The Poor Girl's Primer*, for the use of the charity school in Sheffield, 1789. The prayer is quoted in full in Birchenough, *History of Elementary Education in England and Wales*, p. 7.
[29]"Bishop Butler's Sermon on Charity Schools," *The Schoolmaster*, I, 159 ff.
[30]Kingsley, *Alton Locke*, chap. IV, p. 36.
[31]"The Chimes," Second Quarter, in *Christmas Books*.

house. The kindly, hard-working soul carried on a little home-laundry business, and supplemented her meagre income by taking care of charity children from the workhouse. In the following little dialogue she is explaining to Mrs. Boffin's secretary the presence of the children in her home, which has all the earmarks of a dame school as well:

> "Those are not his brother and sister?" said Mrs. Boffin.
> "Oh dear no, ma'am. Those are Minders."
> "Minders?" the Secretary repeated.
> "Left to be Minded, sir. I keep a Minding-School. I can take only three, on account of the mangle. But I love children, and Fourpence a week is Fourpence. Come here, Toddles and Poddles."
> Toddles was the pet name of the boy; Poddles of the girl. At their little unsteady pace, they came across the floor, hand in hand. . . .
> "And Master—or Mister—Sloppy?" said the Secretary, in doubt whether he was man, boy, or what.
> "A love-child," returned Betty Higden, dropping her voice; "parents never known; found in the street. He was brought up in the———" with a shiver of repugnance, "———the House."[32]

One feels that if the children left in the charge of Old Betty did not learn the rudiments of knowledge, they at least experienced kind treatment and loving care. With this single instance of true charity we leave the various charity schools and turn to two schools that were conducted along the lines of the monitorial plan.

Since the first school attended by Charley Hexam was said to have been "partitioned off into square assortments," it is concluded that Dickens had the monitorial schools in mind; and furthermore, since "squares" and not "semi-circles" are designated, it is suggested that it was a National rather than a British school. Similarly, the mechanical nature of the instruction in the second school to which Charley Hexam eventually graduated—the double school taught by Bradley Headstone and Miss Peecher—also suggests the monitorial system. It must also be admitted that since *Our Mutual Friend*, from which the descriptions of these schools are derived, was published between 1864 and 1865, it is possible that, in the allusion to mechanical teaching, Dickens was probably attacking the Revised Code which was instituted in 1861,[33] but there is no mention of state inspectors or grants; perhaps Dickens was purposely vague. In any event, he was apparently impressed with the dreary monotony of the whole system.

The first school which Charley Hexam attended is described as "a miserable loft in an unsavoury yard," in which the atmosphere was so

<hr>

[32]*Our Mutual Friend*, Bk. I, chap. XVI, p. 242.
[33]See Introduction above.

oppressive that half the pupils either fell asleep or remained in a half-stupid state of wakefulness, while the other half kept up a monotonous droning noise. "It was a school for all ages, and for both sexes. The latter were kept apart, and the former were partitioned off into square assortments."[34] The teachers were not trained; "they were animated solely by good intentions"; and a constant jumble was the result:

And particularly every Sunday night, for then, an inclined plane of unfortunate infants would be handed over to the prosiest and worst of all the teachers with good intentions, whom nobody older would endure. Who, taking his stand on the floor before them as chief executioner, would be attended by a conventional volunteer boy as executioner's assistant. . . . It was the function of the chief executioner to hold forth, and it was the function of the acolyte to dart at sleeping infants, yawning infants, restless infants, whimpering infants, and smooth their wretched faces; sometimes with one hand, as if he were anointing them for a whisker; sometimes with both hands, applied after the fashion of blinkers. And so the jumble would be in action in this department for a mortal hour; the exponent drawling on to "my Dearerr Childerrenerr, let us say, for example, about the beautiful coming of the Sepulchre; and repeating the word Sepulchre (commonly used among infants) five hundred times, and never once hinting what it meant; the conventional boy smoothing away right and left, as an infallible commentary. . . .[35]

Since the whole educational system was in a state of flux (as the *Minutes of the Committee of Council* show), from 1840 onwards there were few examples of schools following either a purely individual monitorial, or a simultaneous group-teaching method.[36] The "inclined plane of unfortunate infants," however, undoubtedly refers to a gallery room with rows of desks, each raised a little higher than the row in front. This was a prominent feature of Stow's and Wilderspin's system.[37] For these "gallery lessons" one teacher instructed all the children simultaneously.

The gallery lesson described above occurred on a Sunday. The following describes what happened throughout the week, and apparently in the evenings—in meting out lessons, these teachers of good intentions failed to make any distinction between the common prostitutes and the infants of tender years:

. . . all the place was pervaded by a grimly ludicrous pretence that every pupil was childish and innocent. This pretence, much favoured by the lady visitors, led to the ghastliest absurdities. Young women, old in the vices of the commonest and worst life, were expected to profess themselves enthralled

[34]*Our Mutual Friend*, Bk. II, chap. I, p. 261.

[35]*Ibid.*, pp. 262–3.

[36]See Birchenough, *History of Elementary Education in England and Wales*, pp. 272 ff.

[37]See chap. v below. Cf. Manning, "Charles Dickens and the 'Glasgow System.'"

by the good child's book, the Adventures of Little Margery, who resided in the village cottage by the mill; [who] severely reproved and morally squashed the miller, when she was five and he was fifty; . . . .[38]

The moral precepts of a calculating virtue are ironically ridiculed as follows:

. . . young dredgers and hulking mud-larks were referred to the experiences of Thomas Twopence, who, having resolved not to rob (under circumstances of uncommon atrocity) his particular friend and benefactor, of eighteen-pence, presently came into supernatural possession of three-and-sixpence. . . . Several swaggering sinners had written their own biographies in the same strain; it always appearing, from the lessons of those very boastful persons, that you were to do good, not because it *was* good, but because you were to make a good thing of it.[39]

Dickens concludes his indictment of the efforts of the church with a condemnation of the use of the Bible as an initial textbook: "Contrari-wise, the adult pupils were taught to read (if they could learn) out of the New Testament; and by dint of stumbling over the syllables, and keeping their bewildered eyes on the particular syllables coming round to their turn, were as absolutely ignorant of the sublime history as if they had never seen or heard of it."[40] This seems a fantastic picture, and yet, Pugh, writing as late as 1908, and after quoting this identical picture of the first school Charley Hexam attended, affirms: "Now I do not know how Dickens became acquainted with the constituents of that picture; but I can vouch for its absolute accuracy, out of my own experience of a church school, down to its last detail of the conventional boy."[41] The *Law Magazine*, July 1, 1849, was of the same opinion: "Nineteen twen-tieths of the instruction we have given the poor is of this sorry fruitless kind; such as reading the Scriptures . . . as a horn-book and reading exercise, catechisms repeated parrot-like without a comprehension of their meaning." Of three hundred and fifty boys in a monitorial school who had read "And Eli had two sons," not one could answer the simple question: "How many sons had Eli?"[42]

In describing the second school attended by Charley Hexam and in which Miss Peecher and Bradley Headstone taught—a double school in which the sexes were segregated—Dickens gives its location in the flat country near the Thames where Kent and Surrey meet. Apparently there

---

[38]*Our Mutual Friend*, Bk. II, chap. I, pp. 261–2.
[39]*Ibid.*, p. 263. Cf. Tuer, *Stories from Old-Fashioned Children's Books*.
[40]*Ibid.*, Bk. II, chap. I, p. 261.
[41]Pugh, *Charles Dickens*, p. 259.
[42]Quoted in Stow, *The Training System*, pp. 150, 119, respectively.

had been a mania for school-building, because the schools were new, dotted all over the country, and all exactly alike; all according to pattern; all according to the latest "gospel of monotony."

Peculiarly enough, in apparent contradiction of his bitter condemnation of the untrained "teachers of good intentions" who taught in the first school depicted above, Dickens makes a withering attack on the duly qualified teachers who taught in the second school which he described. Bradley Headstone, teacher of the boys in this second school, had been a pauper lad who had worked his way up from the bottom by sheer dogged perseverance. He was certainly a member of the type whose main concern in life is respectability; and so, with great play on the word "decent," Dickens paints a word portrait of a decent young man of six-and-twenty, in pepper-and-salt pantaloons, black coat and waistcoat, white shirt, and formal black tie, who possessed a rather stolid intellect and a mass of hard-won facts which he had mechanically stowed away in his mind from his childhood up. "He could do mental arithmetic mechanically, sing at sight mechanically, blow various wind instruments mechanically, even play the great church organ mechanically."[43]

Some of the same measure of scorn is meted out to Miss Peecher, but while there is an undertone of satire, the attack is much more delicate, as befitting a maiden lady who still retains some of her youthful charm:

Small, shining, neat, methodical, and buxom was Miss Peecher; cherry-cheeked and tuneful of voice. A little pincushion, a little housewife, a little book, a little workbox, a little set of tables and weights and measures, and a little woman, all in one. She could write a little essay on any subject, exactly a slate long, beginning at the left-hand top of one side and ending at the right-hand bottom of the other, and the essay should be strictly according to rule. If Mr. Bradley Headstone had addressed a written proposal of marriage to her, she would probably have replied in a complete little essay on the theme exactly a slate long, but would certainly have replied yes.[44]

In spite of her foibles, or perhaps because of them, Miss Peecher is an attractive character; there is a delightful picture of her tripping into her little teacherage, after watering her flowers, to "brush up" such useless intellectual cargo as the length, depth, and height of the principal rivers and mountains of the world;[45] and she was human enough to indulge in an innocent flirtation with the unresponsive Bradley Headstone.

Except for the innuendo of that trick of speech—the repetition of the word "mechanical"—nothing further is revealed of the way in which Bradley Headstone actually taught his classes. But the following dialogue

[43]*Our Mutual Friend*, Bk. II, chap. I, p. 265.
[44]*Ibid.*, p. 267.   [45]*Ibid.*, p. 269.

between Miss Peecher and Mary Anne, one of her pupils, is illuminating; it suggests rather monotonous drill in grammatical construction:

"Oh, Mary Anne, Mary Anne!" returned Miss Peecher, . . . "When you say, *they* say, what do you mean? Part of speech They?"

Mary Anne hooked her right arm behind her in her left hand, as being under examination, and replied:

"Personal pronoun."

"Person, They?"

"Third person."

"Number, They?"

"Plural number."

"Then how many do you mean, Mary Anne? Two? Or more?"

"I beg your pardon, ma'am," said Mary Anne, disconcerted now she came to think of it, "but I don't know that I mean more than her brother himself." As she said it, she unhooked her arm.

"I felt convinced of it," returned Miss Peecher. . . . "Differences between he says and they say? Give it me."

Mary Anne immediately hooked her right arm behind her in her left hand—an attitude absolutely necessary to the situation—and replied: "One is indicative mood, present tense, third person singular, verb active to say. Other is indicative mood, present tense, third person plural, verb active to say."[46]

Mary Anne, no doubt, found this abstraction a little dull; perhaps the personality of Miss Peecher enlivened her lessons.[47] But even this procedure was a decided, even if mechanical, advance on the lessons and classroom procedure which Dickens depicted as usual in the first school attended by Charley Hexam.

If one takes into account the social conditions that existed in England during Dickens's lifetime and the actual practices followed in the charity schools, it is apparent that the general impression he conveys of these schools is on the whole a true one. From all the available knowledge concerning Dickens's own schooldays, it may reasonably be inferred that he had no first-hand experience as a schoolboy of either a church school or a charity school, but when he became a man his genuine interest in the education of the poor made him a frequent visitor to such schools in the London district. On numerous occasions he secured the philanthropic aid of Miss Burdett-Coutts, whose millions were ever at the dis-

[46]*Ibid.*, pp. 268–9.

[47]Conjectures as to the prototypes of this school are fascinating but seldom rewarding. The description fits the private school at Lewisham, attended by Dickens's niece Emily Barrow and her friend Charlotte Lane. At the time of the novel, 1864, Dickens had an apartment near by, at Hatcham Park and New Cross Road. The girls used to visit him and chattered about their schooling. Wright, *The Life of Charles Dickens*, p. 311; Lindsay, *Charles Dickens*, p. 379; and others.

posal of schools and charity, and for whom Dickens acted as investigator and almoner. The same interest was evident even on his trips to North America, when he visited public institutions and charities.[48] The fact of the matter is that Dickens was always ready to speak or to act as chairman at any public meeting organized for the advancement of the education of the poor;[49] and he was often searching for an opportunity to expose the weaknesses of the church schools and charity schools.[50] There is no doubt that Dickens knew both the problems and the issues.

Moreover, other literary men of the nineteenth century are known to have attended schools of this type, and the scattered references they have left behind give ample support to the impression Dickens conveyed. Leigh Hunt (1784–1859), for example, described in his *Autobiography*[51] the conditions that existed at Christ's Hospital when he was in attendance there. Originally designated solely for orphans, this school had eventually reached a semi-charitable status, but it continued to clothe its pupils in the traditional blue cap and "skirt," with yellow stockings and waistcoats. Actually, Christ's Hospital was five schools in one—a grammar, writing, drawing, mathematical, and reading school. Leigh Hunt, in its grammar school, did not know the multiplication table at fifteen years of age! He described how sixty of the six hundred pupils who were in attendance were housed in his dormitory. Canings were frequent. Boyer, the senior teacher, pinched ears and noses till the blood came, and rebuked the boys for eating apples although he munched them in school sessions himself. On one occasion he knocked out Hunt's front teeth with a volume of Homer. He was a notorious flogger, as the poet Coleridge remembered: "Poor J. B.! may all his faults be forgiven; and may he be wafted to bliss by little cherub boys, all heads and wings, with no *bottoms* to reproach his sublunary infirmities."[52] Hunt labours the point that such abuses were actually commonplace, and that Dickens merely demonstrated abuses found in inferior schools.

Charles Lamb (1775–1834), who had also gone to school at Christ's Hospital, testified to blue milk on Mondays and choking pea-soup on Saturdays; to the practice of strapping the six youngest boys as "examples" for unknown culprits who "talked" in the dormitory; to the burning of one boy with a hot iron; and to solitary confinement on bread

[48]For a thorough discussion of the points made in the last three sentences, see chap. VII below.
[49]See chap. VI below.
[50]See chap. VIII below re the *Edinburgh Review*.
[51]Vol. I, 54–119, 75, 81, 92.
[52]Quoted in Lamb, "Christ's Hospital Five and Thirty Years Ago" in *Essays of Elia*, p. 24.

and water with no human contact save a twice-a-week (almost welcomed) chastisement.[53]

Thackeray (1811–1863) attended Charterhouse, another school of a semi-charitable status, in 1822, at the time when Dickens was attending Giles's school in Chatham. The state of flux in the schools is well illustrated by the fact that Dr. Russell of Charterhouse had been able to reduce the required small fee by introducing the monitorial system of Dr. Bell of Madras. Thus, at that time, the school had only eight masters for almost five hundred boys. Thackeray described the monitors as being as coarse as ploughboys, as having snobbish manners, revolting language, and the habit of beginning the study of grammar with the verb "I thrash," which was not intended to be mere idle humour. Thackeray was squeezed into one of the residences on Wilderness Row with fifty other boys, and had to wash publicly at a leaden trough fed by a cistern of ice-cold water, where sporadic glimpses of the cheap yellow soap among the shivering naked bodies of his fellows gave the well-mannered, sensitive boy deep feelings of revulsion.[54] The records of another school, Grey Coat Hospital, tell of girls as well as boys being so cruelly flogged that, in desperation, they set fire to the woodwork and smashed windows to attract attention.[55] Apparently Dickens's description of young Biler's teacher was not overdrawn, since Mandeville described charity-school teachers as "starving wretches" of both sexes.[56]

Of course, there is another side. On paper, at least, the Society for the Promotion of Christian Knowledge, which left the Dissenters out of its jurisdiction, required the teachers in its charity schools to be members of the Church of England, to be temperate, to write a good hand, to cipher, and to be able to expound religious principles.[57] And Thackeray modified his views later in his life. Out of sentiment perhaps, he made it his custom to attend the service for charity schools held in St. Paul's Cathedral, and on one occasion, when four thousand charity-school children with their treble voices drew copious tears from his eyes, he leaned over to whisper huskily to J. L. Motley, a historian from the United States: "It's the finest thing in the world—finer than the Declaration of Independence."[58] Lamb also, in later life, gave a more idyllic picture in "Recollections of Christ's Hospital,"[59] and there are many fond remem-

---

[53]*Ibid.*, pp. 14–26.   [54]Stevenson, *The Showman of Vanity Fair*, pp. 9–12.
[55]Jones, *The Charity School Movement*, pp. 98–103.
[56]See his *Essay on Charity and Charity Schools* (1773).
[57]Dearsley in "The Education of the Poor" discusses the S.P.C.K.
[58]Stevenson, *The Showman of Vanity Fair*, p. 347.
[59]*Gentleman's Magazine*, June, 1813, reprinted in *Charles Lamb and Elia*, pp. 27–42.

brances scattered throughout his letters. Leigh Hunt as well has been recorded as being "grateful to Christ's Hospital."[60] To add to this brighter side, there is Brereton's recollections that, as the pupils sat in church on two forms facing each other, his grandfather's armed butler kept order with a lengthy gad, and to watch this "sergeant-at-arms" make a lunge with his weapon at some youthful miscreant was "as exciting as a man fishing."[61] Furthermore, Greville testified in his diary to the remarkable sale of reading materials as the result of Bell's and Lancaster's new system of teaching children to read; and, on visiting a Bell monitorial school, he doubted whether the children of the wealthy, educated at great expense, could pass the examination given to "these young paupers."[62] In this connection it is interesting to note that when Joseph Lancaster himself arrived in Montreal, Canada, from Albany, New York, in the autumn of 1829, he took varying numbers of backward pupils ranging in age from five to eight years from the schools of Montreal, and although several of them did not even know the alphabet, he claimed in a "Report of the Singular Results of Joseph Lancaster's New Discoveries in Education, Made at Montreal" that he taught them to read in less than six weeks.[63]

In the matter of workhouses and pauper apprentices, there are other factors which merit our consideration if we are to make an accurate appraisal of Dickens's portrayal. When Dickens fell in love with Maria Beadnell and entered the Beadnell circle in 1828, he must have learned about the Bumbledom side of authority in regard to workhouses from Maria's Uncle John, who was a member of the joint vestry board of St. Mary Woolnoth and Woolchurch Haw. This parish "farmed out" its pauper children at four shillings and sixpence each per week, and offered ten pounds sterling as a premium to apprenticeship; Oliver's price was sevenpence halfpenny per week and his premium was five pounds sterling.[64] Again, threads of plot construction should make one chary of drawing close pedagogical inferences. For instance, Smollett's Humphry Clinker, like Oliver Twist, was a workhouse boy, apprenticed and starved, and proved to have former connections with his rescuer. In the Preface to *Oliver Twist*, Dickens himself raises the question whether it might be considered a perversion to have young minds wallow through "the most criminal and degraded" dregs of London; and one could argue

[60]Quoted in *Charles Lamb and Elia*, p. 28.

[61]"Early Education Sixty Years Ago," pp. 464–9.

[62]*The Greville Diary*, I, 149, 312.

[63]Pamphlet no. 370.9714,L12, Public Reference Library, Toronto, Canada (sixteen pages).

[64]Stonehouse, *Green Leaves*, pp. 40–8.

quite logically from the plot that educational environment should be as bad as possible, or at best have little or no effect. Nancy, who was cradled in the gutter and the back alley and schooled in the brothel and the gin-shop, is mistress to a thug and the decoy for Oliver; yet she breaks through all environment and training to rescue the boy she had helped to enmesh. In the same line of thought one could quote Oliver as support, since he appeared to be remarkably unaffected by his environment as an apprentice in the workhouse.

Further consideration of Dickens's presentation of these church and charity schools requires attention to Dickens's sympathy for the poor, to his limitations, and to the power of his art in reforming education. Although Dickens had never attended a charity school, the fertility of his imagination was aided by the memory of the intensity of his own sufferings as a neglected waif at the blacking-warehouse; every time he saw the potential promise of childhood ravaged, he remembered the bitterness that had welled up in his own heart as a twelve-year-old boy.[65] The figure of Oliver Twist reaches straight into the heart of humanity because he is the symbol of the hopes and aspirations which life offers every child. Dickens believed that it was his mission in life to expose the cruelty and oppression in the schools, and to try to make the lot of the poor more livable; as he himself wrote to the Reverend Thomas Robinson: "While you teach in your walk of life the lessons of tenderness you have learned in sorrow . . . I will pursue cruelty and oppression . . . so long as I have the energy of thought and the power of giving it utterance."[66] He despised a school which was at least partly responsible for the slimy abasement and cringing cunning of a Uriah Heep. He was highly indignant at a uniform that branded a child as a pauper. Yet his heart went out to the kindly humanity of old Betty Higden.

But when one has said all this in favour of Dickens, in respect of the faithfulness of his delineation of church and charity schools, and the genuine work (of which this is only a part) that he did for the education of the poor, the fact remains that some qualifications need to be made. Dickens had his limitations. It is amazing that a man who had reported such reforms as the Reform Bill of 1832, the Abolition of Slavery, 1833, the Poor Law Reform of 1834, and the Municipal Act of 1835 did not seem to realize that these schools could not be reformed exclusively by church, state, or benevolent charity alone; he appeared to take little

---

[65]It is interesting to compare Burns and Dickens in this respect. They meet in wit, humour, pathos, satire, and sympathy for the common people (Sloan, "Robert Burns and Charles Dickens," pp. 8–18).

[66]Dexter, ed., *Letters*, I, 314.

account of complex social conditions which had their origins in the industrialization of manufacturing, and which had complicated the problems of charity and education; he did not seem to understand that the curtailment of outdoor relief was necessary in the interests of English society at large, and that the Speenhamland Policy of subsidizing wages was no longer feasible. In his attack on church and charity schools, he does not make sufficient allowance for the difficulty of grouping into classes children of all ages and backgrounds, the problems caused by irregular attendance, lack of buildings and teachers, and inadequate equipment and financial support, not to mention the search for a *modus operandi* to solve the religious contentiousness. During the nineteenth century the social conditions in England were changing so rapidly that sympathy in matters of reform was not enough. Poor-relief, for example, had reached such a state of affairs that it could endure neither the abuse nor the remedy.

Dickens never seemed to suggest any full-scale study of the facts.[67] He seemed to think that everything could be solved by indiscriminate benevolence through which life might become Christmas all the year round. Sibbald once remarked that Dickens was never strong in a reflective sense; like his characters, he did everything but think.[68] This criticism is too harsh, yet it lends some support to the point just made that Dickens's sympathy for the poor had genuine depth and intensity, but that, on occasion, he failed to grasp all the complexities of the situation. Nevertheless, whatever else may be said about his presentation of the schools of the very poor, it was sincere. "Indeed, when he read or spoke, the whole man read or spoke."[69]

Taken as a group, it must be admitted, these descriptions of church and charity schools present a drab and miserable picture; only an occasional ray of sunshine illuminates the gloom—the kindly old pauper schoolmaster, the courageous and unselfish Betty Higden, and the whimsical, precise Miss Peecher. But these schools *were* drab and miserable, and Dickens accurately described them as such. As a matter of fact, he seldom presented a beautiful picture because he described, mainly, the sordid side of life and the habitations of the poor, which had to be por-

[67]Cf. "Thoughts and Experiences of a Guardian of the Poor," pp. 100–5: "A certain section of our labouring poor have been bred up to look upon the poor-rate as a fund specially provided to save them from all care and forethought. . . . What are you to do? There is the pressing need . . . the law supports . . . humanity prompts. . . . There is no alternative but to grant the relief asked for, though in doing so you are helping to perpetuate a great evil. . . . I appeal to all men who have any thought . . . for the poor whether this ought to be."
[68]Sibbald, "Dickens Revisited," pp. 524–34.
[69]H[elps], "In Memoriam," pp. 236–40.

trayed as the ugly, horrible, and miserable places they were. Thus he could be termed the Hogarth of letters. To say that is to infer, of course, that he was master of his craft.

Dickens's portrayals of these church and charity schools reveal, as we have seen, his sincere moral purpose; his use of accurate detail, as in the scene of little Oliver asking for more; his satirical undertone towards the rich, as expressed towards Mr. Dombey in Mrs. Chick's description of Biler's outrageous charity-school uniform; and his revelling in repulsive attributes, physical or moral, as shown by the clammy hands of "umble Uriah Heep." Without hesitancy Dickens takes his readers through the oppressive atmosphere of these schools, but he brings them out again with a perennial interest in what they have observed. This capturing of interest is the result, in part, of Dickens's ability to present a world teeming with characters and personalities. These schools were very commonplace; they were schools for paupers, and children of little account; but through the miraculous power of his art Dickens made them appear like institutions from the Arabian Nights; and their denizens like fairy characters from the works of his friend, Hans Andersen. At times, it is true, his sympathy for the poor, coupled with the educational purpose in his novels, had an inhibiting effect on his art—the character of Bradley Headstone stands as an example. Dickens's art, however, did not suffer as much as it might well have done; fortunately it was saved, not only by his creative ability in characterization and the fairy-tale atmosphere just pointed out, but also by his hilarious humour. Each situation is viewed through the eyes, not of the teachers or of the public, but of the pupils, who see the ridiculous side of every situation. Miss Peecher is a pincushion to them; Bradley Headstone a machine. In the description of the first school Charley Hexam attended, all these features are combined; there is the realistic detail to which Pugh testified; there is the fairyland atmosphere which makes it seem fantastic; there is the humour of that "conventional boy" as he "smooths" the faces of the unfortunate infants; and, finally, there is the emotional appeal to our pity and sympathy. It was the peculiar genius of Dickens to present these realistic details of the schools of the poor, charged with dynamic emotion, relieved of high tension by hilarious fun, and placed in a setting which appeared more like fairyland than Victorian England. The secret is that he set them, not in Victorian England, or in the nineteenth century, or in a world of fairyland, but, by the power of his imagination, within the whole cycle of life.

CHAPTER III

Education through Private Enterprise

Although the schools of the two large societies may have had an imperfect system, they were, nevertheless, controlled and supervised either by the clergy or by public-spirited citizens, who, whatever their prejudices, were educated men; the schools were administered by an enlightened committee at headquarters; moreover, after 1833 they received some government aid; and if they wished to qualify for grants, submitted, after 1839, to some government inspection. But these conditions did not hold for most schools conducted by private enterprise. Of course, some schools of the latter type were good schools, but far too many were conducted by individuals who desired to eke out a few pennies, or by scoundrels relentlessly driven by avarice towards the exploitation of children.

A very common type of elementary private school, if it deserves to be so called, was the "dame school," attended by the youngest boys and girls of the very poor. Because the advent of the Industrial Revolution forced the parents to work at the mills and factories, care or instruction of the children at home became practically impossible. As industrialization increased, dame schools became very numerous.[1] The fee for each child was usually about threepence to fourpence a week, giving a dame an annual income of from seventeen to nineteen pounds. The school was held in the room of a house or shop, often filthy or damp, and was administered by poverty-stricken "dames" who often fell asleep over their charges or who "went out washing," leaving the school in charge of a neighbour. If any instruction was given, it was usually confined to the alphabet, the digits, and the Lord's Prayer printed on a sheet of paper, nailed to a spade-shaped piece of board, and covered with a piece of transparent horn. It was variously known as a horn book, hornen book, horn bat, horn gig, or the criss-cross-row (if symbolic crosses of the

---

[1]Dame schools were either very satisfactory or very few in number in the eighteenth century. Not a single novelist discussed one. See Haar, "Education in the Eighteenth Century English Novel." In contrast, the Statistical Society calculated that there were 230 dame schools in Manchester alone in 1834–7.

church were added), and it cost about three halfpence.[2] A few bright children would progress as far as rudimentary spelling and reading.

For the older children of the poor there was a type of school known as the "common day-school," usually maintained by men. Sixpence to ninepence a week was the usual fee for each pupil, making an annual income of about forty pounds. The masters were, in general, a group of dissolute, ignorant, and brutal men. In addition to the alphabet and the rudimentary reading and spelling of dame school, a little writing and usually some arithmetic were taught. But penmanship was regarded as an "extra," as was also a smattering of geography or grammar. The Hammonds quote one master's reply to a visitor who thought that the pedagogue taught *multum in parvo*: "Yes I teach that: you may put that down too."[3] If the pupils were beyond the stage of the horn book, they might use a "battledore," a folded card constructed on the same principle. It was much more elaborate, however, with woodcuts of a religious or "improving" nature, lists of the vowels and syllables, and additional prayers. The battledore was quite common down to the 1870's and cost about threepence.[4]

If the school boasted textbooks, it probably used those which were familiar in the schools of the societies.[5] *The Robins* by Mrs. Sarah Trimmer, 1786, was a general favourite. It was a delightful book in many ways, but its general tone may be gathered from an illuminating footnote to a story in which the mocking-bird was mentioned: "The mock-bird is properly a native of America but is introduced here for the sake of the moral."[6] *The Lily*,[7] loving "the humble vale" and reading "a silent moral tale," presented twenty-two trifles in verse such as its frontispiece about the boy who would not be dressed until "the rod appeared in sight and his passion soon was cooled." Mrs. Fenwick's *Lessons for Children*[8] introduced such stories as "The Bad Family," concerning Greedy George, Selfish Sarah, Lying Lucy, and Careless Fanny. *Marmaduke's Multiply* and its "cousin" *The Mint*[9] gave a slight acquaintance with figures and money in rhyme and picture. *Town and Country Tales*[10]

---

[2]See Tuer, *History of the Horn Book*, I, 6 f.; and cf. Shenstone, *The Schoolmistress*.

[3]Hammond and Hammond, *The Bleak Age*, p. 141.

[4]See Tuer, *History of the Horn Book*, I, 6 f.

[5]For texts in girls' schools, see chap. IV below.

[6]Darton, "Children's Books," pp. 380 f.

[7]London: J. Harris, St. Paul's Churchyard, 1808.

[8]London: M. J. Goodwin, 1809.   [9]London: J. Harris, 1816.

[10]London: John Territt, and N. Hailes, 1824. See Tuer, *Stories From Old-Fashioned Children's Books*, pp. 28, 117, 148, 333, 386 ff.

doubtfully provided amusement and moral instruction with such tales as "Self-Inflicted Correction." After 1820, Miss Sherwood's edition of Sarah Fielding's *Governess* was commonly used. But Miss Sherwood had "cut out" the two fairy tales because, as she told Sarah Fielding, such stories "can scarcely ever be rendered profitable." "You are, I know," she continued, "strongly impressed with the doctrine of the depravity of human nature," and then explained that such a doctrine could not be introduced to motivate action in fairy tales.[11] Sarah Fielding's belief that children were naturally evil was commonly held. Is it any wonder, then, that the masters of these common day-schools would, on occasion, display their zeal to visitors by stepping into the classroom and administering cuffs all round to show their efficiency?[12] The low status of these schools may be gathered from such customs of the masters as collecting the pupils' fees at the neighbouring tavern, or following another occupation, such as shoe-making, simultaneously with his teaching.

Dry official records of the mid-century, and even those of the closing years of Dickens's life, show that the wretched conditions continued in these private schools until the state intervened. A Royal Commission of Inquiry, set up under the chairmanship of the Duke of Newcastle in 1858, revealed the true state of affairs in a report published in 1861. The following extracts expose the dissolute teachers and the squalid conditions, not in the outlying districts, but in the heart of the nation's capital. It was found, in those districts of London investigated by the Commission, that, of the children who attended school, about one-third went to the type of private day-school under discussion. The teachers were described as follows:

"None are too old, too poor, too ignorant, too feeble, too sickly, too unqualified in any or every way, to regard themselves, and to be regarded by others, as unfit for school-keeping. Nay, there are few, if any, occupations regarded as incompatible with school-keeping, if not as simultaneous, at least as preparatory employments. Domestic servants out of place, discharged bar-maids, vendors of toys or lollipops, keepers of small eating-houses, of mangles, or of small lodging-houses, needlewomen, who take in plain or slop work; milliners; consumptive patients in an advanced stage; cripples almost bedridden; persons of at least doubtful temperance; outdoor paupers; men and women of 70 or 80 years of age; persons who spell badly . . . who can hardly write, and who cannot cipher at all."

The accommodations in the dame schools were said to be so overcrowded that the children tumbled over each other like " 'puppies in a

[11]Darton, "Children's Books," pp. 380–1.
[12]Prideaux, *A Survey of Elementary English Education*, p. 38.

kennel.' " " 'Any room, however small and close, serves for the purpose; the children sit on the floor, and bring what books they please: whilst the closeness of the room renders fuel superfluous, and even keeps the children quiet by its narcotic effects.' "[13]

Twenty years before, another Commission had reported a Yorkshire district of two thousand persons as being blessed with only a mistress of a dame school and an aged cripple who instructed in the common day-school—"the wise man of the county, spoken of with unfeigned reverence by the witnesses, . . . who united the offices of schoolmaster and fortune-teller."[14] One year before Dickens died, Sir Joshua Fitch and Commissioner Feardon found thirty-three children in a room fifteen feet by eight feet where the master of thirty years' experience was preparing the stew for dinner in his shirt-sleeves as he heard individual lessons. Twenty-five other scholars were accommodated in a rough loft. In the small front room of another small home, thirty-five pupils were found idling the time away; eight boys were engaged with copybooks. Their cloth-dresser instructor lamented his lack of vocal abilities to "learn them a few ditties" to pass away the time.[15] Philpott quotes a London dame of seventy, in charge of seven pupils at threepence each, who lived partly on poor-law relief, complained of failing strength due to lack of meat, and looked languidly forward to quitting this earthly existence soon.[16] It would not be difficult to multiply instances given in the official reports of the deplorable conditions in private schools, but it is now time to turn to Dickens's portrayals.

The private schools discussed by Dickens may be roughly grouped into dame schools, common day-schools, and private boarding-schools. These descriptions comprise the bulk of his discussion of school life, and, in many ways, are the most interesting and most widely known.

In the article entitled "Our School," which was discussed at length in chapter I, Dickens mentions a "preparatory" school which was located over a dyer's shop. Everything about the description seems to be hazy, and yet the few little incidents mentioned in it have a definite air of reality: the frequent grazing of a knee on the scraper at the top of the steps, "trying to scrape the mud off a very unsteady little shoe"; the little pug dog, Fidèle, who snapped at people's legs, and who balanced cake

[13]Education Commission, 1861, *Parliamentary Papers*, XXI, 1861, I, pp. 93, 29, 94.
[14]Children's Employment Commission, 1843, *Parliamentary Papers*, XIII, 1843, II, p. 152.
[15]Report on schools for the poorer classes in Liverpool, Manchester, Leeds, etc., 1869, quoted in Curtis, *History of Education in Great Britain*, pp. 161 f.
[16]Philpott, *London at School*, p. 12.

on his nose; and the first impression of death and burial, when "we all three nestled awfully in a corner one wintry day . . . with Miss Frost's pinafore over our heads; and Miss Frost told us in a whisper about somebody being 'screwed down.' " Nothing more is told; everything else is left to conjecture.

In much the same class were three other schools, Mrs. Pipchin's school, Mr. Wopsle's great-aunt's school, and the school taught by the crippled Phoebe. Mrs. Pipchin is symbolic of barbarous methods of controlling children by force, Mr. Wopsle's great-aunt represents mere pretence and incompetence, and Phoebe is probably meant to illustrate what a teacher may accomplish through interest and kindness.

Mrs. Pipchin's establishment was attended by little Paul Dombey of *Dombey and Son*. Mrs. Pipchin was avowedly a heightened portrait of Mrs. Roylance, an elderly lady of reduced means with whom Dickens lodged when he was working as a boy at the blacking-warehouse.[17] She is described as a rather bitter old lady, stooped, hook-nosed, mottle-faced, and evil-eyed, who was spoken of as "a great manager of children"; the whole secret of her management was to force everything on a child which he didn't like, and to take away everything he did like. Dickens made hilarious fun of the whole set-up. So sombre was Mrs. Pipchin's presence that it quenched any number of candles; her "castle" at Brighton was set in an unusually "chalky, flinty, and sterile" soil, which grew nothing but marigolds, and where "the houses were more than usually brittle and thin." Dickens builds up his fantastic picture with numerous snails clinging to the street doors; with specimens of various cacti, writhing "like hairy serpents" around laths or sticking out their spikes in people's faces; and with myriads of spiders, and earwigs in season. Mrs. Pipchin is an ogress in a fairy castle. She took her chops "hot and hot" and her "constitution required rest" afterwards. Buttered toast, in unlimited quantities, greased her face, but never seemed "to lubricate her internally." Naturally, after tea, as all giants or ogresses do, she sat down before the fire with her spectacles and a green book, and "began to nod." Then, with delightful humour, Dickens adds: ". . . whenever Mrs. Pipchin caught herself falling forward into the fire, and woke up, she filliped Master Bitherstone on the nose for nodding too."[18] The picture of bluff Sir Roger de Coverley waking from his nap in church immediately comes to mind. Master Bitherstone knocking his verbal shins against the genealogical Bible-reading from Genesis, and the stories in which the naughty boy was invariably eaten by a ferocious animal

---

[17]Forster, *The Life of Charles Dickens*, I, 65.
[18]*Dombey and Son*, I, chap. VIII, pp. 120 f., 122–4.

both befit Mrs. Pipchin's method of forcing a child's mind open "like an oyster"; and both befit the delightful satirical vein of the whole treatment.

The description of Mr. Wopsle's great-aunt's evening school in *Great Expectations* has also to be read in the same spirit of fun. There is no fierce indignation in either picture; the lesson, if one were intended, is plain enough—the education obtainable in a dame school was chiefly a fiction—and the historical records prove it. But life in such a school is not depicted as being bitter and unendurable; in fact, I think the youngsters must have enjoyed it, especially if they saw the fun in it that Dickens did. The school was an evening school kept by a dame,

. . . that is to say, she was a ridiculous old woman of limited means and unlimited infirmity, who used to go to sleep from six to seven every evening, in the society of youth who paid twopence per week each for the improving opportunity of seeing her do it. She rented a small cottage, and Mr. Wopsle had the room upstairs, where we students used to overhear him reading aloud in a most dignified and terrific manner, and occasionally bumping on the ceiling. There was a fiction that Mr. Wopsle "examined" the scholars once a quarter. What he did on these occasions was to turn up his cuffs, stick up his hair, and give us Mark Antony's oration over the body of Caesar.

In the schoolroom, which was the dame's sitting-room and bedchamber, she also kept a little general store, and she was assisted by an orphan named Biddy. The orphan's hair always needed brushing, her hands needed washing, and her shoes needed mending. Pip describes his experiences at the hands of this dilapidated pair as follows: "Much of my unassisted self, and more by the help of Biddy than of Mr. Wopsle's great-aunt, I struggled through the alphabet as if it had been a bramble-bush; getting considerably worried and scratched by every letter. After that I fell among those thieves, the nine figures, who seemed every evening to do something new to disguise themselves and baffle recognition. But at last I began, in a purblind groping way, to read, write, and cipher, on the very smallest scale."[19]

Obviously Dickens is not in a very serious mood. Yet it is in this novel that he gives perhaps his best picture of a school with the lessons in progress. It is a remarkable account in many ways; while it is simply ludicrous, and such details as there being only one reading-book, but three Bibles, may be exaggerations, the whole general impression gives, nevertheless, a fairly accurate picture of what some of these evening

[19]*Great Expectations*, chap. VII, p. 49. It cannot be too strongly emphasized that this was Dickens's normal manner of expression even in his letters. Consider his remarks when a steward gave up his bed to Dickens: "It was very comfortable, though the engine was under the pillow, and the wall extremely nervous, and the whole in a perspiration of warm oil" (Osborne, ed., *Letters*, p. 136).

schools were like—an empty sham. The school functioned in the following manner:

The educational scheme or Course established by Mr. Wopsle's great-aunt
may be resolved into the following synopsis. The pupils ate apples and put
straws down one another's backs, until Mr. Wopsle's great-aunt collected her
energies, and made an indiscriminate totter at them with a birch-rod. After
receiving the charge with every mark of derision, the pupils formed in line
and buzzingly passed a ragged book from hand to hand. The book had an
alphabet in it, some figures and tables, and a little spelling—that is to say, it
had had once. As soon as this volume began to circulate, Mr. Wopsle's great-
aunt fell into a state of coma; arising either from sleep or a rheumatic
paroxysm. The pupils then entered among themselves upon a competitive
examination on the subject of Boots, with the view of ascertaining who could
tread the hardest upon whose toes. This mental exercise lasted until Biddy
made a rush at them and distributed three defaced Bibles. . . . This part of
the Course was usually lightened by several single combats between Biddy
and refractory students. When the fights were over, Biddy gave out the
number of a page, and then we all read aloud what we could—or what we
couldn't—in a frightful chorus; Biddy leading with a high shrill monotonous
voice, and none of us having the slightest notion of, or reverence for, what we
were reading about. When this horrible din had lasted a certain time, it
mechanically awoke Mr. Wopsle's great-aunt, who staggered at a boy for-
tuitously, and pulled his ears. This was understood to terminate the Course
for the evening, and we emerged into the air with shrieks of intellectual
victory.[20]

The studies became even more difficult during the winter months, as
there was only one candle to illuminate the multi-purpose schoolroom.
After imbibing at this well of knowledge for some years, including the
little comic song from Biddy with the "Too rul loo rul" in the chorus, and
the mauling by Mr. Wopsle in his dramatic performances, Pip finally
graduated from this "course of instruction."[21]

In contrast to the neglect in the Wopsle school and the external
authority of Mrs. Pipchin were the interest and kindness shown in the
little day-school for tiny tots conducted by Phoebe in "Mugby Junction,"
one of the Christmas stories. Published in 1865, five years before
Dickens's death, it may represent some of his maturest thought, but, as
might be suspected, it has none of his early rollicking and hearty humour.
Barbox Brothers, hearing the children singing, and noting the kisses of
farewell which they fling to Phoebe at the window as they leave, goes to
investigate. He finds that the teacher is bedridden for life, but conducts
a little school for tiny tots for the love of it. The situation is preferable

[20]*Ibid.*, chap. x, pp. 82–3.
[21]*Ibid.*, chap. xv, p. 125.

to the forceful methods of a Mrs. Pipchin and the hollowness of Mr. Wopsle's establishment, but, if it represents Dickens's profoundest philosophical thought on education, it leaves much to be desired.[22] True, the children were singing, but what?—the multiplication table! From the modern view it would represent both a poor singing lesson and a bad arithmetic lesson. Obviously, no individual, however sweet and charming, could possibly hope to teach effectively from her bed. However, Phoebe's beautiful personality and the response it awakened in Barbox Brothers have a delicate charm all their own.

One feels that Dickens was not always familiar with the type of school which he purported to describe; besides, by the middle of the nineteenth century the various types of schools had begun to merge into each other. As a result, one is never sure whether Dickens is describing a common day-school or some other type. Mr. Wopsle's great-aunt's school might be considered closer to a common day-school than to a dame school, except for the fact that it was conducted in the evening. Dickens does not deal at any great length with day-schools, but he apparently gives a typical picture of one in *Little Dorrit*, where he tells briefly of Mr. Cripples's Academy, and in *The Old Curiosity Shop*, where he gives a fairly complete picture of the first of Mr. Marton's schools visited by Little Nell and a glimpse of the boys who attended the second one.

When Arthur Clennam went to the house where Little Dorrit's Uncle Frederick lived, he caught a glimpse, behind the blind of the parlour window, of a little pale-faced boy eating a piece of bread and butter and waving a battledore over his head. The window blind displayed the information that instruction might be secured in the evenings as well as in the daytime, and the street door bore evidences of the warped desire of children to scribble people's names in the wrong places. Although, in deference to a stranger, the boys left off cuffing each other for the moment, their yells would have reflected credit on the teaching of an Indian chief. Other than to say that it was here that Little Dorrit managed to secure the rudiments of learning, nothing more is told concerning Mr. Cripples's Academy.[23]

Dickens gave the world no finer picture of peace and contentment than that of Mr. Marton, the old schoolmaster in *The Old Curiosity Shop*, sitting among his flowers in his garden, close to the door of his porch, looking out over his beehives, and smoking his pipe. Rather pale, and shabbily dressed, he did not hesitate to extend the limit of his meagre hospitality in response to Little Nell's timid request for shelter for herself

[22]Cf. Hughes, *Dickens as an Educator*, p. 276.
[23]*Little Dorrit*, I, chap. IX, pp. 111–14.

and her grandfather during the night. As the kindly old man set about preparing something for the weary travellers to eat, Nell looked around her:

> There were a couple of forms, notched and cut and inked all over; a small deal desk perched on four legs, at which no doubt the master sat; a few dog's-eared books upon a high shelf; and beside them a motley collection of peg-tops, balls, kites, fishing-lines, marbles, half-eaten apples, and other confiscated property of idle urchins. Displayed on hooks upon the wall in all their terrors, were the cane and ruler; and near them, on a small shelf of its own, the dunce's cap, made of old newspapers and decorated with glaring wafers of the largest size. But, the great ornaments of the walls were certain moral sentences fairly copied in good round text, and well-worked sums in simple addition and multiplication . . . bearing testimony to the excellence of the school, and kindling a worthy emulation in the bosoms of the scholars.[24]

A teacher might be tempted to question the wisdom of retaining the half-eaten apples on a shelf, and a red-blooded youth might doubt the efficacy of the moral sentences.

There is a sort of idyllic flavour in the description; there is nothing fiercely satirical, nothing hilariously funny. The same tone predominates in the account of so many "white-headed" boys, bowing, hanging up their caps on pegs, and taking their places on the forms; in the drowsy hum of the pupils, conning their lessons by rote; and in the absent-mindedness of the schoolmaster. The thoughts of the kindly old pedagogue were wandering with the little sick pupil whose place was empty:

> None knew this better than the idlest boys, who growing bolder with impunity, waxed louder and more daring; playing odd-or-even under the master's eye, eating apples openly and without rebuke, pinching each other in sport or malice without the least reserve, and cutting their autographs in the very legs of his desk. The puzzled dunce, who stood beside it to say his lesson out of book, looked no longer at the ceiling for forgotten words, but drew closer to the master's elbow and boldly cast his eye upon the page; the wag of the little troop squinted and made grimaces (at the smallest boy of course), holding no book before his face.[25]

Everything is closer to the delicate idealized vein of Goldsmith than to the sterner realistic pictures of Crabbe.[26] For enjoyment, such scenes demand a very "willing suspension of disbelief"; for full appreciation, a certain tautness of the mind. When these conditions are fulfilled, a gentle undercurrent of amused satire and a type of whimsical, kindly humour

---

[24]*The Old Curiosity Shop*, I, chap. XXIV, p. 235.
[25]*Ibid.*, chap. XXV, p. 241.
[26]*The Borough*, XXIV. "Poor Reuben Dixon has the noisiest school."

are apparent. The same benevolence on the part of the master, and the same benign humour are expressed in the following description of a writing lesson:

> The lessons over, writing time began; and there being but one desk and that the master's, each boy sat at it in turn and laboured at his crooked copy, while the master walked about. This was a quieter time; for he would come and look over the writer's shoulder, and tell him mildly to observe how such a letter was turned in such a copy on the wall, praise such an up-stroke here and such a down-stroke there, and bid him take it for his model. Then he would stop and tell them what the sick child had said last night, and how he had longed to be among them once again; and such was the poor schoolmaster's gentle and affectionate manner, that the boys seemed quite remorseful that they had worried him so much, and were absolutely quiet; eating no apples, cutting no names, inflicting no pinches, and making no grimaces, for full two minutes afterwards.
>
> "I think, boys," said the schoolmaster when the clock struck twelve, "that I shall give an extra half-holiday this afternoon."

The half-holiday occasioned murmurings among the parents; and the ultimate death of the little sick scholar brought forth the complaint that there was not much good in learning.[27]

Little Nell and her grandfather are thought to have overtaken the old schoolmaster again at Warmington, five miles from Banbury.[28] Nothing but the ruins remain of the two dwellings, at the western end of the church at Tong, which served as cottages for the schoolmaster and the pair of travellers.[29] Actually, we are told nothing more about this school than about the first one, except for the delightful introduction to each of the pupils given by the Old Bachelor. Whether the Old Bachelor's method of approbating the boys is sound pedagogy is a nice point, but there is no doubt that the blithe-hearted critic was "with the boys."

It is an amazing fact that, throughout Forster's whole discussion of *The Old Curiosity Shop*, and the record of the conversations and correspondence between Forster and Dickens, the old schoolmaster does not form a topic of consideration. As a side remark, Dickens says that he was not able to take the philosophy of the old master to himself, but that is all, in an account which extends to twenty-three pages. Unless Forster is at fault then, it may be assumed that Dickens was not greatly concerned about Mr. Marton, who could not in any case be termed a major character in *The Old Curiosity Shop*. In *Nicholas Nickleby*, on

[27]*The Old Curiosity Shop*, I, chap. xxv, pp. 242–4.
[28]Dexter, *The England of Dickens*, p. 179.
[29]The route of Little Nell and her grandfather is thought to have been through the Midlands, via Aylesbury, Banbury, Warwick, Birmingham, Wolverhampton, and Shifnal, to Tong in Shropshire, where Nell died (*ibid.*, chap. viii).

the other hand, until Dickens let the adventures of Nicholas run away with him in the manner of Fielding's Tom Jones, he intended to make the schoolmaster, Squeers of Yorkshire, the major instrument of the rapacious uncle's schemes. This statement is borne out by Dickens's journey to Yorkshire, his Preface to the novel, a letter of his (quoted later in this chapter), and by the manner in which Dotheboys Hall dominates the whole novel. Mr. Marton and his school were nothing like as important in the pages of *The Old Curiosity Shop*. It was little Nell who was uppermost in the mind of Dickens, as the closing chapter of Forster's first volume shows: "Nobody will miss her like I shall," wrote Dickens to Forster. It has been said, however, that Mr. Marton and Mr. Squeers were drawn to illustrate the same truth.[30] If this is so, it is strange that there is no reference to the fact in Forster's biography or among the thousands of extant letters of Dickens. It is more probable that Dickens, after the trenchant portrayal of Mr. Squeers, desired to portray a more benevolent schoolmaster. Is it possible that Dickens had the large-hearted and benevolent John Pounds of Portsmouth in mind when he described the benign Mr. Marton? *The Old Curiosity Shop* was written in 1840–1; John Pounds had died just the year before, in 1839, and his school became much publicized on his death.[31]

Dickens's descriptions of private boarding-schools in England are among the best known in his works. Although Dotheboys Hall, Salem House, Doctor Blimber's and Doctor Strong's establishments are not the household words that they were a half-century ago, they are not unfamiliar names in English literature. Before discussing them, however, mention ought to be made of Mr. Crisparkle, Old Cheeseman, and Mr. Pecksniff.

The Reverend Septimus Crisparkle, one of the minor canons at Cloisterham Cathedral in *Edwin Drood*, was tutor to Neville Landless. He was good-natured, kind, and a lover of boys; to young Landless he was all that his name implies. He was probably meant to illustrate the influence of a Christian gentleman in the educational process, and was definitely a superior tutor to Mr. Matthew Pocket in *Great Expectations*, at whose

[30]Hughes, *Dickens as an Educator*, p. 259.

[31]John Pounds (1766–1839) was a benevolent cobbler of Portsmouth, who encouraged the poor children of the neighbourhood, both boys and girls, to visit his workshop. He was companion, nurse, doctor, and schoolmaster to them, teaching them to read and write from handbills, to cook their own meals, and to mend their own shoes—all free of charge. The date of his death, January 1, 1839, and the resultant publicity about his school, supports the conjecture that Dickens had a particular school and schoolmaster in mind. Dickens was in Petersham and London in 1839, and, because of his interest in ragged children, would have been attracted by the account of Pounds's work on their behalf.

house Pip studied for a time. Old Cheeseman, in "The Schoolboy's Story,"[32] had risen from a poor pupil to become second Latin master, and finally fell heir to a large fortune; he continued, however, to visit the school, to take home the boys who were forced to spend their holidays at school (as he had been forced to do), and to give the boys an annual feed. Pecksniff's school for architects, in *Martin Chuzzlewit*, was an empty sham. Pecksniff had never designed anything, nor surveyed anything, unless it was the view of Salisbury Cathedral from his window. He exploited people by advertising for resident apprentices from whom he collected a premium and whom he then left to their own resources, except for the mere detail of filching anything that a pupil designed which had marketable value. This hypocrite might be termed a whitened sepulchre but for the fact that he dressed in black, and that there was no bottom to his shameless deceit.

The three most infamous schools which Dickens depicted were of three types. Dotheboys Hall was a school to which unwanted boys were banished to get them out of the way. Salem House was also a villainous school, but it was near London, not in far-away Yorkshire, and its brutality chiefly consisted in giving stripes instead of lessons. Doctor Blimber's Establishment had a much higher status than either of these. It was an expensive and fashionable private boarding-school for boys, located in the vicinity of Brighton, to which little Paul Dombey was sent to be educated, or, rather, to be "brought on." It was a very fine house, overlooking the sea. But it was not so majestic inside; the curtains were drab, fires were rarely lighted, visitors were few, and there was so little sound of life that the monotonous ticking of the great clock in the hall could be heard all over the house.[33]

Dickens's account of the school seems to have been quite accurate. At any rate, Mary Boyle had no difficulty in recognizing Rev. Dr. E. Everard's school at Brighton as a school of the same type; it was known locally as the "Young House of Lords," and its pupils used to dance with Mary and her classmates at Miss Poggi's Brighton School.[34] A generation later, T. B. Powell made out a good case for considering Dr. Everard's school ("for the education of the sons of the nobility") as the original of Doctor Blimber's Establishment.[35]

There were three teachers at Doctor Blimber's Academy: the doctor

[32]In *Christmas Stories* (first appearing in the Christmas number of *Household Words* for 1853).
[33]*Dombey and Son*, I, chap. XI, p. 173. The immediately following page references in the text are to this same volume and chapter.
[34]*Mary Boyle: Her Book*, pp. 85–7. (Cf. *Dombey and Son*, I, chap. XIV.)
[35]Powell, "Dr. Blimber's Establishment," pp. 90–4.

himself, his daughter Cornelia, and Mr. Feeder, B.A. "The doctor was a portly gentleman in a suit of black, with strings at his knees, and stockings below them. He had a bald head, highly polished; a deep voice; and a chin so very double that it was a wonder how he ever managed to shave into the creases. He had likewise a pair of little eyes that were always half shut up, and a mouth that was always half expanded into a grin, as if he had, at that moment, posed a boy, and were waiting to convict him from his own lips." (p. 172) He always had one hand in the breast of his coat and the other behind his back, and when he walked he turned a sort of semi-circular sweep as he put each foot forward. He accepted only ten pupils at a time, but he gorged them with enough facts for a hundred. His wife always lamented that she had never known Cicero, and always liked to dress the boys in "the largest possible shirt collars, and the stiffest possible cravats" (p. 173), because it was *so* classical.

Their daughter, Miss Cornelia Blimber, "although a slim and graceful maid, did no soft violence to the gravity of the house. There was no light nonsense about Miss Blimber. She kept her hair short and crisp, and wore spectacles. She was dry and sandy with working in the graves of deceased languages. None of your live languages for Miss Blimber. They must be dead—stone dead—and then Miss Blimber dug them up like a Ghoul." (p. 173) Miss Blimber was possibly suggested by the daughter, a thoroughly competent scholar, of the master of a school in St. John's Wood where Dickens's son Charley attended.[36]

As for the Doctor's assistant, Mr. Feeder: "He was a kind of human barrel-organ, with a little list of tunes, at which he was continually working, over and over again, without any variation. . . . it was his occupation to bewilder the young ideas of Doctor Blimber's young gentlemen. . . . They knew no rest from the pursuit of stony-hearted verbs, savage noun-substantives, inflexible syntactic passages, and ghosts of exercises that appeared to them in their dreams." (pp. 173 f.) At the end of the first year, Doctor Blimber's pupils had the firmly fixed idea that all poetry and literature were nothing more than a mere collection of words and grammatical syntax.

These three pedagogues administered the school by what Dickens aptly calls "a system of forcing," a sort of hot-house cultivation, which brought forth flowers prematurely. Little Paul Dombey,[37] aged only six years, was quickly initiated into the system, and given a pile of new books, duly marked, to be perused before breakfast, and to be assimi-

---

[36]Kitton, *Charles Dickens*, pp. 163 f.
[37]Paul is said to represent Dickens's nephew, Harry Burnett, a crippled child who died at the age of ten.

lated before Miss Cornelia Blimber returned from her "constitutional." These books "comprised a little English, and a deal of Latin—names of things, declensions of articles and substantives, exercises thereon, and preliminary rules—a trifle of orthography, a glance at ancient history, a wink or two of modern ditto, a few tables, two or three weights and measures, and a little general information" (p. 196). It was no wonder that little Paul did not know, when he had waded through this deep pond of knowledge, whether "*hic haec hoc* was Troy weight," or whether a verb "agreed with an Ancient Briton" (p. 196). Young Toots, it was said, after enduring a course of this instruction, left off having brains when he began to have whiskers (p. 172). The boys talked Latin and Greek in their dreams; they were regaled with the lore of antiquity at their meals (pp. 190 ff.). This is the only novel in which Dickens attacks the forcing of children in classical pursuits. In *Hard Times* he attacks the overloading of children with facts, but the school in that case is of an entirely different sort.

Some rather rash statements have been written about the great peda-gogical lessons which Dickens meant to convey in *Dombey and Son*.[38] Beneath the ridicule there *is* certainly a satirical attack on any such system of "cramming." But, in the first place, one has to keep a sense of proportion and to realize that Dickens expected his readers to have a sense of humour. It is impossible, for instance, to take the following description of Doctor Blimber's system very seriously:

In fact, Doctor Blimber's Establishment was a great hothouse, in which there was a forcing apparatus incessantly at work. All the boys blew before their time. Mental green peas were produced at Christmas, and intellectual asparagus all the year round. Mathematical gooseberries (very sour ones too) were common at untimely seasons, and from mere sprouts of bushes, under Doctor Blimber's cultivation. Every description of Greek and Latin vegetable was got off the driest twigs of boys, under the frostiest circum-stances. Nature was of no consequence at all. No matter what a young gentleman was intended to bear, Doctor Blimber made him bear to pattern, somehow or other. (pp. 171–2)

The futility of forcing children to memorize facts, the danger to the health of frail or nervous children, and a debasement of the true meaning of education are certainly implied, but the whole picture is distorted for

---

[38]Cf. Hughes, *Dickens as an Educator*, pp. 106 f., where he writes: "Toots is an illustration of the destruction of mental power by the 'hard mathematics' and other subjects, when they are taught improperly." Cf. also Jackson, *Charles Dickens*, p. 71, where the overloading of six-year-old Paul with Latin, orthography, and ancient and modern history—obviously meant by Dickens to be ridiculously funny—is seriously labelled the "most perverse, the most irrational, and the most comprehensively cruel and unjust" system.

the amusement of Dickens's readers; no reasoned argument is presented, but rather a scene of fancy and mirth.

In the second place, since it is Mr. Dombey who is to be brought down, not Paul, there is the construction of the plot to be considered. All Mr. Dombey's plans and hopes were to be shattered, starting with the heavy blow at the death of little Paul. Yet the process of disintegration had to be gradual. As the realization came that the boy, his father's favourite, preferred his sister Florence to attend him, Mr. Dombey's indifference to Florence turned into jealousy and then into bitter hatred. But Mr. Dombey deeply loved his son; therefore little Paul had to be killed with kindness. What better way of killing him, then, than to let Mr. Dombey's kind intentions overload the frail child with academic work? Although Paul was three or four years younger than the other pupils (see Dickens's instructions to Hablôt Browne[39]), the masters were urged by his father to set him at greater and greater tasks, to make him take all the courses possible. A system of education which would allow such a thing to happen was open to censure, and Dickens attacked it as a matter of course. His main concern, however, was with the character of Paul[40] and with the unfolding of the plot of the novel. The school needs a master, hence Doctor Blimber; Doctor Blimber needs some more pupils, especially one who will show the effect of such a system on a weak mind in the same manner as Paul shows its effects on a weak body, so we get Toots and others, who will prove very useful also at the end of the story to marry stray feminine characters and to produce a happy ending.

It was in his descriptions of school life and his creation of child characters that Dickens excelled. He loved the children he created in his books as he loved real children, and that is why his child characters make such a poignant appeal to his readers. The story of Paul's schooling may be enjoyed without the consideration of any moral or pedagogical lesson; its delightful humour and playful fancy place it among some of the best literature that Dickens ever wrote. But we must now leave Doctor Blimber's Establishment for Dotheboys Hall.

If one were to hazard a guess as to the most widely known books in English literature that deal with school life, *Nicholas Nickleby* would be among them, surely. The infamous master, Mr. Wackford Squeers, is numbered among the immortal creations in English fiction, while his Dotheboys Hall has become symbolic of any institution where children

---

[39]Dexter, ed., *Letters*, I, 770 f., 824 f.

[40]Edgar, *The Art of the Novel*, p. 119, terms Paul "one of the generative figures in the book."

are maltreated, half-starved, and brutally punished. As the many claimants to a personal acquaintance with Squeers, or *a* Squeers, show, there existed in Yorkshire a type of school to which unwanted children were sent to get them out of the way, and to keep them as cheaply as possible[41] —step-children, orphans, illegitimate children, or children whose presence hindered their parents from securing desirable positions. Isolation in the wilds of Yorkshire and the long expensive journey of two hundred miles to London ensured that no vacations would be allowed and that few complaints would reach the capital. These schools were a diabolical convenience for callous parents, guardians, and brutal exploiters of defenceless youth.

Evidence as to the existence of such schools is furnished by Richard Cobden who, in 1814, was sent by his mother's brother-in-law to a school in Yorkshire, where, from his tenth to his fifteenth year, the unfortunate lad was "ill-fed, ill-taught, and ill-used," and where he "never saw parent or friend."[42] Quarterly letters were dutifully sent home by young Richard, but as they were dictated by the teacher, his father remained blissfully ignorant of his son's maltreatment. Additional evidence is contained in a pamphlet entitled *Old Yorkshire Schools*, published in 1884 by J[ohn] B[rooks], who had been a pupil at a Yorkshire school kept by Mr. Clarkson at Bowes. Brooks is very detailed in his description, yet at the same time he is very matter-of-fact and apparently bears no grudges. He describes breakfast at Clarkson's school as consisting of sour milk and brown bread, and dinner of salted, fatty, unpalatable beef. The boys caught young crows, split them open, seared them on the schoolroom stove, and then devoured them. Brooks attests to the dearth of soap and towels, to copious amounts of fresh air through the broken window panes, and flea-infested blankets. Later, in the *Newcastle Weekly Chronicle*, December 24 and 31, 1884, Brooks described a beating he had received from the hands of an usher named Alderson. When Brooks went to Newcastle on a visit to relatives, his scars and bruises were discovered by a servant, and the boy was withdrawn from Clarkson's school.[43]

In 1834, James Abernethy recorded his experiences at John Smith's

41Cf. "Mr. Pickwick and Nicholas Nickleby," p. 654: "As a matter of fact, the schoolmasters were not alone to blame for these outrages on humanity. Some refuge was demanded for repudiated children. . . . And those who demanded such a place, where they might hustle out of sight and memory the poor little waifs at the least possible expense to themselves, were equally guilty with those who supplied the demand." See also Hardy, "Yorkshire Schools," pp. 218–20.

42Morley, *The Life of Richard Cobden*, p. 3.

43Clinton-Baddeley, "Benevolent Teachers of Youth," pp. 375–8.

school, located a scant four miles from Barnard Castle at Cotherstone, to which his father, captivated by Smith's advertisement and moderate annual charge of twenty pounds sterling, had sent young James and his brother George in 1829. Smith met the boys' father at the Belle Sauvage Inn, Ludgate Hill, somewhat in the manner of Squeers in *Nicholas Nickleby*, and the two boys set off in a brig for Stocton-on-Tees where Smith was met by his wife with a horse and rig. Schoolmaster and wife became fortified against the cold with so much brandy that the horse was left to find the way home to the academy. The building—it had originally been used as a nunnery—accommodated fifty boys. Surrounded by these hardened and miserable wretches, the brothers were first locked in, then relieved of their clothes, for which the workhouse variety were substituted, and allotted a straw mattress with a couple of blankets. They were forced to eat their scant rations standing up: breakfast consisted of black bread, with milk and water; dinner of more milk and bread, and soup containing about an ounce of putrid meat for each boy; and supper of more black bread and milk. The two Abernethy boys endured this treatment, rising at five, retiring at seven, with no holidays, no visitors, for about two years, until an unexpected visit of an uncle resulted in their withdrawal from the school.[44]

The *Methodist Recorder*, May 22, 1919, gives the experiences of young Bold Cooke, who in 1804 had been packed off to Mr. Edward Simpson's school, Wodencroft Lodge, at the tender age of six years. Like Dotheboys Hall, Wodencroft Lodge had a farm in connection with the school, and like John Smith's school it was only a short distance from Barnard Castle in Yorkshire. The boys were able to wash at a near-by well but were provided with neither soap nor towels. They worked on the farm, were forced to knead the dough for their bread with their feet, were given poor and insufficient food, and slept three to five in a bed. One miserable runaway, who was subsequently captured, was stripped naked, tied to the door of each dormitory in turn, and flogged mercilessly for the edification of its occupants. It is scarcely surprising, therefore, that a number of Yorkshire schoolmasters recognized themselves in Mr. Squeers, and considered taking libel action against Dickens after the publication of *Nicholas Nickleby*; Clarkson, who by this time had moved his school from Bowes to Yarm, was among them.[45]

The manner in which these schools were operated is clearly evident from the examples described. The masters of such schools customarily advertised in the newspapers for new pupils. Dibelius mentions an

[44]*Ibid.*, pp. 369–71.
[45]*Ibid.*, pp. 374–5.

example in the *Norfolk Chronicle* of April 29, 1775;[46] Clinton-Baddeley gives a facsimile of several examples from *The Times* of July 17, 1826;[47] the earliest example I have seen is given by Hardy from the London *Advertiser* of September, 1749.[48] Among the advertisements in a periodical instalment of the novel, *Nicholas Nickleby* itself, the following was found: "Fairlawn House, Classical and Commercial Academy, Hemmington Lane, Kennington, conducted by Mr. W. Owen. Young gentlemen are boarded . . . for thirty guineas per annum. . . . Instruction . . . in any accomplishment on the usual terms. The domestic comforts under the discretion and indulgent care of Mrs. Owen."[49] Even this advertisement of a southern school is as smooth as Sam Slick's soft sawder. The fee is one and a half times as high as those in the north, and the number of subjects offered is fewer. The word "any" and the "indulgent care of Mrs. Owen" could prove very elastic. Such advertisements usually made extravagant claims concerning the delightful surroundings of the respective academies, the absurdly large number of subjects taught, and the offering of "extra" subjects such as French for an additional two guineas or so, and attested to the liberality of the board and lodging and the eminent qualities of the education afforded. "NO VACATIONS" was usually equated with "EDUCATION"—both in block letters! The masters announced that they would make semi-annual visits to London and could be interviewed at designated inns. In this manner appointments were made to pick up new victims.

Aside from the accuracy and justness of Dickens's description of these schools in general, much speculation has arisen, naturally, as to the identity of the Yorkshire schoolmaster who formed the prototype of Mr. Squeers, and of the Yorkshire school that was the original of Dotheboys Hall. Squeers has been said to have been modelled on a certain Mr. Shaw, or Sowerby, or Squires, or some other infamous Yorkshire pedagogue. In the Preface to a later edition of *Nicholas Nickleby* we have Dickens's own testimony that he and Hablôt Browne went to Yorkshire to investigate conditions there before he began his book; Forster says this visit took place in 1837, but he must have been in error, for we have the record of Dickens's letter[50] and of the entry in his diary for February 3, 1838, which reads: "Shaw, the school master, we saw today is the man in whose school several boys went blind some-

[46]Dibelius, *Charles Dickens*, pp. 119–20.

[47]Clinton-Baddeley, "Benevolent Teachers of Youth," p. 360.

[48]Hardy, "Yorkshire Schools," pp. 218–20.

[49]Darwin, *The Dickens Advertiser*, pp. 80–3.

[50]Jan. 25, 1838: "I start on my pilgrimage to the cheap schools of Yorkshire (a mighty secret of course) next Monday" (Dexter, ed., *Letters*, I, 154).

time since, from gross neglect. The case was tried and the verdict went against him. It must have been between 1823 and 1826. Look this out in the newspapers."[51]

The trial to which Dickens refers took place in October, 1823, and actually there were two cases: Jones *versus* Shaw, and Ockaby *versus* Shaw, both of which were decided before Mr. Justice Park in the Court of Common Pleas on October 30 and 31. Shaw, of Bowes School, was ordered to pay damages of 300 pounds the first day and another fine of 300 pounds the next day. The trial revealed some interesting things about the school. The entry fee was twenty guineas per annum, and when the pupils arrived their clothing was confiscated. There were some three hundred boys. They slept three to five in a bed, and each morning the poor little wretches had to undertake a flea chase. Soap was a luxury, provided once a week only, and solely to the older boys. Towels were a luxury also, for there were only two to be shared among the three hundred pupils. Every Sunday afternoon the boys were fed skimmings of the pots, often containing maggots, and the usher used to offer a penny for every maggot.[52]

It is apparent then, that Dickens knew there was an institution in Yorkshire kept by Mr. Shaw at Bowes, and that Shaw had been convicted of ill treating his pupils; secondly, that Dickens made a journey to Yorkshire and made the acquaintance of Shaw. Dickens also visited other schools in the neighbourhood of Barnard Castle armed with introductions given him by Richard Barnes, an attorney at that place. From Dickens's diary, quoted above, it is obvious that he drew on the newspaper accounts of Shaw's trial—probably the account in *The Times*. It is also likely that Dickens saw one of Shaw's cards when he was at Barnard Castle. A comparison of Shaw's card of terms and the card attributed by Dickens to Squeers reveals a remarkable similarity. Here is Shaw's card:

At Bowes Academy near Greta Bridge, Yorkshire; youth are carefully instructed in the English, Latin, and Greek languages, Writing, Common and Decimal Arithmetic, Bookkeeping, Mensuration, Surveying, Geometry, Geography, and Navigation, with the most useful branches of the Mathematics, are provided with Board, Clothes, and every necessary at twenty guineas per annum each. No vacations except by the parents' desire. N.B. The French

[51]Kitton, *Charles Dickens*, p. 63. See also Dexter, ed., *Letters*, I, 147, 157, 185, 193, for the diary entry and also for letter to Mrs. Dickens, Feb. 1, 1838, and to Mrs. Hall, Dec. 29, 1838.

[52]Dibelius, *Charles Dickens*, pp. 119–20; *Yorkshire Herald*, Oct. 30, 1823. The trial at the Court of Common Pleas, London, is quoted in full in Lambert, *When Victoria Began to Reign*, pp. 227 ff.

Language Two Guineas per annum extra. Mr. Shaw attends at the George and Blue Boar, High Holborn, the first three weeks in the months of January and July.[53]

Across the extant copy of Shaw's card, Cumberland Clark found the following words written: "Mr. Shaw leaves the Saracen's Head, Snow Hill, at half past six o'clock." Note the place where Mr. Squeers "attends daily" in Dickens's advertisement:

EDUCATION. At Mr. Wackford Squeers's Academy, Dotheboys Hall, at the delightful village of Dotheboys, Near Greta Bridge in Yorkshire, Youth are boarded, clothed, booked, furnished with pocket-money, provided with all necessaries, instructed in all languages living and dead, mathematics, orthography, geometry, astronomy, trigonometry, the use of globes, algebra, single stick (if required), writing, arithmetic, fortification, and every other branch of classical literature. Terms, twenty guineas per annum. No extras, no vacations, and diet unparalleled. Mr. Squeers is in town, and attends daily, from one till four, at the Saracen's Head, Snow Hill. N.B. An able assistant wanted. Annual salary 5 pounds. A Master of Arts would be preferred.[54]

Clinton-Baddeley has ably demonstrated that Shaw's card was not wildly exceptional but was similar to those found in the advertisement columns of *The Times* during the 1820's, thirties, and forties, and it is almost certain that Dickens had seen Shaw's card, for the list of clothing recited to Mr. Snawley by Squeers at the Saracen's Head is similar to that found on the reverse of Shaw's card.[55]

The character Smike may also be traced to Bowes. Dickens may again be quoted as authority: "There is an old church near the school and the first grave-stone I stumbled on, that dreary winter afternoon, was placed above the grave of a boy, eighteen long years old. . . . I think his ghost put Smike into my head on the spot. . . . The identical scoundrel you speak of I saw—curiously enough. His name is Shaw . . . another action was brought against him by the parents of a miserable child, a cancer in whose head he opened with an inky penknife, and so caused his death."[56] Mr. Robert Lamb of Durham, England, assured the *Newcastle Weekly Chronicle* that he knew the true story of Smike[57] and that Shaw had been grossly maligned in Dickens's account. Lamb contended that Dickens had been misinformed by a dismissed usher.

[53]As quoted in Clark, *Charles Dickens and the Yorkshire Schools*, pp. 23–4.
[54]*Nicholas Nickleby*, chap. III.
[55]Clinton-Baddeley, "Benevolent Teachers of Youth," pp. 360–82.
[56]Letter to Mrs. S. C. Hall, Dec. 29, 1838, in Dexter, ed., *Letters*, I, 185 f.
[57]My source was a reprint in the Toronto *World*, Jan. 4, 1892. Wright, *The Life of Charles Dickens*, quotes the Newcastle *Weekly Chronicle* (May, 1889), with a slightly different version by J. M. R., p. 125.

This claim is partly confirmed by the rest of Dickens's letter to Mrs. Hall, which shows that he called on Shaw and saw him for a few moments, but was refused admittance to the school. Moreover, Dickens did have an introduction to a man named McKay, who at that time had a school of his own but had formerly been an usher at Shaw's school at Bowes.

Another point to be considered is that there is a memorial window in the church at Bowes which pays respect to Shaw's integrity. The fact that so many different persons have been recorded as the original Squeers[58] merely supports the statement which Dickens made in his Preface to the book: "Mr. Squeers is a representative of a class and not of an individual." The newspaper reports of the court evidence, however, the cards, Dickens's letters to Mrs. Hall, his visit to Yorkshire and his conversations there, must all be taken into account.

An article on "Mr. Pickwick and Nicholas Nickleby"[59] illustrated by Vanderhoof and Rimmer supports the claim that the description of Dotheboys Hall is a fairly faithful description of Mr. Shaw's school at Bowes. Dickens located Dotheboys Hall three miles from the George and New Inn, Greta Bridge. It was not considered a Hall in that neighbourhood, for it consisted of a long, one-storey, low-straggling building, very cold-looking, and had several straggling outbuildings, such as a barn and stable, in a rather large rambling yard.[60] The schoolroom itself was a long, low, dirty room. Most of the glass was missing from its two windows, and the apertures were stuffed with copy-books. The room, very much like a barn, had a ceiling supported with cross-beams and rafters, and was so dilapidated that it was impossible to determine whether paint or whitewash had ever been applied. There was a desk for Squeers and one for his assistant, and a couple of long, rickety forms for the boys; the desks were marked, notched, and ink-stained; in the corner nearest the master's desk drooped a small stove.[61]

Mr. Shaw did not correspond in appearance to Squeers, who is described as a villainous-looking fellow with only one eye, and a sinister smile that puckers up one side of his face. He is introduced to the reader at a coffee house in London, where, dressed in an academic suit of black, the sleeves too long and the trousers too short, and a white neckerchief around his garrote neck, he awaits prospective clients in accordance with the terms of the advertisement. By this time, he has already secured one little victim for his school. He boxes the little boy's ears for doing

[58]See, e.g., Toronto *Mail*, May 14, 1895; Toronto *World*, Jan. 4, 1892; and Adrian, "Nicholas Nickleby and Educational Reform," pp. 237–41.

[59]*Scribner's Monthly*, XX (Sept., 1880), 641–56.

[60]*Nicholas Nickleby*, chap. VII, pp. 98 f.   [61]*Ibid.*, chap. VIII, pp. 104 f.

nothing, knocks him off the trunk on which he is seated, and, for daring to sneeze, knocks him on again. When a visitor enters the inn, Squeers pretends to be mending a pen and offering kindly advice to the little boy. But the visitor proves to be another character as villainous as himself, Snawley, who disposes of his two step-children to Squeers; he is anxious to get rid of them at a cheap distant school with no holidays, and no writing home.[62] Next morning, the master, after breakfasting well himself, permits the boys a few swallows of milk and water—mostly water—and deliberately times the operation so that the poor little ravenous devils cannot finish before the coach-horn blows.[63] This introduction, not without its humour, effectively prepares us for the meanness and brutality of the "trader in human flesh."

In his Preface, Dickens describes Nicholas Nickleby as an impetuous young man of little experience, who, having been left penniless and thrown on the bounty of his villainous uncle, secures the position of tutor at the Squeers school. The first night at the school he sleeps on the floor. He is provided with a bit of soap but no towel,[64] and in any case washing is out of the question because the pump is frozen. His first glimpse of the children in the schoolroom next morning reveals emaciated, deformed wretches, sullen, vicious, and neglected, from whose hearts every trace of sympathetic emotions and thoughts has been flailed out or starved out. Mrs. Squeers feeds the boys brimstone and treacle and Squeers flogs sundry unfortunates as he peruses certain alleged letters from home.[65] After enduring the school for some time, the young assistant interferes at the unmerciful flogging of the half-starved drudge, Smike, beats the master thoroughly; and then, accompanied by Smike, sets out for London.[66]

The similarity of the details in Dickens's account to those given by the boys who actually were in attendance at Yorkshire schools such as Bowes Hall, John Smith's school, or Wodencroft Lodge are apparent even to the casual reader. Ingram Dawson attended a school of this type at Gainford, just across the Yorkshire border in the county of Durham. There were only half enough leather breeches to go round, so half the boys remained at home when the other half went to church. From Dawson we get another glimpse of the actual conditions at Shaw's school. The headmaster of the school at Gainford sent a delegate to the auction sale of Shaw's Academy; the sale was to have been conducted in the dining room but there was such a deposit of potato peelings on

[62]*Ibid.*, chap. IV, pp. 36–41.
[64]*Ibid.*, chap. VII, pp. 100–1.
[66]*Ibid.*, chap. XIII, pp. 177 f.
[63]*Ibid.*, chap. V, pp. 56–7.
[65]*Ibid.*, chap. VIII, pp. 104 f.

the floor that the sale had to be moved out into the yard.[67] And apparently the runaway from Wodencroft Lodge was not the only "Smike" in real life, for the Burial Register at Bowes church lists some twenty-nine unmarked graves in the churchyard—pupils of tender years who died between October 10, 1810, and March 30, 1834. At least ten of these twenty-nine pupils had belonged to Shaw's school, and the rest to other schools near by—all within the parish of Bowes.[68]

Although Shaw's school at Bowes probably provided the setting for Dotheboys Hall, it was not necessarily the scene of all the incidents Dickens described, and if there had been libel laws with teeth in them, he might well have been not a little embarrassed. Dibelius, a noted German Dickensian scholar, could find no basis for ascribing the well-known brimstone-and-treacle scene to Shaw's school, and suggested that Dickens probably secured his material for that episode from some other school.[69] In support of this theory, it was of great interest to uncover authoritative evidence of a similar scene in the *Military Reminiscences of Captain J. H. Cooke*, a boarder at Garden House Academy, Kentish Town:

At the spring and fall of the year, the same female was again at her post *sine die*, a living statue, her left hand resting on a huge brown jar of brimstone and treacle, the fingers of the other mechanically coiling around the long handle of an iron spoon, its bowl rivalling those seen in gravy dishes. The boys were placed in a long string, or Indian file, one hugging the other's back, and so on, awaiting the direful moment; while some of the bigger boys acted as turnkeys to hinder a bolt and to cut off all hope of escape, as a general panic of this sort had been known to occur more than once. Then, in succession everyone tamely crept up to the starched and erect personage, when the well-known hand crowned the scalp or headpiece, the fingers sometimes stopping one eye, and often bunging up both; so that the patient taker of brimstone and treacle was made as blind as a bat, his jaws expanding to an awful extent, the unhappy head no longer resting as it was wont to do, erect on the trunk, but pushed back between the shoulders; and with such quickness was it placed in this position, that the most expert tooth-drawer could not have transfixed a head in the like position more to advantage for the extraction of any tooth. Then followed the stately spoon into the orifice; I will not say how far it entered, as it signified little whether Dame Nature had given jaws expanding wide or not, for the ruthless spoon found a passage, leaving the overflowing residue of brimstone and treacle rolling down each side of the mouth, which, as quick as thought, was scraped up right and left with the spoon, and given a second edition; and if all this was not kindly taken, or there was any spluttering, coughing, or sneezing, or the like, a good sound box on the ear closed the operation.[70]

[67]Croyden, "Film Prospecting among the Yorkshire Schools," pp. 121–5.
[68]Cooper, "Burial of Boys in the Delightful Village of Dotheboys," pp. 107–12.
[69]Dibelius, *Charles Dickens*, pp. 119–20.
[70]Moncrieff, *A Book about Schools*, p. 240.

Some remarkable similarities become evident if Cooke's vigorous description is placed tentatively beside Dickens's, though Dickens's has a lighter touch and less straining for effect:

Mrs. Squeers stood at one end of the desks, presiding over an immense basin of brimstone and treacle, of which delicious compound she administered a large instalment to each boy in succession; using for the purpose a common wooden spoon, which might have been originally manufactured for some gigantic top, and which widened considerably every young gentleman's mouth; they all being obliged, under heavy corporal penalties, to take in the whole of the bowl at a gasp. In another corner, huddled together for companionship, were the little boys who had arrived on the preceding night. . . . Besides these there was a long row of boys waiting, with countenances of no pleasant anticipation, to be treacled; and another file, who had just escaped from the infliction, making a variety of wry mouths indicative of anything but satisfaction. The whole were attired in such motley, ill-sorted, extraordinary garments, as would have been irresistibly ridiculous but for the foul appearance of dirt, disorder, and disease, with which they were associated.

"Now," said Squeers, giving his desk a great rap with his cane which made half the little boys nearby jump out of their boots, "is that physicking over?"

"Just over," said Mrs. Squeers, choking the last boy in her hurry, and tapping the crown of his head with the wooden spoon to restore him. "Here, you Smike; take away now. Look sharp."[71]

Moncrieff, writing in 1925, gave no exact dates for Cooke's account, but remarked that the diary had been compiled four generations ago. Obviously, then, Cooke's description preceded Dickens's, if a "generation" is given the common reckoning of thirty years, but I do not know for sure whether Dickens knew of this particular diary or not. At any rate, the diary shows that Dickens had no need to exaggerate. Cooke also gives a graphic description of other miseries the children endured. The process of combing their hair was "a downright carding"; and they were washed with "such muscular application" that it was often very difficult "to get rid of the effects of the soft soap, from what aperture or crevice it might have found ingress"; a poor boy finally emerged with his "neck well-nigh dislocated, and glowing like an ember."[72]

Little is told about the manner of conducting lessons at Dotheboys Hall and little about the books. In chapter VIII Squeers is depicted conducting a class in philosophy and spelling in the practical mode of teaching: a pupil spells the word window, w-i-n-d-e-r, then goes out to clean the parlour window; another spells botany, b-o-t-t-i-n-e-y, then is in-

---

[71]*Nicholas Nickleby*, chap. VIII, pp. 108–9.
[72]Moncrieff, *A Book about Schools*, pp. 239–40.

structed to go outside and begin weeding the garden; another defines a horse as a quadruped, and then goes out to rub the horse down. Nickleby then hears some dull reading from some filthy, dog-eared, antiquated spelling-books, and the rest of the boys are sent out to fill up the coppers for washing day. Great pains have been taken to point out that the story illustrates the wrong approach to a sulky boy, the cruelty of corporal punishment, the devilish philosophy of coercion, and the pulling of the heart-strings on the part of Smike.[73] On the other hand, others have urged the recognition, in this description of the lessons, of some educational practices which are considered basic today:[74] for example, the merging of the theoretical with the practical. But surely it is vain to look for pedagogical lessons either for or against a system of education which is meant to be taken seriously in one respect only—as an exposure of the vile practice of banishing unwanted boys to inhuman Yorkshire schools. The account must in its other aspects be read with some of the gusto and in the light-hearted spirit in which it was written, or what is left? If it was a direct satirical attack, then Dickens permitted sound educational practice to be ridiculed. But these things were *not* practical: the pupil could not have weeded the garden since it had snowed the night before; it was so cold that the pump had frozen and Nickleby could not even wash. To a critical reader the weeding and the water-carrying do not ring true. The lessons are excellent comedy. This is Dickens, writing sparkling comic episode, at the height of his powers.

The immediate result of the exposures in *Nicholas Nickleby* was public indignation followed by the gradual disappearance of the cheap, far-away Yorkshire schools. This was evident to Sir Joshua Fitch, Assistant Commissioner of the Schools Inquiry Commission, 1864, who testified: "I have wholly failed to discover any example of the typical Yorkshire School with which Dickens had made us familiar; I have seen schools in which board and education were furnished for twenty pound and even eighteen pound per annum, but have been unable to find evidence of bad feeling or physical neglect."[75] The advertisements of the nefarious schools that had been operating around Bowes and Barnard Castle in 1838 soon disappeared from the advertising columns of *The Times*: Shaw's appeared for the last time in 1840, and only Simpson of Earby survived by 1848.[76] There is an extant letter dated Streatland Castle, September 27, 1861, testifying that a former usher at Shaw's school, now in want

[73]Hughes, *Dickens as an Educator*, pp. 29 ff.
[74]Nicoll, *Dickens's Own Story*, p. 133, and Ewing, "Squeers as a Model," p. 233.
[75]Quoted in Curtis, *History of Education in Great Britain*, p. 86.
[76]Clinton-Baddeley, "The Benevolent Teachers of Youth," pp. 381–2.

of a place, was in dire poverty since "Mr. Dickens's misguided volume, sweeping like a whirlwind over the North caused Mr. Shaw to become a victim to paralysis, and brought Mrs. Shaw to an untimely grave."[77]

Dickens's avowed purpose of reform raised the artistic problem of reconciling the presentation of suffering with an optimistic outlook on life. He resolved the problem by depicting the hideous results of rapacious brutality in one brief paragraph.[78] Without dwelling on this horrible picture, he immediately passed on to the mirth-provoking brimstone-and-treacle scene with its excellent comedy, refreshing humour, and human interest. For, with all their moral and physical repulsiveness, Squeers and his wife are interesting characters. Morally we loathe them, but we are nevertheless interested in them. The people of the nineteenth century became interested in them too, interested enough to destroy them. As Chesterton remarked, Dickens had to make men like Squeers live, in his novels, before he forced them to die.[79] It is this quality that has saved the novel from oblivion, not the moral or ethical purpose of the book or the pedagogical lessons that may be ascribed to it. It is not the appeal to the emotion of pity that makes the novel live, for the pathetic figure of Smike fails to achieve artistic effect; rather, it is the quality of that exquisite delight which the refreshing humour of Dickens imparts to his readers.

We now are forced, however, to leave Dotheboys Hall for another private boarding-school. Salem House, in *David Copperfield*, was a private school near London for the children of the middle class. It was unthinkable, of course, that any school to which the austere, arrogant, coercive Mr. Murdstone would consign a boy could be other than a place of wretchedness over which an ignorant and ferocious brute presided; but Matthew Arnold asserted that it was typical of England's middle-class schools.[80] After that wonderful first journey alone,[81] punctuated with the peculiar statement that "Barkis is willing," and enlivened by the sharp practice of the waiter at Yarmouth and the flute-playing of the sallow-faced junior master who met him at the inn,[82] David ultimately arrived at Salem House, a bare brick building surrounded by a high brick

[77]Hare, *The Story of my Life*, I, 4.
[78]*Nicholas Nickleby*, chap. VIII, p. 108: "But the pupils—the young noblemen!" etc.
[79]Chesterton, *Charles Dickens*, p. 284.
[80]Fitch, *Thomas and Matthew Arnold*, p. 230.
[81]Cf. chap. I above, for Dickens's own journey from Chatham to London.
[82]Cf. chap. I above, re the two ushers. Dickens knew of the incident in Holcroft's *Memoirs* in which young Holcroft was swindled out of his supper (as was Copperfield), because he remarked to Forster that his biography "might go on the same shelf with Holcroft."

wall, where Mr. Tungay, a close-cropped, bull-necked man with a wooden leg answered the clanging bell and admitted him through the imposing gate. David arrived in holiday time as a punishment for biting Mr. Murdstone's hand and for other alleged misdoings, and was forced to wear a placard inscribed: "Take care of him. He bites." His spirits were not raised by the sight of the schoolroom:

> I gazed upon the schoolroom into which he took me, as the most forlorn and desolate place I had ever seen. I see it now. A long room, with three long rows of desks, and six of forms, and bristling all round with pegs for hats and slates. Scraps of old copy-books and exercises litter the dirty floor. Some silkworms' houses, made of the same materials, are scattered over the desks. Two miserable little white mice, left behind by their owner, are running up and down in a fusty castle made of pasteboard and wire, looking in all the corners with their red eyes for anything to eat. A bird, in a cage very little bigger than himself, makes a mournful rattle now and then. . . . There is a strange unwholesome smell upon the room, like mildewed corduroys, sweet apples wanting air, and rotten books. There could not well be more ink splashed about it, if it had been roofless. . . .[83]

Eventually, David made the acquaintance of the headmaster, Mr. Creakle, who was to "file his teeth," and who began by twisting his ear. The following description of Mr. Creakle illustrates the genius of Dickens in disclosing types through particular traits, and in arousing terror through the senses—the strained whisper, the visible bulging of the thick veins. (Dickens awakens a similar repulsion through the senses by concentrating attention on Uriah Heep's clammy hands, Bounderby's metallic laugh and stretched forehead, and Pumblechook's fish-like mouth.)

> Mr. Creakle's face was fiery, and his eyes were small, and deep in his head; he had thick veins in his forehead, a little nose, and a large chin. He was bald on the top of his head. . . . But the circumstance about him which impressed me most was, that he had no voice, but spoke in a whisper. The exertion this cost him, or the consciousness of talking in that feeble way, made his angry face so much more angry, and his thick veins so much thicker, when he spoke, that I am not surprised, on looking back, at this peculiarity striking me as his chief one.[84]

As Creakle himself said, he *was* a tartar; he warned the boys to be prepared for punishment, because he had come up to the beginning of term very much refreshed. "It will be no use rubbing yourselves; you won't rub the marks out that I shall give you. Now get to work, every boy!"[85]

[83]*David Copperfield*, I, chap. v, p. 92.

[84]*Ibid.*, I, chap. vi, p. 98.

[85]*Ibid.*, I, chap. vii, p. 106. Cf. *Nicholas Nickleby*, chap. viii: "There," said Squeers, when he had quite done, "rub away as hard as you like, you won't rub that off in a hurry." Also note Forster, *Life*, I, 94 f., and Langton, *The Childhood and Youth of Charles Dickens*, p. 96.

He was as good as his word, for he had half the boys writhing and crying from the effects of his ruler before the day was over, while the rest pored over their books in fear and trembling. He made mouths, cast his eyes about the room for a chubby little boy, or cracked a joke before he caned an unfortunate urchin, at which the boys could not refrain from laughing: "miserable little dogs, we laugh, with our visages as white as ashes, and our hearts sinking into our boots."[86]

Mr. Tungay, the man with the wooden leg, was supposed to have assisted Mr. Creakle in some dishonest work in the hop-business, and on graduating with Creakle into the academic field, maliciously decided that all the boys were his natural enemies. The first assistant master was Mr. Sharp, a rather delicate-looking man with a large nose and a wig of wavy hair. Mr. Mell, the other master, who had met David at the inn and taken him to his mother's humble apartments in the alms-house, was rather good to the boys.

It is a pedagogical truism that pupils accustomed to strict discipline tend to take advantage of milder teachers. Yet from the literary viewpoint, since the "inevitability" of the plot did not demand it, one is surprised that the boys should bear-bait Mr. Mell so unmercifully in return for his kindness to them: "Boys started in and out of their places, playing at puss-in-the-corner with other boys; there were laughing boys, singing boys, talking boys, dancing boys, howling boys; boys shuffled with their feet, boys whirled about him, grinning, making faces, mimicking him behind his back, and before his eyes; mimicking his poverty, his boots, his coat, his mother, everything belonging to him that they should have had consideration for."[87] Perhaps Dickens secured hints from Forster's *Life of Goldsmith* (or even the usher in *Roderick Random*) in conjuring up the character of Mr. Mell. In any case, following Steerforth's insolence, and his revelation to Mr. Creakle that Mr. Mell's mother is the recipient of charity, the gaunt, sallow-faced, rusty-headed master is peremptorily dismissed. The boys cheered—all except one. The picture of chubby Tommy Traddles in tears over Mr. Mell's departure gladdens the heart like a rainbow. And it is true that poetic justice is meted out to Mr. Mell at the end of the story—he becomes Doctor Mell, head of his own school in Australia. Yet the incident is a curious one, and, save for giving another glimpse into the character of Steerforth, adds very little to the story. Moreover, from an artistic view, it is more than probable that the whole sub-plot connected with Steerforth would be as well left out of the novel.

[86]*David Copperfield*, I, chap. VII, p. 108.
[87]*Ibid.*, p. 114.

In the midst of this scene, the unexpected arrival of Mr. Creakle carries a hint, perhaps, of the ill-timed nap of Mr. Blinkins in "Our School." Aside from this incident, little more is told of the activities at Salem House. A few scant rays of bright sunshine are cast on the gloom by the account of David's telling stories to the group each evening in bed, the clandestine feeds provided by Steerforth—from Copperfield's money— and the visit of Mr. Peggotty and Ham. For the rest, until David is called home at his mother's death, his schooling at Salem House is shrouded "in a dirty atmosphere of ink," "tear-blotted copybooks," and "canings."[88]

It will be remembered that Dickens's many happy days at Mr. Giles's school in Chatham rendered his later experiences at the blacking-warehouse in London all the more bitter; and then, as if by the waving of a fairy wand, he was sent to school again, this time to Mr. Jones's academy. Similarly, in *David Copperfield*, we find David attending another school after he runs away from the winery of Murdstone and Grinby to the home of his Aunt Betsey Trotwood. But, whereas the boy Dickens found Mr. Jones a far less amiable instructor than Mr. Giles, David Copperfield certainly found Doctor Strong a more gracious schoolmaster than brutal Mr. Creakle of Salem House.

According to the novel, Doctor Strong's school was located at Canterbury. There was a series of great stone urns on the high brick wall which surrounded the courtyard, and the rather grey-looking building could be glimpsed through the rusty iron railings of the gate. On the inside, it was found that: "The schoolroom was a pretty large hall, on the quietest side of the house, confronted by the stately stare of some half-dozen of the great urns, and commanding a peep of an old secluded garden belonging to the Doctor, where the peaches were ripening on the sunny south wall. There were two great aloes, in tubs, on the turf outside the windows; the broad, hard leaves of which plant (looking as if they were made of painted tin) have ever since by association, been symbolical to me of silence and retirement."[89] The Doctor was a quiet, amiable old gentleman (David thought he looked as rusty as the iron gates outside his school) who had married a woman many years his junior. Mr. Wickfield and David found him in the library "with his clothes not particularly well-brushed, and his hair not particularly well-combed; his knee-smalls unbraced; his long black gaiters unbuttoned; and his shoes yawning like two great caverns on the hearth-rug."[90] His eye had little lustre; his manner was contemplative and a little awkward, perhaps because he was

[88]*Ibid.*, pp. 106–8.   [89]*Ibid.*, I, chap. xvi, p. 271 f.
[90]*Ibid.*, p. 272.

compiling a dictionary of Greek roots, which at the rate of the learned gentleman's progress was calculated to take over a thousand years. But, for all his peculiarities, he was beloved by all the boys because of his simple-hearted faith in them. When David and the Doctor entered the classroom on David's first day at the school, all the boys rose to say good morning, and one boy, Adams, showed the new boy to his place and introduced him in a gentlemanly manner to the masters.

Nothing is recorded of the lessons studied; no books are mentioned; no other masters are described; only one pupil is named. The whole stress is laid on the far-reaching influence of the personality of Doctor Strong. The boys did not wish to disgrace his reputation or that of their school when they were outside its walls, and wished to secure his good-will by diligence in their studies when they were in the schoolroom. "Doctor Strong's was an excellent school; as different from Mr. Creakle's as good is from evil. It was very gravely and decorously ordered, and on a sound system; with an appeal, in everything, to the honour and good faith of the boys, and an avowed intention to rely on their possession of those qualities, unless they proved themselves unworthy of it, which worked wonders. We all felt that we had a part in the management of the place, and in sustaining its character and dignity."[91]

For an appraisal of Dickens's interpretation of education through private enterprise, some recorded reminiscences of such schools may be added to the general historical facts presented in the opening pages of this chapter. Brereton described the dame school kept by Mrs. Margesson which he attended for a penny a week, and at which he was taught numeration and a smattering of addition and subtraction, and drew pot-hooks on a slate. When he was inattentive, he was crowned with a shovel-shaped dunce's cap and made to stand in a corner, and when he misbehaved he was chastised with a stick, or shut up in a closet by his nurse.[92] Thackeray recalled the little school at the Polygon in Southampton that he attended before his seventh birthday. Besides chilblains, scant victuals, and terrifying canings, Thackeray remembered one occasion when the wretched schoolmaster ordered all the little pupils out of bed in the middle of the night; each boy had to go alone to a back garden shed, find a bench in the dark, and put his hand into a sack that was on the bench. The sack had been filled with soot, and as each boy came back, he was examined to see whether his hand was clean or dirty. The reason for all this was that an article had been stolen from the school, and the headmaster's theory was that the boy guilty of the theft would

[91]*Ibid.*, p. 282; cf. Davis, *The Creation of Dickens's David Copperfield*, p. 20.
[92]Brereton, "Early Education Sixty Years Ago," pp. 464–9.

be afraid to put his hand into the sack.[93] A. L. Hayward tells of the town of Framlington, which in 1841 had 2,523 inhabitants, where education "lay mostly in the hands of Miss Boult, a straight-backed, rather fierce old lady whose stock of knowledge extended little beyond Deportment, the elements of the three R's, and a choice collection of fancy stitches." John Wright also eked out a poor living in Framlington, combining bookbinding, conducting a band, and teaching poor children. Framlington was more fortunate than most towns since it had a good school in addition to these poor ones.[94] Anthony Trollope, in the opening pages of his *Autobiography*, tells of being selected at Mr. Drury's private school at Sunbury as one of four who were to be punished for perpetrating some unknown crime. Entirely innocent, he was ordered to write out a long sermon, to be helped last at every meal throughout the term, and to refrain from entering the playground.[95] There are more diabolical punishments than flogging! Goldsmith warns in *The Vicar of Wakefield* that to be an usher in a school, one must be bred to the business, have had the smallpox, be prepared to sleep three in a bed, and have a good stomach. Thomas Creevey remembered Newcome's School at Hackney where swearing was commonplace, where acting almost excluded the three R's, holidays were declared on every possible occasion, and where the master once rang for a carving knife when a boy threatened to kill himself.[96] Stow recorded cases of cockfighting in private schools.[97] Twenty-five years after Dickens's death, all private schools were still not "select." Hugh Walpole, as late as the middle of this century, remembered Marlow school-terrors, especially the evening hour from eight-thirty to nine-thirty, when the bigger boys held "circus," forcing smaller boys to swing on the gas brackets, to fight each other, to jump off lockers, to be tossed from boy to boy, to stand stripped for public appraisal of their physical deficiencies, and to be jabbed with pen-nibs in tender places.[98]

It should be realized that these private schools—both the worst and the best—were beyond the control of any educational authority. Many of them were better than the ones that have been described. The school of Rev. Robert Dawes at King's Somborne, with its library, object lessons, and evening adult attendance was pronounced "the best in the land";[99]

[93]Stevenson, *The Showman of Vanity Fair*, p. 7.
[94]Hayward, *The Days of Dickens*, pp. 251, 256.
[95]Trollope, *Autobiography*, pp. 6 ff.
[96]*Creevey Papers*, pp. 397–401.
[97]Stow, *The Training System*, p. 115.
[98]Hart-Davis, *Hugh Walpole*, pp. 17–18.
[99]Smith, *The Life and Work of Sir James Kay-Shuttleworth*, p. 167.

another good school was kept by the Hill family in Birmingham; Disraeli and Newman attended a good school at Ealing.[100] At Enfield, Middlesex, John Clarke kept an "airy" and "commodious" school with two acres of playing-field, where the Abbé Béliard was "esteemed and even loved" and the usher, Dyer, corrected classics for publishers. Among Clarke's pupils may be mentioned Keats, Captain Marryat, and Edward Cowper.[101] At Hazelwood was found a form of student government, and a printing-shop and other manual activities. The school of John G. Dyne, Turnham Green, attended by Sala, was a "Pestalozzian one" where corporal punishment was unknown.[102] Midst other much poorer schools, the school of Mr. Hill, the staunch Dissenter of Framlington, was inherited from his father and "prepared" its pupils well "for the larger schools of Botesdale."[103] Some pupils, like Charles Dibdin, even found some pleasure and learning in the North Country school of Master Bowman at Starforth, in Durham, where he spent five years.[104] To these examples may be added the more widely known schools of Robert Owen, Wilderspin, Dr. Mayo, Wood, and Stow.[105]

It is clear that the conditions Dickens described actually existed in certain privately kept schools, but it does not necessarily follow that *all* private schools were reprehensible. It does not follow either, as has sometimes been implied (by Frieser for example), that since conditions in the great public schools are known to have been bad, conditions in private schools must have been worse; nor that the methods followed in the great public schools were identical with those in academies such as Doctor Blimber's Establishment; nor that the reforms which Thomas Arnold carried out in the public schools are attributable to Dickens.[106]

Throughout Dickens's descriptions of private schools, everything seems to focus on the personality of the teachers—on Mr. Wopsle's great-aunt, Pecksniff, Mrs. Pipchin, Squeers, Creakle, and Doctor Blimber on the one hand, and on Phoebe, Mr. Marton, and Doctor Strong on the other. Subtract the personality of the teacher from any or all the descriptions, and what is there left? This circumstance is striking, doubly so. In the first place, it testifies to Dickens's possession of the power to create characters whose personalities are visualized in the imagination and whose speech and actions are retained in the memory. In the second

[100]Moncrieff, *A Book about Schools*, pp. 235 f.
[101]Clarke and Clarke, *Recollections of Writers*, pp. 2–12.
[102]Sala, *Life and Adventures*, I, 133–41.
[103]Hayward, *The Days of Dickens*, pp. 251 f.
[104]Clinton-Baddeley, "Benevolent Teachers of Youth," pp. 379–80.
[105]See chap. v below.
[106]See Frieser, *Die Schulen bei Dickens*, pp. 5, 81, 87, 134.

place, it appears to emphasize a general pedagogical lesson which Dickens meant to imply: that method, equipment, system, and curriculum count for little unless all are reinforced by the sympathy and the personality of adequate teachers. That is the main lesson, surely, which Dickens meant to convey when he drew such characters as Phoebe, Mr. Marton, and Doctor Strong. Any attempts to draw up rules from Dickens for governing the process of learning and teaching in the light of more modern pedagogy are likely to stick fast amid his satire, humour,[107] sentiment, and plot-construction.

It is evident that Squeers, Creakle, and Blimber are somewhat distorted and enlarged for the sake of fun. They are displayed dramatically and even theatrically at times. But the many letters from people who asserted they went to school to the original Squeers show that any charge that these characters are improbable is false. They lived both in the reality of English life and in the fairyland between the covers of Dickens's novels. Historical accounts of conditions in many of the private schools of England confirm the wretchedness and the squalor, the brutality of the masters, and the inadequacy of the education given. It is to the credit of Dickens as a humanitarian that he exposed the vicious practices which existed in the Yorkshire schools. Even if men like Shaw were only partially guilty, public opinion decided the ultimate fate of the schools they operated.

Dickens, however, just as he had no concrete solution for the problem of Oliver Twist, had no solution for Dotheboys Hall but disbandment. The portrayal of this nefarious institution, masquerading as a school, administered by a devilish business man who exploited the frailings of mankind and dealt in human flesh, was well calculated to set Dickens's readers on fire, but it did not resolve the problem of private schools. Dickens apparently did not wish to abolish all private institutions. When he wished to present good schools in his novels, he depicted private institutions—but under good masters.

[107]See chap. VI below.

CHAPTER IV

The Education of Girls

Although such early thinkers as Juan Luis Vives (1492–1540) and Comenius (1592–1670), and the early journalist, Defoe (*c.* 1659–1731) advocated some educational training for women and girls, little came of their theories on co-education for many years. Education was not considered necessary for girls until comparatively modern times. Of course, a few women, such as the versatile Queen Elizabeth of the sixteenth century and Mary Godwin of the nineteenth, did secure a scholarly education. Occasionally we read of such a well-educated woman as the dazzling Lady Mary Wortley Montagu, or that brilliant woman of the theatre, Aphra Behn, who scandalously won her way to Westminster Abbey. A few years before the birth of Charles Dickens, about 1800, Jane Austen was working unobtrusively at her manuscripts. As the nineteenth century wore on, there were others: the Brontë sisters, Harriet Martineau, Mrs. Elizabeth Gaskell, and George Eliot. But they were exceptions; good fortune had given them a well-educated father or an exceptional tutor, or placed them among a select group of writers and advanced thinkers. Most girls and women in the days of Dickens still occupied a very inferior position in life. The parents of the wealthy, in the name of education, made an attempt to prepare their daughters for the marriage market. But even when attained, the status of a well-to-do married woman in the nineteenth century was far from enviable. The law debarred her from direct political power, considered her a chattel of her husband, permitted her to be treated with violence, and waived any rights she might claim to the custody of children or to the disposal of real estate.[1] Even so, the smattering of schooling which the girls of gentle birth did receive led them to assume a superior attitude to girls of more humble birth. Fanny, in the opening pages of Jane Austen's *Mansfield Park*, even though she was able to read and write and work well at domestic tasks, was considered very ignorant by her aristocratic cousins because she was unable to name the rivers of Russia, put parts of the map of Europe together, or distinguish between crayon and water-colour. It may be recalled that Maggie Tulliver of George Eliot's *The Mill on*

[1]Brailsford, *Shelley, Godwin, and Their Circle*, p. 190.

the Floss was regarded as "quick but shallow" (Book Four) and secured little from the feeble literature and dry history meted out to her at Miss Furniss's boarding-school at Laceham; and later (Book Five), when she went back to this dreary school to teach "amid the watery rice pudding, spiced with Pinnock," the move was considered as "going into service again." This thread of feminine inferiority in life and education may be observed reaching down the years to Wells's *Joan and Peter*, in the satirization of the School of St. George and the Venerable Bede, as Peter and Sydney "spoon" all the while Miss Murgatroyd dilates on the ideal advantages of co-education.

In England up to about 1850, the education of girls, such as it was, may be divided into four main divisions. The daughters of noble families were educated privately, at home, as ladies, under the care of governesses. The daughters of the well-to-do middle class, the second group in the social scale, would probably attend one of the better private boarding-schools for girls. The daughters of the lower middle class (sometimes much lower)—daughters of families reduced to "genteel poverty," or of poor clergymen—formed the third group, and would more than likely attend one of the semi-charitable boarding-schools for girls which, because it was partially supported by some benevolent individual, could accept much lower fees. Finally, for the fourth group, the very poor, there was no provision at all, unless they were able to attend a dame school, a monitorial school, or a charity day-school.

The first group, who were educated at home, left the nursery at the age of seven or eight years to enter the schoolroom, faced with the prospect of staying in this cloistered life for about ten years, when they could hope to take their places in life beside their emancipated sisters who had "come out." Usually the younger sisters did not come out before the elder ones were married. Lady Catharine de Burgh in Jane Austen's *Pride and Prejudice* was positively flabbergasted to find that the *five* Misses Bennet were all out at once. And well she might be, for young ladies of the schoolroom simply did not exist in the social world; they neither accepted nor received any invitations; and polite visitors were expected to ignore them. The schoolroom was tucked away in some little-used section of the house. There, surrounded with shabby furniture, seated on ink-stained chairs beside deeply scratched tables, confronted with tattered maps and faded revolving globes, young girls kept daily company with a governess.

The governess was usually a submissive, unprotesting person, of unimpeachable morality, but of little practical wisdom, and of still less scholarship. She was usually a gentlewoman of reduced fortune. She might be an orphan or a widow, or perhaps the wife of a ruined gentle-man or a ne'er-do-well. Forced by circumstances to earn her own living, she would be obliged to turn to teaching, as the only "respectable" occupation open to a woman of good birth. Governesses were kept in a sort of perpetual isolation, because the reserve and decorum of English aristocratic society demanded that they be kept both busy and at a distance. As a result, a governess was more or less "declassed," because she, in her turn, could not, even if she were so inclined, associate with the low-born servants and trades-folk. Charlotte Brontë in *Jane Eyre* set Jane's salary at thirty pounds per annum (chap. x); but when Charlotte Brontë herself entered the service of Mr. and Mrs. John White of Upperwood House, Rawdon (near Leeds), her salary, in 1841, was only twenty pounds per annum, with deductions for laundry.[2] Before that, Charlotte had been governess to the children—"riotous, perverse, un-manageable cubs"—of Mrs. Sidgwick of Stonegappe (near Skipton). The "pampered, spoilt, and turbulent" children got on her nerves; on one occasion she had a huge Bible hurled at her; and on all occasions she was overwhelmed not only with schoolwork but with "oceans of needle-work, yards of cambric to hem, muslin nightcaps to make, and above all things, dolls to dress."[3]

One of the chief sources of information about the education of girls in nineteenth-century England is the English novel, from which the qualifications of the governesses can be inferred. Apparently, ladies of reduced fortune, or orphans about to enter adult life, either advertised for situations as governesses or managed to secure recommendations to or from friends. Miss Pinkerton, in *Vanity Fair*, when recommending two of her pupils to Mrs. Bute Crawley in 1814, claimed that the said young ladies were able to instruct in Greek, Latin, Hebrew, Spanish, French, and Italian; in geography, science, music, and the use of the globes; and that one of the girls could teach "the Syriac language, and the elements of Constitutional Law." Miss Pinkerton cynically added that perhaps the youthfulness and pretty appearance of one of the prospective gover-nesses might be objectionable (chap. xi). This list of scholarly accom-plishments is surprising indeed, and it is probable that Thackeray wrote with tongue in cheek. At any rate, scepticism on his part would have been justified, considering that Miss Mangnall, author of one of the most popular textbooks of the time, thought that Mahomet was Emperor of Persia.

The Brontë sisters, who had served as governesses themselves, are

[2]Hanson and Hanson, *The Four Brontës*, p. 92.
[3]*Ibid.*, pp. 69–79.

likely to be far more reliable sources. Anne Brontë pictures the genuine and sincere Agnes Grey, in her novel of the same name (chap. VI), offering music, singing, drawing, French, Latin, and German. Charlotte Brontë's Jane Eyre was more modest. Her advertisement offered the following: "A young lady, accustomed to tuition . . . is desirous of meeting with a situation in a private family where the children are under fourteen. . . . She is accustomed to teach the usual branches of a good English education, together with French, Drawing, and Music. . . ." (chap. X)

But, to be brief, it is fairly well established that the curricula, both of girls at home and at private boarding-schools, consisted of two parts: elegant accomplishments and a little solid knowledge. The elegant accomplishments took most of the time by far; Maria Edgeworth, author of *The Parent's Assistant* (1796), speaks of going through all the tortures of the back-board and iron neck-collar to produce grace and carriage, and to draw out the neck.[4] Nevertheless, Maria's education at the school of Mrs. Davis in Upper Wimpole Street, London, was better than most, and her French had been well grounded at Mrs. Lataffiere's school at Derby.[5] The aim was to prepare the girls for the marriage market by enabling them to acquire polish and gracefulness through such media as Italian and French, music, dancing, and embroidery. The solid knowledge consisted of geography, botany, and history; the history, designated "ancient and modern," might better have been described as superficial. There was also a very vague but rather comprehensive course of instruction known as general knowledge.

An examination of the books that were used adds greatly to our knowledge of the girls' studies. Along with Mavor's *Speller*, perhaps the most commonly used book was *Mangnall's Historical and Miscellaneous Questions for the Use of Young People*, commonly known as *Mangnall's Questions*. It was published in 1800[6] by Miss Richmal Mangnall, a Yorkshire schoolmistress, whose school is to be described later. The Preface made the proud boast that the book was "intended to awaken a

[4]Cf. Dickens, *Martin Chuzzlewit*, chap. IX, p. 166: "Mr. Pinch's sister was at that moment instructing her eldest pupil—to wit, a premature little woman of thirteen years, who had already arrived at such a pitch of whalebone and education that she had nothing girlish about her."

[5]Mood, "Maria Edgeworth's Apprenticeship," chap. II.

[6]By 1815, this Stockport printing had run to eleven editions; its author, originally a teacher in Mrs. Wilson's School for Girls, near Wakefield, and who subsequently took over the school herself, sold out her rights to Longmans for 100 guineas (see Gardiner, *English Girlhood at School*, p. 476). The following references in the text, however, are to the London: Wm. Tegg and Co., edition of 1851. For other texts and story books see the early pages of chap. III above.

laudable spirit of curiosity in young minds." But the lumps of hetero-geneous knowledge which it contained were enough to cloy and bewilder any young mind, and seemed, on the contrary, to be exquisitely designed to quench any such spirit of inquiry. A burning interest was assumed in such questions as these: Where do nutmegs grow? What are the duties of the Justices of the Peace? How are candles made? And in what manner did the Ancient Brahmins live? A section on British and general bio-graphy was attached. Rabelais was alloted four lines (p. 381). Three pages on "Questions on Common Subjects" (pp. 435–8) assumed an unquenchable thirst for knowledge concerning the manufacture of gin and brandy, an insatiable hunger to know the composition of starch and gunpowder, and a dynamic interest in the definition of common oil. Concerning the "Elements of Astronomy," the number of comets was deemed crucial, as was the time-span of the planetary orbits (pp. 410–14). Ancient history demanded a repetition of the names of all the Roman emperors with their virtues and vices, the battles of antiquity, the most celebrated queens, and the customs of the Gentoo women (pp. 61–3, 87). Still, the Preface insisted that the author "meant well."

The fourth edition of *Etiquette for Ladies* (1837) laid down eighty maxims on accomplishments, dress, and manners: gloves should always be worn in public but not at dinner; the use of a knife as spoon or fork was vulgar indeed—the conveyance of food to the mouth on a knife, warned the text, carried "the imminent danger of enlarging the aper-ture"; music or drawing—but not morning work—should be laid aside when visitors called; loud talk was Plebeian; short dresses were not in accordance with good etiquette, nor were coloured shoes; and references to persons by initial was "heathenish."[7]

Another book was Blair's *Preceptor on the Arts and Sciences*; but more common was the dry "classic," Gray's *Memoriatechnica*, which gave the names of all the Roman kings and emperors with their respec-tive dates. The naughty boy in *Carols of Cockayne* mentions Pinnock's *Catechism*, which, apparently, was common in boys' schools also:

> When they taught him how to spell, he showed his wicked whims,
> By mutilating Pinnock and mislaying Watts's hymns.[8]

One is inclined not to blame him very much. *Conversations in Natural Philosophy*, by Joan Marcett, claimed to verse its readers in every science

[7]Sections quoted in Lambert, *When Victoria Began to Reign*, pp. 196–200.

[8]Quoted in Cruse, *The Englishman and His Books in the Early Nineteenth Century* (to which I am indebted for various details in this paragraph). Cf. Sala, who claimed he was "pitchforked" into a French school before he had been "through Pinnock or knew one out of five rules of Lindley Murray's Grammar" (Straus, *Sala*, p. 30).

except mathematics. Butler's *Exercises on the Globe* covered a very wide field of knowledge, encompassing such a wide variety of topics as Robert Burns, whalebone, Lazarus, and sirens.[9] Murray's *English Grammar* was very widely used. It had been written in 1795, by a gentleman of York, a close friend of the poet Gray. The book contained a crass amount of moral sentiment embedded in the rule-of-thumb grammar which was to be memorized.[10] There was another book in four volumes which must have been a welcome relief from this dry, pious, factual material; it was a *History of England* by Oliver Goldsmith, written with all the charm and picturesque detail which one would expect from the whimsical and kindly Goldsmith; Jane Austen used one when she was a girl. To conclude this glimpse at the books used by the girls, three popular reading-books may be added: *The English Reader* by Murray, published in 1800; *Elegant Extracts* by Knox; and *The Speaker*, by Dr. Enfield, which was said to be bowdlerized—expurgated of anything calculated to call a blush into the cheek of a young maiden.[11]

If the formidable mass of knowledge which remained did not bring a blush to the cheek of the nineteenth-century girl, one strongly suspects that it brought many an ache to her head. If the girl, privately instructed at home by her governess, was able to assimilate one-tenth of the miscellaneous and useless knowledge suggested in the books which she studied, she certainly, in the language of little Miss Jellyby, "knew a quantity."[12]

In the better class of boarding-schools for the daughters of parents who were able to pay the full expense of education, the instruction was not greatly different from the instruction given in private homes by governesses. When she was fourteen, Elizabeth Gaskell went to a boarding-school at Stratford-on-Avon, and remained there for three years. The annual fee was 148 pounds. The school was kept by three Byerley sisiters, who, because of financial difficulties, had turned to the teaching of French, Italian, music, and deportment. As was so often the case, one of the sisters was greatly beloved. Another was as deaf as a

[9]Cf. ". . . she is half supposed to hint, 'So I myself came into the world, completely up in Pinnock, Mangnall, Tables, and the use of the Globes'" (Dickens, "Tom Tiddler's Ground" in *Christmas Stories*, pp. 280–1).

[10]Cf. *The Old Curiosity Shop*, chap. xxix, p. 277. Mrs. Jarley had taken "great pains to conciliate" the young ladies from the boarding-schools "by altering the face and costume of Mr. Grimaldi as clown [one of the wax figures] to represent Mr. Lindley Murray as he appeared when engaged in the composition of his English Grammar. . . ."

[11]Emily Shore, in her *Journal*, 1831–9, said she read *Bowdler's Selections* and *Pickwick*, and made history charts (Percival, *The English Miss*, pp. 69–74).

[12]Dickens, *Bleak House*, I, chap. iv, p. 53: "But knows a quantity, I suppose? Can dance, and play music, and sing? She can talk French, I suppose, and do geography, and globes, and needlework, and everything?"

post. Elizabeth Gaskell was one of the best-educated women of the age, but just how much she was indebted to this school for her education is difficult to estimate. She had studied French, botany, and dancing prior to her residence there, and studied Latin, French, and Italian after she left. She also lived for two years in the home of Rev. William Turner, and it is to be inferred that she obtained valuable training from him, for he was an enlightened scholar, active in founding Sunday schools and literary and philosophical societies.[13]

If any school should reveal the highest standards of education in the better class of boarding-schools for girls, surely it would be that of Miss Mangnall, author of the famous *Mangnall's Questions*. Fortunately, an authentic account of the conditions in this noted Wakefield school is given in the diary of Elizabeth Firth, a close friend of the Brontës, who was one of the pupils. A summary of its contents was given by Miss F. Gadeson in an address at Cambridge in August, 1900, and quoted, in part, the next year, by R. D. Roberts. From this document, we discover that the "ladies" under Miss Mangnall's direction read *Rokeby*, *The Vicar of Wakefield*, and *The Lay of the Last Minstrel*. They studied the use of the globes, learned latitude and longitude, and after two long hours of investigation decided that Mahomet was Emperor of Persia! Those who had failed to learn a list of rivers by heart were dismissed. Miss Firth must have learned them, for she was awarded the gift of an inkstand from the celebrated Miss Mangnall for proficiency in geography. The diary also mentions the task of memorizing the names of the English kings. The "ladies" indulged in "poking," impertinence, gossip, stealing, lying, fighting, and untidiness, not to mention the bad spelling of the diary. They were rewarded with gifts, food, or walks, and were punished with whippings, threats, delayed baths, or enforced transcription of lines and verses. Failure in spelling resulted in being "sent to bed."[14]

Girls at the fashionable boarding-schools did not seem to suffer such gross neglect and be given so few material comforts as the pupils at the semi-charitable schools for girls. An example of the latter type is the school located at Cowan Bridge, two miles from Kirkby Lonsdale, which was attended by the Brontë sisters. Maria and Elizabeth entered this school in July, 1824, and Charlotte and Emily followed in August and November of the same year. This boarding-school for the daughters of poor clergymen had been founded, a little over a year before, by the benevolent rector of Willington, the Reverend William Carus Wilson.

---

[13]Haldane, *Mrs. Gaskell and Her Friends*.
[14]Roberts, ed., *Education in the Nineteenth Century*, chap. v. See also the *Modern Language Quarterly*, Aug., 1900, for a reprinting of the diary itself.

The low fee of fourteen pounds a year was levied for education, clothing, and lodging, with extra charges for frocks, pelisses, bonnets, and books. It is possible to give the bare facts about this school without entering the controversy over the picture given of it by Charlotte Brontë in *Jane Eyre*. The building was a disused bobbin-mill. The ground floor had been converted into schoolrooms and the upstairs into dormitories. The rooms had low ceilings, paved stone floors, and small windows. At one end of the mill was a cottage which served both as teachers' room and dining-room.[15]

The purpose here is to discover the conditions in semi-charitable schools, and it must be admitted that the picture of Cowan School in *Jane Eyre* was probably heightened and exaggerated.[16] But even if the porridge was not often burnt, the beef high, the stew full of rancid fat, and the discipline quite so humiliating as Charlotte Brontë depicted it, the rigour of the condemnation expressed in *Jane Eyre* leaves no doubt about the emphasis laid, in these schools, on the doctrine of the utter depravity of children; and obviously there must have been sufficient neglect, unkindness, harsh discipline, and coercion for the novelist to have produced such a picture. These two facts stand out: the girls *did* spend unpleasant and strenuous Sundays, and, throughout the winter during which the Brontë sisters attended the school, there *was* a great deal of sickness. Every Sunday, without fail, and no matter what the weather, the girls were forced to walk two miles to Tunstall Church to attend the morning service. In a vacant and otherwise unused room, while they waited for another long service held during the afternoon, they ate their cold dinners which they had brought with them. Before the year was over, the two elder Brontë girls, Maria and Elizabeth, had developed tuberculosis, and each of them in turn found a quiet grave in the chancel of Haworth Church. Charlotte and Emily were eventually taken home.[17]

It should be added that some girls of the nineteenth century attended the monitorial day-schools, and some went to the full charity schools, which were discussed in chapter II. Such was the educational provision for girls in nineteenth-century England. The instruction given in the semi-charitable boarding-schools was little better than the artificial

[15]The details were gathered from Benson, *Charlotte Brontë*, pp. 21–7.

[16]But see Hanson and Hanson, *The Four Brontës*, p. 12, where it is stated that the writings of the founder, the Rev. W. Carus Wilson, "testify that Charlotte, in her savage indictment of him in *Jane Eyre* 'exaggerated nothing.' "

[17]Benson, *Charlotte Brontë*, pp. 22–3; Hanson and Hanson, *The Four Brontës*, pp. 11–13.

training that was given to the daughters of the nobility at home and the daughters of the wealthy middle class at the fashionable boarding-schools, and for the very poor there was, as I have said, practically no provision at all.

Dickens gave five glimpses of the life led by private governesses, and described seven boarding-schools and day-schools for girls (besides the girls' school taught by Miss Peecher which was described in chapter II). Of the five governesses, Miss Lane received only casual mention. She was in the employ of Mr. Borum, to whom Nicholas Nickleby, accompanied by Miss Snevellicci, applied to "bespeak" a new play for the benefit of Mr. Crummles's daughter, otherwise known as "the infant phenomenon." Mr. Borum's children, having been brought from the nursery in order to get a good look at the child prodigy, began to poke their fingers into her eyes to see if she were real, tread upon her toes, pinch her, filch her parasol, and use her as the rope in a game of tug of war; whereupon Miss Lane, the governess, was entreated to "see to the children."[18] Inasmuch as the child prodigy was lucky to escape without being torn limb from limb, it may be inferred that Miss Lane, or any other governess in similar circumstances, lived a very unenviable existence.

Another governess whom Dickens depicted was Ruth Pinch, a sister of the trustful Tom Pinch in *Martin Chuzzlewit*. In this novel, Dickens caught the snobbish discrimination that society practised against governesses, even chatty, harmless, trim, and cheerful ones like Miss Pinch. The footman managed to announce Ruth's visitors in a tone befitting the social station of a governess—half way between the deferential, respectful tone in which he announced visitors for his master and the more intimate tone reserved for the servants. The attitude of wealthy young pupils and their parents is well shown by the fact that the pupils, in order to satisfy their mother's curiosity, were encouraged to spy upon the governess and report everything that took place. The nineteenth-century custom of treating little girls as miniature adults is revealed in the delightful description of Miss Pinch's eldest pupil: a "premature little woman of thirteen years old, who had already arrived at such a pitch of whalebone and education that there was nothing girlish about her." The fawning condescension of Pecksniff and the haughty arrogance of his daughters completed the submission of Miss Pinch to her position in the social scale. Perhaps Dickens seeks to imply her true worth when he has her marry young John Westlock. But there is no doubt about the position

[18]*Nicholas Nickleby*, chap. XXIV, p. 379.

she occupied in the eyes of masters and servants in the lofty and wealthy brass-and-copper merchant's house.[19]

A third governess is Mrs. General in *Little Dorrit*. She was a widow of forty-five who was said to have been qualified by birth, accomplishments, and position in society for the situation of governess, matron, and chaperon in the family of Mr. Dorrit. She was no ordinary governess, this woman, as she insisted herself. She was to "form the mind" and manners of her charges only on conditions of equality, and as a companion and friend. At the outset, she delicately hinted at a remuneration of 400 pounds a year, and inwardly conceived designs on the whole of Mr. Dorrit's fortune through the simple expedient of bringing him to the altar.

> In person, Mrs. General, including her skirts, which had much to do with it, was of a dignified and imposing appearance; . . . she was a chalky creation altogether, . . . a cool, waxy, blown-out woman, who had never lighted well. . . .
> Her way of forming a mind was to prevent it from forming opinions. . . .
> Mrs. General was not to be told of anything shocking. Accidents, miseries, and offences, were never to be mentioned before her. Passion was to go to sleep in the presence of Mrs. General, and blood was to change to milk and water.[20]

Dickens cannot forbear giving her a peculiar mania for "varnishing" everything in sight. She complains that Little Dorrit—who, as a child, had been the old man's strength and stay, and a mother to her brother and sister in the Marshalsea—has no self-reliance of character. Little Dorrit is not to wonder at Venice, and she must call her father "Papa" because, like such words as prunes, prism, and potatoes, it gives such a pretty formation to the lips. Her sister, Fanny, does not escape censure either; she forms too many opinions, whereas good breeding should form none.[21] But the pretty, vivacious, and frivolous Fanny is almost a match for this "ghoul in gloves"[22] who is trying to feel her way into the Dorrit family, and the cold hand of death reaches out to seize the hand of Mr. Dorrit before the gloved hand of Mrs. General can clasp it tenderly in hers.

Perhaps a more acute treatment of the sense of shame, inferiority, and either meek submission or sullen resentment which such treatment aroused in the hearts of these dependent women is that given later in *Little Dorrit* (chap. XXI), where the sullen and self-tormenting Miss

[19]*Martin Chuzzlewit*, chap. IX, p. 166.
[20]*Little Dorrit*, Bk. II, chap. II, p. 25.
[21]*Ibid.*, chap. v, p. 53; chap. VII, p. 89 f.
[22]*Ibid.*, chap. xv, p. 223.

Wade recounts in her long letter the writhing agony which her proud spirit underwent during her experience in the dependent and inferior position of governess in several wealthy families. In "Astley's,"[23] Dickens catches the general attitude of the nineteenth century again, to a nicety. When the family at the play discovered that one of their little cherubs who was seated behind a pillar could not see what was taking place, the boy was lifted into the governess's place and she was unceremoniously pushed in behind the offending pillar!

A searing line was also drawn between the daughters of the wealthy and those of the less fortunate who occupied a lower station in life. This discrimination is well illustrated by the little incidents that took place during Nell's visit to Miss Monflathers's Boarding and Day Establishment, as depicted in *The Old Curiosity Shop*.[24] Little Nell had been sent by Mrs. Jarley with a package of handbills setting forth the merits of the wonderful wax-works, and just as the little girl reached the front of the school property, the large iron gates swung slowly open to permit the passage of a long procession of girls, walking two by two, accompanied by their headmistress, who was carrying her lilac silk parasol. The presentation of the handbills gave Miss Monflathers an irresistible opportunity to impress a "moral" lesson on the minds of her youthful charges, and to drive home Little Nell's duty as a social inferior. Assuming a tone of ridiculous hauteur, Miss Monflathers proceeded to lecture the child on her wickedness in being a wax-work child at all, instead of nobly assisting in the great manufacturers of her country for the munificent sum of three shillings a week. Nothing could be more illustrative of the philosophy then current of keeping all impolite and inferior noses to the grindstone, and the insistence that the lower classes should stay in that station in life in which Providence had seen fit to place them.

Little Nell was in tears at the force of Miss Monflathers's invective and, in her confusion, let fall her handkerchief. One of the pupils, Miss Edwards, good-naturedly glided forward and timidly picked it up. Poor, orphaned Miss Edwards was not a paying pupil in the school, but only an apprentice, and she was constantly made to feel her inferiority. Because she yielded to a kindly impulse on this occasion, she was severely upbraided by Miss Monflathers for taking the part of "every grovelling and debased person" who came in her path, and was sent to her room with orders not to leave it for the rest of the day. The unfor-

---

[23]"Scenes," *Sketches by Boz*, p. 120.
[24]Chap. XXXI, pp. 295–306. The original of Miss Monflathers's School, and also of Miss Twinkleton's Academy in *Edwin Drood*, is thought to have been Eastgate House, a girls' school at Rochester (Dexter, *The England of Dickens*, p. 181).

tunate girl, in her haste to carry out this injunction, forgot to gratify Miss Monflathers's ego with a curtsy, and was arrested by a cry of mortification from the headmistress. "The young lady turned and curtsied. Nell could see that she raised her dark eyes to the face of her superior, and that their expression, and that of her whole attitude for the instant was one of mute but most touching appeal against this ungenerous usage. Miss Monflathers only tossed her head in reply, and the great gate closed upon a bursting heart." Dickens had no hesitation in blandly remarking that Miss Edwards was the object of her teacher's spite solely because she—an apprentice and a dependant—had been endowed by nature with a keen intellect and a pretty figure, whereas the baronet's daughter, who paid for all the extras and was "the gayest feather in Miss Monflathers's cap," had unaccountably been endowed with few brains and very plain features.

Esther Summerson was also set apart from other children, though at a different type of school—a neighbourhood school where she was a day-pupil—and for a different reason.[25] Her first week was crowned with joy at an invitation to a birthday party; her godmother, however, snubbed the invitation; there were holidays at school and parties at home on other children's birthdays, but none on hers. When Esther pleaded with her godmother to tell her why she was so different from other children, the narrow-minded old lady told her that it would have been better if she had never been born. "Your mother, Esther, is your disgrace, and you were hers. . . . For yourself, unfortunate girl, orphaned and degraded from the first of these evil anniversaries, pray daily that the sins of others be not visited upon your head. . . . You are set apart."[26] Thus Esther lived the life of a social outcast, a victim of stringent Victorian morality.

But eventually her godmother died and Esther was sent to a boarding-school at Greenleaf, which was conducted by the two Miss Donnys. Her life was far different there, for two reasons: in the first place, a benevolent guardian was paying for her tuition; in the second, since she was to qualify as a governess, she was given an opportunity to instruct the other children. Losing herself in helping each newly arrived pupil, she gave up thinking that it would have been better if she had never been born, and her birthdays became happy anniversaries. Dickens tells nothing of the lessons that were taught, the books that were used, or the methods that were followed by the teachers in either of the schools Esther attended; he contents himself by assuring his readers that Esther's

[25]*Bleak House*, I, chap. III, pp. 19–21.
[26]*Ibid.*, p. 21.

accounts at Greenleaf were paid regularly throughout six quiet years, and then passes on to a description of Esther's leave-taking. There is no doubt that Esther had won her way into all hearts; indeed, the whole scene is almost suffocating in its sentiment; there are too many "dear Esther's," too many clinging arms, too many tears leaping to the eyes, and too much lavender water; furthermore, the idea of a *gardener* presenting her with a nosegay of *geraniums* is grotesque,[27] and there is no suggestion that this incident was a stroke of humour. If Esther had become a governess of the usual sort, instead of a companion to the youthful ward of her benevolent guardian, she would no doubt have been treated as a social inferior, as her godmother had caused her to be treated at her first school, and as Miss Edwards was treated at Miss Monflathers's fashionable establishment.

Dickens described four other fashionable girls' schools besides Miss Monflathers's: the Ladies' Seminary at Chelsea, which was a day-school conducted by Mrs. Wackles; Miss Pupford's Establishment; Minerva House, Chelsea, conducted by the Misses Crumpton; and the Nuns' House at Cloisterham, under the direction of Miss Twinkleton.

A comparison of the buildings is interesting. There was the little school at Chelsea where

Miss Sophia Wackles resided with her widowed mother and two sisters, in conjunction with whom she maintained a very small day-school for young ladies of proportionate dimensions; a circumstance which was made known to the neighbourhood by an oval board over the front first floor window, whereon appeared in circumambient flourishes, the words "Ladies' Seminary": and which was further published and proclaimed at intervals between the hours of half-past nine and ten in the morning by a straggling and solitary young lady of tender years standing on the scraper on the tips of her toes and making futile attempts to reach the knocker with a spelling-book.[28]

It is regrettable that we do not receive so much as a glimpse of the interior of this flourishing place of learning, for this very life-like scene of the late arrival arouses speculation as to the reception she received on the other side of that door with the high knocker. The description of Miss Pupford's school is even more concise: "Miss Pupford's establishment for six young ladies of tender years is an establishment of a compact nature, an establishment in miniature, quite a pocket establishment. Miss Pupford, Miss Pupford's assistant with the Parisian accent, Miss Pupford's cook, and Miss Pupford's housemaid, complete what Miss Pupford calls the educational and domestic staff of her Lilliputian Col-

[27]*Ibid.*, p. 33.
[28]*The Old Curiosity Shop*, chap. VIII, pp. 79–80.

lege."[29] A little later in the same story we are given a peep at a sampler, hanging on the college wall; the date has been carefully picked out, but the two peacocks remain, "terrified to death by some German text that is waddling downhill after them out of a cottage." A third description, that of Minerva House, is a little more informative:

The house was a white one, a little removed from the roadside, with close palings in front. The bedroom windows were always left partly open, to afford a bird's-eye view of numerous little bedsteads with very white dimity furniture, and thereby impress the passer-by with a due sense of the luxuries of the establishment; and there was a front parlour hung round with highly varnished maps which nobody ever looked at and filled with books which no one ever read, appropriated exclusively to the reception of parents, who, whenever they called, could not fail to be struck with the very deep appearance of the place.[30]

Finally, there is the description of the Nuns' House in *Edwin Drood*.[31] It is difficult to imagine the superficial instruction, which masqueraded as education for girls in the nineteenth century, being imparted in the quiet old cathedral town, with its stately spires, storied cathedral crypt, narrow streets, old-fashioned yards, muffled bells, monastery, convent, and ivy-covered chapels, all betokening an age that was past. Yet Dickens blended the young ladies' establishment into the sombre and brooding tones of antiquity, as he speculated whether the patient nuns were in the habit of bending their submissive heads to avoid the beams in the low ceilings, or sat in the long, low windows telling their beads, or were so unfortunate as to have been "walled up alive" in one of the many nooks beneath the "jutting gables" for some fleshly misdemeanour. There was a certain amount of incongruity, as Dickens noted, because the new and shining brass plate did not blend with the greying tone of the old stone walls. "On the trim gate enclosing its old courtyard is a resplendent brass plate flashing forth the legend: 'Seminary for Young Ladies. Miss Twinkleton.' "

Dickens has comparatively little to say about the curriculum that was followed in these girls' schools. He hardly mentions it in *Edwin Drood*, except to point out that Miss Twinkleton was guilty of some rather prudish frauds when reading novels to her pupils: she had the habit of omitting the love scenes and inserting short moral saws of her own.[32]

[29]"Tom Tiddler's Ground" in *Christmas Stories*, pp. 280–90.
[30]"Sentiment" in *Sketches by Boz*, pp. 375–80.
[31]Chap. III, pp. 19–20.
[32]Chap. XXII (closing paragraphs), p. 276. This would suggest that Dickens did not approve of the bowdlerized versions commonly found in the school readers, but his reputation for the "unsullied page" forbids one from expanding this suggestion.

There is little more about the studies in the description of Miss Pupford's Establishment, except the hint that Miss Pupford had come into
the world "completely bound up in Pinnock, Mangnall, Tables, and the
use of the Globes." Since her assistant was said to have "a Parisian
accent," acquired when she was "pickling in brine" and undergoing a
"clear-starching derangement" at the bottom of a boat two miles off
Margate, it may be inferred that French of a sort was misunderstood.[33]
Instruction in Minerva House was dismissed with a scant sentence which
remarked that the establishment was a place where "some twenty girls
of the ages of from thirteen to nineteen inclusive, acquired a smattering
of everything and a knowledge of nothing; instruction in French and
Italian; dancing lessons twice a week; and other necessaries of life."[34]
From the description given earlier in this chapter of the heterogeneous
lumps of knowledge which actually were studied, it may be readily seen
that Dickens's remark was very much to the point. Perhaps the clearest
statement of what was studied is that given for Mrs. Wackles's Seminary:
"The several duties of instruction in this establishment were thus discharged. English grammar, composition, geography, and the use of the
dumb-bells, by Miss Melissa Wackles; writing, arithmetic, dancing,
music, and general fascination, by Miss Sophy Wackles; the art of
needle-work, marking, and samplery, by Miss Jane Wackles; corporal
punishment, fasting and other tortures and terrors, by Mrs. Wackles."[35]
If the subject of spelling is added—the little girl who arrived late used
her spelling-book to reach the door-knocker—this is almost a complete
list, but little insight is given into the methods or the books that were
used. Obviously, since Dickens had never attended a girls' school, and
was not of an aristocratic family, he had little first-hand knowledge of
these details. The inclusion of arithmetic in the list may, or may not,
be an error; it is at least unusual to find girls' being taught arithmetic
so early in the nineteenth century as 1840–1, when *The Old Curiosity
Shop* was published.[36]

The most delightful reading in connection with these schools, however,
is Dickens's descriptions of little incidents that took place during preparations for a ball or for the Christmas vacation. What preparations there
were at Minerva House for the half-yearly ball! How lovely were the

[33]"Tom Tiddler's Ground" in *Christmas Stories*, p. 280.
[34]"Sentiment" in *Sketches by Boz*, p. 375.
[35]*The Old Curiosity Shop*, chap. VIII, pp. 79–80.
[36]I found only one other instance, but that is fairly authoritative—in Charlotte
Brontë's account of Jane Eyre's first day at Lowood School, published in 1847.
Dickens may have recalled that arithmetic was included in the studies of his sister
Fanny when she was in attendance at the Royal Academy of Music, 1823–7.

decorations of blue calico roses and plaid tulips! How the linen drapers were astonished at the unprecedented demand for blue ribbons and white gloves! Then there is that ludicrous purchase of geraniums for bouquets again—perhaps intentional here. What a lacing of stays and scorching of hair there was in the evening! Dickens gave his humour and imagination full play:

"How do I look, dear?" inquired Miss Emily Smithers the belle of the house, of Miss Caroline Wilson, who was her bosom friend, because she was the ugliest girl in Hammersmith, or out of it.
"Oh! charming, dear. How do I?"
"Delightful! you never looked so handsome," returned the belle, adjusting her own dress, and not bestowing a glance on her poor companion.[37]

There is a whimsical touch in Dickens's humour as he describes the tears that come into Miss Pupford's eyes, and the air of mystery with which she imparts the secret to her assistant that a former pupil of the Lilliputian College has distinguished herself to the extent of getting her name in the birth or marriage column of the morning paper; or when he relates how the housemaid, Bella, of the same establishment, works on the good nature of little Miss Kimmeens who, forced to spend her holidays at the school because her father is in far-off India, has been left in the housemaid's care; all the feminine wiles at Bella's command are used to exploit the child's innocent heart to induce her to urge Bella to go away for a holiday too.[38]

But nothing equalled the clandestine preparations which indicated that the Christmas vacation was drawing near at Miss Twinkleton's establishment.[39] There was the corruption of the attendants and housemaids by the free distribution of hairpins, cold cream, pomatum, ribbons, and down-at-heel shoes; all this was justified to ensure secrecy and to avoid possible awkward questions about crumbs in the beds. How naughty and elated the young ladies felt as they sipped cowslip wine out of the little medicine glass! What a flavour the dressed tongue, cut with a pair of scissors, must have had as it was served around on the curling tongs! And how delicately Miss Twinkleton bestowed a kiss on each young lady's cheek, as she presented her with an envelope that contained the bill with the governess's compliments on the corner! The vacation break-up at Miss Pupford's is almost equally delightful.

Dickens usually took great pains to describe the teachers of his schools; often this was the place where his satire was keenest and his

[37]"Sentiment" in *Sketches by Boz*, p. 380.
[38]"Tom Tiddler's Ground" in *Christmas Stories*, p. 282.
[39]*Edwin Drood*, chap. XIII, pp. 151–3.

humour most sparkling. He seemed to take a diabolical delight in his ridicule of the teachers but with such zest and merriment did he expose their oddities that only the bubbling humour is remembered and the sting of the satire is forgotten: "Miss Melissa might have seen five and thirty summers or thereabouts, and verged on the autumnal; Miss Sophy was a fresh, good-humoured, buxom girl of twenty; and Miss Jane numbered scarcely sixteen years. Mrs. Wackles was an excellent but rather venomous old lady of three-score."[40] Mrs. Wackles expressed her venomous personality by the administration of "corporal punishment, fasting and other tortures and terrors." Then there were the two Miss Crumptons, who were tall, upright, skinny, and yellow, very much like a pair of bean poles: "Miss Amelia Crumpton owned to thirty-eight and Miss Maria Crumpton admitted she was forty; an admission which was rendered perfectly unnecessary by the self-evident fact of her being at least fifty. They dressed in the most interesting manner—like twins; and looked as happy and comfortable as a couple of marigolds run to seed. They were very precise, had the strictest possible ideas of propriety, wore false hair, and always smelt very strongly of lavender."[41] It may be added that Miss Maria had the habit of appearing in the schoolroom with her false hair in curl-papers to convince the pupils that it was real, and also of pronouncing every new pupil to be "a most charming girl," no matter whether she resembled Helen of Troy or one of Cinderella's stepsisters.

As a mark of chivalry, perhaps, two other portraits were drawn in a more gracious manner, with a humour that was whimsical rather than mocking: "Miss Pupford is one of the most amiable of her sex; it necessarily follows that she possesses a sweet temper, and would own to the possession of a great deal of sentiment if she considered it quite reconcilable with her duty to parents. Deeming it not in the bond, Miss Pupford keeps it as far out of sight as she can—which (God bless her!) is not very far."[42] But Dickens could not forbear to add, slyly, that it was difficult to imagine Miss Pupford without mittens, without a front, without some gold wire around her teeth, or without some little dabs of face powder. Seldom, however, did he reach the lightness and gracefulness which prevail in the following:

Miss Twinkleton has too distinct phases of being. Every night, the moment the young ladies have retired to rest, does Miss Twinkleton smarten up her curls a little, brighten up her eyes a little, and become a sprightlier Miss

[40]*The Old Curiosity Shop*, chap. VIII, p. 80.
[41]"Sentiment" in *Sketches by Boz*, p. 375.
[42]"Tom Tiddler's Ground" in *Christmas Stories*, p. 280.

Twinkleton than the young ladies have ever seen. Every night at the same hour, does Miss Twinkleton resume the topics of the previous night, comprehending the tender scandal of Cloisterham, of which she has no knowledge whatever by day, and references to a certain season at Tunbridge Wells, . . . notably the season wherein a certain finished gentleman . . . revealed a homage of the heart, whereof Miss Twinkleton, in her scholastic state of existence, is as ignorant as a granite pillar.[43]

Such a picture has some of the naturalness and charm of the kindly, amiable Goldsmith. But in the very next sentence, Dickens reverts to the vein of the theatre as he describes Mrs. Tisher, assistant at the Nuns' House, as a "deferential widow, with a weak back, a chronic sigh, and a suppressed voice."

If Dickens's interpretation of the education of girls in England is placed beside the composite picture of girls' education given earlier in this chapter, it may be seen that, in some respects, his treatment was rather superficial. He gave very little information about the books that were used, being content merely to mention the names of a few of them. We never get, as we did in his account of the church schools, a satisfying look at the girls' schoolrooms when a lesson is in progress. We are given a picture of the buildings, the pupils, the teachers, and the activities of the schools as an outsider viewed them. Yet Dickens was no ordinary outsider: he was a keen observer, with a fertile imagination, an originality of expression, and a sparkling humour. In its essence, the superficiality of his treatment was a sound one, because he was describing a superficial system of schools.

Dickens's conception of the humble governesses of the nineteenth century was as varied as human personality, ranging from the gentle and inoffensive Ruth Pinch to the embittered and revengeful Miss Wade. And his view of the position accorded governesses by society is supported by other novelists of the period, for instance by Mrs. Gaskell in her *Wives and Daughters* (1866). The governess, Mrs. Kirkpatrick, had been a sort of companion-governess in the Duke's family in her maiden days. Following the death of her first husband, she turned to school-teaching; on her second marriage with the country doctor, she was forced to use part of the money intended for her trousseau to pay off the debts of her school. Pity is often expressed for her during her days as governess and teacher, and envious contempt after her marriage: "I remember the time when Mrs. Kirkpatrick wore old black silks and was thankful and civil as became her place as a schoolmistress, and as having to earn her bread. And now she is in satin. . . . Mrs. Dempster . . . sent her a

[43]*Edwin Drood*, chap. III, pp. 20–2.

new breadth for her lilac silk gown, in place of one that had been spoilt
by Mrs. Dempster's servant spilling the coffee over it the night before;
and she took it and was thankful, for all she's dressed in pearl-grey satin
now." So speaks Miss Hornblower, while Mrs. Kirkpatrick's daughter
testifies that it was necessary to keep up appearances in the "great dreary
house where Mamma kept her school" and to breathe no word of their
poverty for fear of injuring the school.[44] Here snobbish society, depicted
in realistic details, is pitted against a rather exotic and intelligent woman.

As for Dickens's scheming Mrs. General, we have a counterpart in
Thackeray's scheming hussy, Becky Sharp, who, when Sir Pitt Crawley
kneels before her, is, for once in her career, discomfited, and confesses
through her tears that she is married already. Thackeray grips us with
sheer human interest to prevent us from considering Becky utterly despicable; Dickens uses humour to moderate our reaction to Mrs. General.
Perhaps there were few such spirited governesses, and it is interesting to
note that both novelists interpose obstacles to thwart the ambitions of
these two grovelling yet dominating women. Again, the attitude of servility that the charity schools pounded into girls from the lower ranks of
society is well caught in Mrs. Gaskell's *Wives and Daughters*, where
charity uniforms with white caps and checked aprons must be worn,
and obsequious curtsies and humble "please ma'ams" are rigidly demanded of Molly Gibson. The earlier humble status of women is seared
by the same author in *Sylvia's Lovers* (1863) where she hints that farmers regarded their sheep dogs with more deference than they did their
women.[45]

Does an echo of a realist intrude with the argument that what the
novels depict and what actually took place may be far from identical?
That could be. Biographies of the period, however, suggest little disparity, thus adding weight to the delineations in the novels. Gladys Storey
related how a governess, purple-faced with Victorian prudery, shocked
into portraying that indignation which only a schoolma'am could express, haughtily bundled her feminine flock from the hall in which
Dickens was giving a reading on Pecksniff and Mrs. Gamp, in order
that their innocent girlish minds should be no further violated.[46] Sala
describes the education his mother got at a school in Kensington: her
employment of her younger schoolmates to scratch her chilblains as she
conned her lessons; her endurance of the stocks and the backboard; and
how she had to practise entering and alighting from an old ramshackle

[44]*Wives and Daughters*, chaps. XXVI, XLIII.
[45]London, 1910, chap. VIII, p. 78.
[46]Storey, *Dickens and Daughter*, p. 114.

yellow chariot in the back court of the school in order to develop that
superb dignity and languid grace that would be needed if she meant to
marry a wealthy man.[47] Mary Boyle's description of her early schooldays
at fashionable Brighton, 10 Regency Square, convincingly recounts the
strictness of Miss Poggi, the slates smudged with tears, the dreary parsing
of words, the juvenile dissipation at the dances with the boys of Dr.
Everard's Establishment, and the redolence of curling tongs and the
searching reek of singed hair that emanated from the school throughout
the whole preceding afternoon.[48] Charlotte Brontë went to teach at
Margaret Wooler's School, Roe Head, Huddersfield, in July, 1855. Her
diary reveals that her heart was not in the teaching, the exercises, or the
themes. Exclaiming at the futility of explaining the difference between
an article and a noun, she resents her "wretched bondage" and the "idleness," the "apathy," and the "asinine stupidity of these fat-headed oafs,"
the "dolts" who are her pupils.[49] As the century opened, Maria Edgeworth, who relied on "practice and experience" and laid her experiments
or their results before the public, had nothing but disdain for the "female
accomplishments" which masqueraded as education for girls.[50] And
towards the close of the century, after Dickens's death, Mrs. William
Grey testified before the "Society of Arts" in 1871 that the aim was not
how to become desirable wives but rather how to catch desirable hus-
bands.[51] Mrs. John Sandford, in *Women in Her Social and Domestic
Character*, condemned the education given to adolescent girls, urging
that it be "more solid and less flashy," that it rid itself of its excessive
exhibitionism in the form of childish sketches, piano repertoires, faint-
ings, hysterics, sighings, and "improvements."[52]

These pieces of evidence are supported by the dry conclusions of the
Schools Inquiry Commission, 1864–7. Because they inculcated false
values and employed the monotonous method of teaching by rote, "the
female teachers in girls' schools" were "not fully equal to their tasks."
The Commission condemned girls' education in general for "want of
thoroughness and foundation, want of system; showy superficiality; inattention to rudiments; undue time given to accomplishments and those
not taught intelligently."[53] In the House of Lords, as late as May 31,

[47]Sala, *Life and Adventures*, pp. 4–6.
[48]*Mary Boyle: Her Book*, pp. 80–1.
[49]Hanson and Hanson, *The Four Brontës*, pp. 44–9.
[50]Edgeworth, *Practical Education*, pp. v–vi, 579, ff.
[51]Percival, *The English Miss*, p. 77.
[52]See the excellent abstract in Lambert, *When Victoria Began to Reign*, pp.
204–10.
[53]Education Commission, 1864, *Parliamentary Papers*, XX, XXI, 1864, I,
pp. 548–61.

1880, Lord Norton affirmed the searing lines still drawn in the schools between wealth and its lack, referring to the "nine-penny respectables" and the "two-penny slums" who, in far too many cases, were taught in separate rooms and similarly stigmatized in the playgrounds.[54]

It is apparent, therefore, that Dickens gave a reasonably correct delineation of the education of girls. He adjudged the inferior social position of the governess correctly; pilloried the unjust treatment meted out to non-paying pupils like Miss Edwards; ridiculed the utterly artificial veneer of dress, dancing, deportment, music, and mispronunciation of French and Italian which masqueraded as girls' education; and poked fun at the absurdities and pious frauds of some of the preposterous teachers in girls' schools. In one of his speeches about the sort of schools he did not like, he derided that type of girls' school where the young ladies seemed to be always in "new stays and disgrace," or "pinioned by an instrument of torture called a backboard."[55] It must be granted, then, that even if he did not have an accurate knowledge of details, or of the many problems involved, he was certainly conscious of the need for improvement in the education of women and girls.[56]

But Dickens did more than tug at public emotions in his exposure of Miss Monflathers's pitiless venom and her snobbish vilification of the unfortunate schoolgirl, Miss Edwards. He placed the power of his art and genius at the service of educational advance. In doing so he ran a grave risk of sacrificing his art (which he took very seriously) to didacticism. If we pause to compare him with Maria Edgeworth, we see that didacticism won out with Miss Edgeworth, and her literary art declined. The genius of Dickens, however, lies in the fact that he successfully served both art *and education*. He drew such interesting pictures of life at these schools for girls, that, in a sense, he made it appear more interesting than it actually was. He probably never gave a portrait of a really complete woman. All the teachers in these girls' schools of his are preposterous, with their gold teeth, lavender water, and false hair in curl-papers.[57] But where else in English literature can one find such another group of fussy old creatures? If one were to add such a fantastic talker as Mrs. Gamp, or Mrs. Todgers, whose "gravy adds ten years to one's

[54]Hansard, *Parliamentary Debates*, Third Series, vol. 252, c. 749.

[55]At London, Nov. 5, 1857; see *Speeches by Charles Dickens*, pp. 290–6; also chap. VI below.

[56]Cf. his indirect appeal for better divorce laws in *Hard Times*.

[57]The history of the period has to be considered also: in 1851, *Punch* was full of "Bloomers" and "Bloomerisms" poking fun at the notions of Mrs. Lydia Bloomer, newly arrived from America, on the wearing of trousers by women; the *Saturday Review*, in 1868, ran a series of articles attacking the dyeing of hair, the painting of the face, and attempts by women to secure more education.

life," one would have one of the greatest group of comic characters since Shakespeare. The general treatment of the education of girls is mainly satirical; there is little bitterness, however; all is dilated in a spirit of hilarious fun. The teachers are described as they appeared to the young girls themselves, mythical and yet humorous denizens of a world of fancy, ogresses who made their lives miserable with *Mangnall's Questions*, or fairy-godmothers who transported them to fairyland on the wings of the annual ball. That Dickens became theatrical, his teacher-characters mere cartoons, was part of the imaginative humour of the man himself. On one of his numerous theatrical ventures, for instance, a participant resorted to the chintz cover of a sofa for a disguise; at this moment, Dickens to the amazement of the company, suddenly remarked: "He has the general appearance of going to have his hair cut!"[58] In so far as it is the cartoonist who succeeds in leaving a dominant impression, Dickens may be said to have been truly educative.[59] Let those who would peevishly dismiss these pictures as mere caricatures not forget the effect which their vividness would have in the formation of public opinion.

A clearer perspective of Dickens's vital contribution to education through the power of his art is obtained if a comparison is made with the interpretation of school life given by Charlotte Brontë. Cowan Bridge School, which Charlotte attended as a girl, was the model for Lowood School described in *Jane Eyre*. In the novel, Jane Eyre is Charlotte Brontë, and Helen Burns is Charlotte's sister Maria. It is interesting to note that much of the life at Lowood was depicted as Charlotte saw it through her own eyes as a child. Her first impression of the archdeacon, for instance, was that of "a black pillar" that frowned ominously. "What a great nose! and what a mouth! and what large prominent teeth!"[60] This is the same manner in which Dickens describes his characters, for example: "The child glanced keenly at the blue coat and stiff white cravat, which with a pair of creaking boots and a very loud ticking watch, embodied her idea of a father."[61] But there is none of the laughter of Dickens in Charlotte Brontë's description of her teachers:

Seen now, in broad daylight, she looked tall, fair, and shapely; brown eyes, with a benignant light in their irids, and a fine pencilling of long lashes round, relieved the whiteness of her large front; on each of her temples her hair, of a very dark brown, was clustered in round curls, according to the fashion of those times, when neither smooth bands nor long ringlets were in vogue; her dress, also in the mode of the day, was of purple cloth, relieved by a

[58]"Mr. Dickens's Amateur Theatricals," p. 211.
[59]Beresford, "Successors of Dickens," pp. 374–6.
[60]Chap. IV.
[61]*Dombey and Son*, I, chap. I, p. 4.

sort of Spanish trimming of black velvet; a gold watch (watches were not so common then as now) shone on her girdle. Let the reader add, to complete the picture, refined features; a complexion, if pale, clear; and a stately air and carriage, and he will have, at least as clearly as words can give it, a correct idea of the exterior of Miss Temple—Maria Temple, as I afterwards saw the name written in a prayer-book entrusted to me to carry to church.

As for the other teachers, "the stout one was a little coarse, the dark one not a little fierce, the foreigner harsh and grotesque, and Miss Miller, poor thing! looked purple, weather-beaten, and overworked. . . ."[62]

Both Dickens and Charlotte Brontë were, for many years, singularly silent about their early schooldays. In 1850, Dickens incorporated in *David Copperfield* some few pages of biographical material which he later gave to Forster. Charlotte Brontë kept her own counsel until 1846, but she had lost none of the bitterness in her heart, and in *Jane Eyre* she pilloried some of the administrators of the school which she had left at the age of nine. The rigour of her condemnation, written in language of fire, contrasts strongly with the more kindly ridicule of Dickens. There were no clandestine bedroom suppers at Lowood, no half-term balls with ribbons, flowers, and lacing of stays. There were scanty rations, harsh punishment, sickness, and death there. The porridge was burnt, according to the novel, the beef high, and the stew full of rancid fat. For slatternly habits, Helen Burns was sent to get "a bundle of twigs tied together at one end. This ominous tool she presented to Miss Scatcherd with a respectful curtsey; then she quietly, and without being told, unloosed her pinafore, and the teacher instantly and sharply inflicted on her neck a dozen strokes with the bunch of twigs."[63] In relating the child's death, Charlotte Brontë is swift and incisive, speaking with a brief but impassioned eloquence which goes straight to the heart of the reader:

"Good-night Helen."
"Good-night Jane."
She kissed me, and I her; and we both soon slumbered.
When I awoke it was day: an unusual movement aroused me, I looked up; I was in somebody's arms; the nurse held me; she was carrying me through the passage back to the dormitory. . . .
A day or two afterwards I learned that Miss Temple, on returning to her own room at dawn, had found me laid in a little crib; my face against Helen Burns's shoulder, my arms around her neck. I was asleep, and Helen was—dead.[64]

There are hints of Dickens's satire in *Jane Eyre* too, but Charlotte Brontë's touches are more bitter, with some veiled irony. One catches a

[62]*Jane Eyre*, chap. v.   [63]*Ibid.*, chap. vi.
[64]*Ibid.*, chap. ix.

glimpse of it in the grimaces given by the orphan as Mr. Brocklehurst has them turn their faces to the wall to examine their hair and orders it to be cut off. How angry he was! And how his cane shook in his hand because hair which was *naturally* curly did not conform to the regulations concerning straight hair! There is irony in the entrance, just at that moment, of his wife and daughters, who wear their hair in an elaborate arrangement of curls. There is bitter indignation in the picture of Jane, perched on a stool, being publicly branded as an infamous little liar.[65]

Charlotte Brontë tells a little more about the lessons than does Dickens. The periods were apparently of an hour's duration. Miss Temple gives a lesson in geography with the aid of the globes; the other teachers give lessons in history and grammar, followed by writing, arithmetic, and music. Miss Smith teaches sewing, and Madame Pierrot instructs in French. A fairly comprehensive account is given of a history lesson on Charles I, taught by Miss Scatcherd.[66]

The only ray of sunshine to lighten the drab, oppressive existence at Lowood was the sympathy of Miss Temple, who quietly but firmly shielded the girls from the Spartan treatment and the humiliating abuse whenever possible. On frosty mornings, in her plaid coat, she would pass along the line of insufficiently clad children, with their numbed ungloved hands, their stiff chilblained feet, to urge them to keep up their courage like "stalwart soldiers." Occasionally she would take them up to her study to share her own meagre rations and to read an old classic.

Allowances must be made for the different types of schools for girls which each novelist described—chiefly fashionable boarding-schools in the case of Dickens, and a semi-charitable institution in the case of Charlotte Brontë. But the tone of each is very different: Dickens adopts a tone of light ridicule mixed with hilarious fun; Charlotte Brontë's tone is oppressive, bitter, and a little ironical. She never uses the comic relief of Dickens, even in her pathos. She has no fear that the pathos will collapse; her feeling of strong passion is too intense. She is expressing revolt, chastened and disciplined by religious training. Dickens's humour sweetened the bitter truth. The feminine novelist's direct frontal attack raised a storm of protest, but Dickens's humour, like the Trojan horse, took the citadel from within.

[65]*Ibid.*, chap. VII.
[66]*Ibid.*, chap. v.

CHAPTER V

Educational Theory and Practice

This presentation and assessment of what Dickens had to say about education in his novels and short stories has reached almost full circle. The method of organization was selected because it appeared to do least violence not only to the schools of nineteenth-century England but also to Dickens's descriptions of them, but it has not permitted distinctions to be made among educational administration, theory, or method. Questions naturally arise whether Dickens was attempting to present the views of some prominent educationist, or whether he had worked out a coherent philosophy of his own, or further, whether he had formulated logical and far-reaching educational administrative reforms.

A few observations need to be made in regard to one or two pioneers in British educational thought. We begin with R. L. Edgeworth (1744–1817) and his daughter Maria (1767–1849), two of the advanced educational thinkers at the turn of the century. On religion and politics they remained silent, because, as they said, they had no desire to secure partisans.[1] They concentrated on schooling, and urged that it should be based on the spirit of play and on observation, and should be related to the activities of life. In contrast to the generality, who accepted the necessity of harsh punishments, as witness Lancaster in his school manual, the Edgeworths urged that punishments should be intelligible to the children, "inducing useful and agreeable habits, well-regulated sympathy, and benevolent affections."[2] They advised that spelling should be taught by writing rather than by mere drill, science by observation rather than by mere rote, and arithmetic by proceeding from concrete examples such as cubes, globes, or coloured objects, and then to abstractions later. Maria outlines a lesson on "one and one are two," for example, beginning with the words: "One cube and one cube are called two. Two what?" The children are naturally expected to reply: "Two cubes." The same process is repeated with glasses and raisins and other articles. Then one glass is added to one cube, and the answer "two *things*" is elicited,

---

[1]Edgeworth and Edgeworth, *Practical Education*, pp. vii–viii.
[2]*Ibid.*, p. vii.

and finally the abstract "*two*."[3] Such ideas and methods are common enough today, but they were revolutionary when the Edgeworths were advocating them.

Robert Owen (1771–1858) was another educational pioneer. When he rose to become owner of the factory in which he had started to work as a boy, he reduced the working day of the children in his employ to ten hours, and would not hire children under the age of ten. In 1816 he opened a school at New Lanark for the children of his workmen. Monotonous drill on the three R's was abandoned and was replaced by little oral lessons in nature study, and by story-telling, singing, dancing, and the playing of games. A girl in her teens, Molly Young, and a kind-hearted weaver, James Buchanan, were placed in charge. Theoretically at least, and to a great extent in practice, dreary tasks, mechanical instruction, dire punishments, and questionable rewards were abandoned in favour of a new spirit and a more liberal daily programme.[4]

Similar ideas of instruction were developed a little later by Wilderspin, who opened a school at Spitalfields in 1820. He rejected the mechanical method of instruction by pupil-monitors, and used teachers instead. Emphasis was laid on interest and amusement and the playing of games as aids to learning. Sometimes one teacher would instruct the whole school in a raised gallery-room, and at other times the school would be divided into groups.[5] A certain amount of general information appears to have been injected into the lessons. For example, in Wilderspin's alphabet, the letter M stands for mouse, and a mouse is useful because he forces indolent servants to put candles out of his reach, and because his smell forces people to clean their cupboards occasionally![6]

Another pioneer, David Stow, began to apply even more modern ideas in an infant school which he opened in Glasgow in 1826. He even developed Owen's and Wildespin's theories in a training-school for teachers. His chief contribution was a stress on "training" as contrasted with mere reading or telling. He thought that individual methods of teaching, that is, teaching one child at a time, were inferior to group teaching, that is, oral instruction in the form of questions which were answered in chorus by a large group of children. The children were seated in tiers in a room known as a gallery-room, and the lessons were conducted by a method that was termed "picturing out." The teacher or

[3]*Ibid.*, pp. 430 ff.
[4]See Owen's evidence to Education Commission, 1816–18, *Parliamentary Papers*, **IV**, 1816, i, pp. 238–41.
[5]Wilderspin, *The Infant System*, pp. 76–107, 162–99.
[6]*Ibid.*, p. 228.

"trainer" proceeded from questions about concrete objects to questions about ideas and then about terms; and it was hoped that by this method the unknown would become "visible to the mind's eye."[7] Moral "training" was given in this setting by appealing to what Stow termed "the sympathy of numbers." In his manual, for example, he outlined a gallery-room lesson centring on a boy who had stolen a toy from another pupil in the playground: social pressure was exerted on the culprit by the oral discussion of whether this was his first offence, whether he should be cuffed, more severely punished, or forgiven.[8] It is evident that Stow realized the need of training teachers for their work, so that they would study not only the subjects they were to teach but also the pupils. In their teaching, they were responsible both for training minds and for building character. It is apparent, further, that in his advocacy of learning by doing; in his realization of the importance of developing hidden ideas; in his association of history and geography; in his faith in play and fun in the open air, where he thought half the school time should be spent; in his emphasis on singing, religious exercises, and moral training; in his abolition of rewards; and in his substitution of oral instruction for learning by rote, Stow was very modern indeed. Obviously, such theories are a far cry from the cramming at Doctor Blimber's, or the mechanical memorization of Mr. Wopsle's great-aunt's school, or the callous physical punishment inflicted by Mr. Creakle at Salem House.

The Mayos were among those responsible for the introduction into England of the so-called "object lessons," based on the ideas of Pestalozzi. Dr. Charles Mayo had been interested enough to visit Pestalozzi's school at Yverdon in 1819, and afterwards he sought to popularize the ideas of Pestalozzi that are well known today. The system was infused with a sympathetic interest in the welfare of children, and the discipline was fatherly. Instruction was to be based on a child's natural experiences and suited to his abilities and his stage of development. By proceeding from a study of concrete objects to a study of more difficult and abstract ideas, it allowed for the progressive unfolding of his mind. In time, of course, the logic of the steps of the carefully graded subject-matter was found not to be always sound psychologically.

The "object lessons" introduced into England went through a steady

[7]*Ibid.*, pp. 182 ff. and 405 ff. The "Glasgow system" referred to in Johnson, ed., *The Heart of Charles Dickens*, p. 51, which the editor was unable to identify, undoubtedly had reference to the Glasgow Training School of David Stow. See Manning, "Charles Dickens and the 'Glasgow System,'" pp. 202–6.

[8]Stow, *The Training System*, pp. iv–v, 205 f.

process of deterioration. Indeed, Dr. Mayo himself observed in his preface to his sister's manual[9] that endeavours were being made in certain
quarters to adopt and adapt the *form* of the Pestalozzian method. Unfortunately, the form was already overshadowing the true Pestalozzian
spirit. That this was so was evidenced even in the manual, not only by
such phrases as those which affirmed that the lessons had "the solid
advantage of ascertained practicability and demonstrated usefulness"
over "ideal beauty" or "ingenious imagination," but also by some of the
actual lessons described. Lesson XVI, for example, describes an oyster
as "an animal, opaque, marine, natural. The valves are circular, stiff,
pulverable; the outside is rough, scaly or laminated, irregular, dull,
dingy, brown, uneven. The inside is pearly, bright, smooth, slightly
concave, iridescent, cold. The mollusc is soft, eatable, nutritious, cold,
smooth, lubricious." Even that much must have made a child's head as
heavy as lead, and the "Remarks on Words" that followed were not
calculated to make it any lighter. For example:

> Lamin *ated* is derived from Lamin *a*, a plate.
> Lub *ricious* is derived from Lub *ricus*, slippery.[10]

The lessons were "intended to be preparatory to instruction in natural
history." According to the manual, the teacher was supposed to hold
up an object before a class of children, and then elicit from them its
name, physical characteristics, usefulness, and so on. However, in her
introductory remarks the author pointed out that she had already seen
the lessons misused through the practice of *telling* the pupils the qualities
instead of presenting the object to them. The steps in the deterioration
are apparent: first the Pestalozzian sequence from objects to definitions
became reversed; next, the definition usurped the rightful place of the
object, which was left out of the procedure; and the process ended with
the giving-out by the teacher of pat definitions to be learned by rote.

The ease with which untrained teachers could slip into this formaliza-
tion and distortion of the Pestalozzian method (which was supposed to
proceed through language, number, and form) may be inferred from the
procedure suggested by Miss Mayo herself at the end of the fourth series
of lessons on liquids. The pupils are expected to define the properties
"common to all" the liquids and "peculiar to each," and Miss Mayo provides a list of definitions. Here are a few items from the list: "Oil is
yellowish, thick, emollient, semi-transparent, greasy, inflammable. Beer

[9]*Lessons on Objects*, published in 1830. In his preface, Dr. Mayo described the
principles of Pestalozzi. He and his sister collaborated in another complete book
on the subject, entitled *Pestalozzi and His Principles*.
[10]Mayo, *Lessons on Objects*, pp. vi, vii, 59 f.

is orange-coloured, bitter, spirituous, artificial, fermented. White wine is bright, yellowish, intoxicating, stimulating, fermented. Vinegar is acid, orange-coloured, semi-transparent. Water is transparent, colourless, tasteless, inodorous, bright."[11] It would obviously be difficult for a teacher to keep a supply of these liquids (except the water) to show the pupils. And it is apparent that if the object that is being defined is absent, a pupil's ability or inability to repeat the definition by rote is no proof of his familiarity or unfamiliarity with the object, as Dickens demonstrated so convincingly in *Hard Times* in the persons of Bitzer and Sissy Jupe.

Pestalozzi's influence was not by any means confined to the Mayos. His school was visited not only by Owen, Brougham, and Kay-Shuttleworth, but also by Friedrich Froebel, who first spent two weeks and then two years at Yverdon, in 1805 and 1808–10 respectively. There would be little need to discuss the educational ideas of Froebel were it not that a study of the novels of Dickens, published in 1900, sought to interpret what Dickens had to say about education in terms of Froebelian thought;[12] and that its premises and conclusions were drawn on by two other closely related studies[13] a few years later, not to mention numerous other acceptances and repetitions.[14] It is imperative, therefore, to discuss this interpretation.

It was James L. Hughes, the initiator of the kindergarten in Ontario, Canada, who in 1900 published a treatise which purported to show that Dickens was a conscious exponent of the philosophy of Froebel.[15] The first chapter was of a general nature, and the second chapter quoted in full an article entitled "Infant Gardens," which had first appeared in *Household Words*, July 21, 1855. Mr. Hughes, in his introduction to the quotations, said that: "Dickens wrote the following article for *Household Words* in 1855 . . . to direct attention to the work of the Baroness Von Bülow, who had come to England to introduce the kindergarten system. Dickens's works show clearly that he had long been a close student of Froebel's philosophy."[16] The rest of the monograph attempted to interpret Dickens's delineation of school life in terms of Froebelian philosophy.

The article, "Infant Gardens," did give a fairly comprehensive account of the philosophy of Friedrich Froebel, and showed that its author was

[11]*Ibid.*, p. 92.   [12]Hughes, *Dickens as an Educator.*
[13]Booth, *Charles Dickens und seine Werke*, sec. 2, Part B; and Frieser, *Die Schulen bei Dickens*, pp. 134 ff.
[14]See, for example, Adamson, *English Education*, p. 340; or Armytage, "Friedrich Froebel," p. 113.
[15]*Dickens as an Educator.*   [16]*Ibid.*, p. 15.

sympathetic to the work of the kindergartens. But the present writer was sceptical not only of Hughes's thesis but also of the claim that Dickens was the author of the article. The style did not appear to be that of Dickens. A re-examination of Dickens's correspondence failed to uncover any mention of the article in his letters to his associate editor, W. H. Wills, or even the name of Froebel throughout eight or ten thousand letters, or throughout his speeches, articles, novels, and short stories. Neither did a work of Froebel, or of any other educational writer for that matter, appear in T. W. Hill's study "Books that Dickens Read"; and a further perusal of Hughes's study failed to find any evidence to show that Dickens had written the article. But to be brief, it may be asserted, from evidence that is considered to be conclusive, that Dickens did not write the article "Infant Gardens" but that it came from the pen of Henry Morley.[17]

The argument might of course be advanced that even if Dickens did not write the article in question, he would certainly be aware of the ideas in it, and that the very fact that it was published in his journal would imply that he knew Froebel's philosophy and was in sympathy with it. Dickens was very conscientious, and he felt it was his duty to read as many as he possibly could of the manuscripts that were submitted to the journal before they were accepted for publication. He collaborated with his associate editor, Wills, even when abroad, on most of the copy editing of *Household Words* and was careful to correct inaccuracies.[18] Therefore, there need be little hesitation in saying that Dickens probably did read "Infant Gardens" and agree to publish it, and that he probably checked the manuscript to make sure that its details were accurate. The article uses the editorial "we," and it is admitted that from July, 1855—the date when the article was published—Dickens and his collaborators had some acquaintance with the educational ideas of Froebel. However, the important consideration in determining Froebel's influence on Dickens's personal views on education is the length of time Dickens had been acquainted with Froebel's work *before* that date. In that respect the researcher is fortunate, for there is evidence in the article itself to show that Dickens and his editorial staff had known of Froebel and his educational work for only a few months prior to the date of publication:

. . . we will end by a citation of the source from which we have ourselves derived what information we possess.

At the educational exhibition in St. Martin's Hall last year, there was a large display of the material used and the results produced in Infant Gardens

[17]See Appendix C.
[18]Grubb, "Charles Dickens: Journalist."

which attracted our attention. The Baroness Von Marenholtz, enthusiastic in her advocacy of the children's cause, came then to England, and did very much to procure the establishment in this country of some experimental Infant Gardens. By her, several months ago—and about the same time by M. and Madame Rongé who had already established the first English Infant Garden—our attention was invited to the subject. We were also made acquainted with M. Hoffman, one of Froebel's pupils, who explained the system theoretically at the Polytechnic Institution.[19]

From this internal evidence, it is obvious that there could have been little or no conscious exposition of the educational philosophy of Froebel in any of Dickens's work before the educational exhibition of 1854. But Dickens's major delineations of schools and school life—*Oliver Twist, Nicholas Nickleby, The Old Curiosity Shop, David Copperfield, Bleak House*, and *Hard Times* (Aug. 12, 1854)—had all appeared before then.

Some knowledge of Froebel's philosophy is necessary in order to determine the extent of Froebel's influence on the works of Dickens after 1854. For our purposes here, a bare outline will suffice. To Froebel, the fundamental purpose of all existence, man on the one hand, and nature on the other, was to reveal God. "Education should guide man to the understanding of himself; to peace with nature; and to union with God."[20] There was, for Froebel, a fundamental unity of all existence. God was in man; God was in nature; both man and nature, therefore, revealed divine laws. The purpose of education was to bring out the divinity in children, and to bring into children from without the divinity found in nature, thus achieving a unity. If God was in man, it followed that children were fundamentally good, not evil; hence self-expression was encouraged through such media as song, language, drawing, music, and gesture; Froebel termed this "making the inner outer." If God was in nature, it followed that nature should be studied to discover the divinity which nature reveals to children; hence the necessity of experimental and manual activities; Froebel termed this "making the outer inner." From this philosophy, Froebel conceived the idea of the kindergarten, which had as its dominant aim the development of each child as an individual through self-activity and motor-expression directed towards social and moral ends. Froebel's influence on the course of educational development, therefore, extended to the introduction of more manual activities (education by doing), more games and play (education through

[19]The first introduction of the kindergarten system into England was by Miss Praetorius, at Fitzroy Square in 1854. In the same year Madame von Marenholtz Bülow went to England to lecture and write in support of kindergartens. About the same time, 1854, Madame Rongé introduced the kindergarten system into Manchester. (Froebel, *Autobiography*, p. 143.)

[20]*Die Menschenerziehung*, quoted in *The Student's Froebel*, ed. Herford, I, 39.

play), more music and song, and milder methods in discipline. It follows that, to Froebel, as to Pestalozzi, the children were the first consideration, not the teachers (as to Herbart), or even the curriculum (as to Hegel); to Froebel, a school was a miniature society, and education was a child's active participation in the life around him, not merely a preparation for a life to be lived later on. As Froebel said himself: "My plan is very simple; what I want is a happy family school, and a peaceful life with nature around me."[21] When Superintendent Zeh visited Keilhau in 1825 he reported: "I found . . . a thoroughly and intimately united family of at least sixty members living in quiet harmony. . . . What the pupils know . . . is immediately applied in life."[22] With this background we may turn to the works of Dickens that have not been examined in previous chapters.

In 1863 and 1864, Dickens published two Christmas stories entitled "Mrs. Lirriper's Lodgings" and "Mrs. Lirriper's Legacy." Mrs. Lirriper was a warm-hearted lodging-house keeper. A young woman lodging in her house had given birth to a baby boy, born, apparently, out of wedlock. Shortly afterwards the young mother died, and Mrs. Lirriper and Major Jackman, another lodger, adopted the baby. Before the child's head could be seen above the table, the Major stated his intentions of "cultivating" the child's mind "on a principle that will make it a delight." Dickens, however, cannot forgo the temptation to indulge in a little burlesque when he has Mrs. Lirriper answer:

"Major" I says "I will be candid with you and tell you openly that if ever I find the dear child fall off in his appetite I shall know it is his calculations and shall put a stop to them at two minutes' notice. Or if I find them mounting to his head" I says "or striking anyways cold to his stomach or leading to anything approaching flabbiness in his legs, the result will be the same, but Major you . . . love the child . . . and if you feel a confidence in trying try."[23]

The Major, unabashed, secured permission to borrow various cooking utensils from the kitchen for a number of half-hour periods during which he and little Jemmy repaired to the front parlour. Eventually, Mrs. Lirriper received an invitation to the front parlour one evening "to witness a few slight feats of elementary arithmetic." The kitchen utensils were arranged on a table spread with old newspapers; the youngster, with flushed face and sparkling eyes, was stood on a chair. (The dramatic presentation reminds one of the boy Dickens, flushed and eager, standing

[21] Armytage, "Friedrich Froebel," p. 109.
[22] *Ibid.*, p. 110.
[23] "Mrs. Lirriper's Lodgings" in *Christmas Stories,* p. 387.

on a chair to recite at the Mitre Inn.) Mrs. Lirriper then described what happened:

... picture my admiration when the Major going on almost as quick as if he was conjuring sets out all the articles he names, and says "Three saucepans, an Italian iron, a hand-bell, a toasting-fork, a nutmeg-grater, four potlids, a spice-box, two egg-cups, and a chopping-board—how many?" and when that Mite instantly cries "Fifteen, tut down tive and carry ler 'toppin-board" and then claps his hands draws up his legs and dances on his chair. . . .
The pride of the Major! (*"Here's* a mind ma'am!" he says to me behind his hand.) . . .
"We have here a toasting-fork, a potato in its natural state, two potlids, one egg-cup, a wooden spoon, and two skewers, from which it is necessary for commercial purposes to subtract a sprat-gridiron, a small pickle-jar, two lemons, one pepper-castor, a blackbeetle-trap, and a knob of the dresser-drawer—what remains?"
"Toatin-fork!" cries Jemmy.
"In numbers how many?" says the Major.
"One!" cries Jemmy.
(*"Here's* a boy, ma'am!" says the Major to me behind his hand.) . . .
But my dear to relate to you in detail the way in which they multiplied fourteen sticks of firewood by two bits of ginger and a larding-needle, or divided pretty well everything else there was on the table by the heater of the Italian iron and a chamber candlestick, and got a lemon over, would make my head spin round and round and round as it did at the time.[24]

There are one or two hints of Froebel here: there is certainly the idea of learning through play as well as the use of concrete objects. But let us examine it closely in the light of a Froebelian lesson in numbering—assuming, for the moment, that Major Jackman and Mrs. Lirriper are meant to be taken seriously.

According to Froebel, a child should first be taught to add one object to another object of the same type (an apple, say), and to repeat out loud: "One apple, another apple, again another apple." When this step had been mastered, the next step was to count objects, speaking the proper numeral: "One pear, two pears, three pears," and so on. The third step was to group objects in sets of ones, twos, threes, and fours; but the grouping was never to exceed five objects. Finally, the child was required to count objects aloud: "One, two, three, four, five blocks," and so on with other objects. This method appears to make sense. But the idea in Dickens's "Mrs. Lirriper's Lodgings" of teaching division and multiplication to so young a child seems a bit weird—Jemmy could not yet speak plainly, and his head could not be seen above the table, so he

[24]*Ibid.*, pp. 388 f.

must have been about five years old, or perhaps less. Furthermore, such absurdities as the attempt to teach the method of "carrying," in arithmetical addition, by adding "three saucepans, an Italian iron, a handbell, a toasting-fork, a nutmeg-grater, four potlids, a spice-box, two egg-cups, and a chopping-board," and the solemn acceptance of the answer "Fifteen, tut down tive and carry ler 'toppin-board,'" is so bizarre that this writer cannot take it seriously.[25]

Dickens carried through the same idea in his next Christmas number, "Mrs. Lirriper's Legacy." In that story, learning was carried out through amusement by an appeal to the boy's instinct for play. The Major and Jemmy managed a toy railroad line. They bought and sold stocks, made monthly reports of the rolling stock and of the upkeep of the roadbed, made surveying excursions, planned passenger rates, and had collisions.[26] The concreteness of the project, and its similarity, on a miniature scale, to conditions in real life were certainly in the tradition of Froebel.

Suppose one disregarded the burlesque in both these short stories, and seized, for the sake of argument, on the use of concrete objects, learning through play, and the manipulation of the miniature railroad. What then? It is obvious that Dickens had no need to go abroad to Germany, or elsewhere, to become acquainted with these ideas. The Edgeworths, Owen, Wilderspin, Stow, the Mayos, and others, could well have provided him with this educational theory and spirit, and with even a more advanced study of method.

Besides, admirable as these two sketches are, it is evident that they by no means incorporate the whole of Froebelian philosophy. True, the emphasis is on the child. The teacher, the Major, had no training; the lessons were carried on at home, not at school. Dickens, throughout all his works, did not place much stress on the curriculum. On the other hand, as we have seen, he laid great emphasis on the personality of the teacher. Again, there is practically nothing about the study of nature, either here in the Lirriper stories, or in the earlier novels. Dickens never stressed Froebel's idea that nature reveals God to the child. Indeed, seldom in his novels does he stress the divine purpose; even in his Christmas stories one seldom feels that his characters, aside from Tiny Tim, experience the eternal behind the temporal blessings.[27] Dickens

[25]Dickens received some sharp criticism at the time concerning the sentimental aspects of the stories in regard to both the boy and Mrs. Lirriper, with the suggestion that Dickens was "beginning to tread on ashes" ("Mrs. Lirriper's Lodgings," *Saturday Review*, pp. 759 f.; and "Mrs. Lirriper's Legacy," *ibid.*, 724 f.).

[26]In *Christmas Stories*, pp. 405 f.

[27]Even though Peggotty, Little Nell, and Sarah read the Bible often. See "Charles Dickens's Use of the Bible," pp. 225–34.

agrees with Froebel, nevertheless, that children are born with a fundamental, if incomplete, goodness at heart. In the novel *The Old Curiosity
Shop*, for example, Kit remarks to his mother: ". . . If I was to see your
good-humoured face that has always made home cheerful, turned into a
grievous one, and the baby trained to look grievous too, and to call itself
a young sinner (bless its heart) and a child of the devil (which is calling
its dead father names); if I was to see this . . . I should go and 'list for a
soldier, and run my head on purpose against the first cannon ball I saw
coming my way."[28] Of course, Kit had been remonstrating with his
mother about her attendance at an evangelical chapel known as "Little
Bethel," a circumstance which suggests that this is probably as much an
instance of Dickens's attitude to hypocrisy and cant as a condemnation
of the doctrine of the depravity of children.

Care must be taken, nevertheless, not to attribute too much credit to
Dickens's knowledge and understanding of educational theory. It has just
been demonstrated that, after 1854, Dickens had a certain acquaintance
with Froebel's theory; and that in the Lirriper stories he illustrated the
use of the spirit of play and of a situation taken from real life as part of
the process of learning. But if one pauses to reflect that in the very first
novel he wrote, *Oliver Twist* (1838), Dickens gave, probably uncon-
sciously, a good example of learning through play, the danger of gener-
alization is all too apparent. Fagin's school for thieves was certainly
conducted along admirable pedagogical lines:

When the breakfast was cleared away, the merry old gentleman and the
two boys played at a very curious and uncommon game, which was performed in this way. The merry old gentleman, placing a snuff-box in one
pocket of his trousers, a note-case in the other, and a watch in his waistcoat
pocket, with a guard-chain round his neck, and sticking a mock diamond pin
in his shirt: buttoned his coat tight round him, and putting his spectacle-case
and handkerchief in his pockets, trotted up and down the room with a stick,
in imitation of the manner in which old gentlemen walk about the streets any
hour in the day. Sometimes he stopped at the fireplace, and sometimes at the
door, making believe that he was staring with all his might into shop-
windows. At such times, he would look constantly round him for fear of
thieves, and would keep slapping all his pockets in turn, to see that he hadn't
lost anything, in such a very funny and natural manner, that Oliver laughed
till the tears ran down his face. All this time, the two boys followed him
closely about: getting out of his sight, so nimbly, every time he turned round,
that it was impossible to follow their motions. At last, the Dodger trod upon
his toes, or ran upon his boot accidentally, while Charley Bates stumbled up
against him behind; and in that one moment they took from him, with the
most extraordinary rapidity, snuff-box, note-case, watch-guard, chain, shirt-

[28]Chap. XXII, p. 213.

pin, pocket-handkerchief, even the spectacle-case. If the old gentleman felt a hand in any one of his pockets, he cried out where it was; and then the game began all over again.[29]

Fagin, villain as he was, certainly knew the most efficacious method of instruction. This crafty receiver of stolen goods had learned much in his systematic training of boys for the "trade" of pilfering. The "merry old gentleman" entered into the spirit of fun, humoured the boys, rewarded them, and encouraged their efforts. After Oliver made his attempt, Fagin patted him on the head and gave him a shilling. Here we find activity, play, interest, motivation, and a situation from real life. Dickens seems to have stumbled on the right method, only to put it into the hands of a villain with criminal intent, and then never to refer to it again for twenty-five years!

It is clear that one ought not to conclude from these instances that Dickens had a professional knowledge of educational theory. It will be interesting to discover how much he knew of administrative practice and, in particular, what his views were on the training of teachers. It was pointed out in the Introduction of this book that drilling on facts was encouraged by the practices introduced by the Revised Code of 1861-2, which in turn had stemmed from the educational report of the Newcastle Commission. There is always a lag between the demands of the public and the carrying out of those demands by administrative authorities, and it would appear that Dickens was astute enough to see the trend of elementary education as early as 1854 when *Hard Times* was first published. He pointed out, a little later, that his purpose in writing the story was to level satire against those people who could see nothing else beyond figures and averages; the "addled heads," as he termed them, who would take the yearly average temperature in the Crimea "as a reason for clothing a soldier in Nankeen on a night when he would be frozen to death in fur."[30] (Incidentally, Froebel would probably have replied that the "human intellect is as inseparable from the mathematic as the human heart is from religion."[31]) *Hard Times*, in the story of Mr. Bounderby, also attacks certain industrialists in the north of England. The novel has been the subject of some harsh criticism,[32] but as the criticism was not concerned with the novel's educational aspects, it may be passed by.

[29]Chap. VIII, pp. 76 f.   [30]Dexter, ed., *Letters*, II, 619.
[31]*The Student's Froebel*, ed. Herford, I, 84.
[32]Leacock, *Charles Dickens*, p. 143; Langton, *The Childhood and Youth of Charles Dickens*, p. 208; Baker, "Charles Dickens" in *The History of the English Novel*, VII, 297; Chesterton, *Charles Dickens*, p. 176; also Ward, Bagehot, and others.

Dickens had already attacked the "hot-house system" of forcing children to memorize lumps of heterogeneous knowledge when he depicted Doctor Blimber's school for young gentlemen in *Dombey and Son*. Doctor Blimber's Academy, however, was a fashionable private school where classics were taught. In *Hard Times*, therefore, Dickens returned as it were to his more usual field—the elementary schools for the lower classes. Here, in Mr. Gradgrind's model school, taught by a man with the significant name of Mr. M'Choakumchild, he introduces a state inspector of schools and ridicules an administrative system which forces little children to endure a monotonous grind of memorization. Facts and more facts were choked down the children's intellectual throats without any draught of imagination to wash them down. Dickens is careful to point out that M'Choakumchild had been given some training in teaching by the state, and he is not at all complimentary about the efforts of the state to provide trained teachers. Here is his description of M'Choakumchild:

He and some one hundred and forty other schoolmasters had been lately turned at the same time, in the same factory, on the same principles, like so many pianoforte legs. . . . Orthography, etymology, syntax, and prosody, biography, astronomy, geography, and general cosmography, the sciences of compound proportion, algebra, land-surveying and levelling, vocal music, and drawing from models, were all at the ends of his ten chilled fingers. He had worked his stony way into Her Majesty's Most Honourable Privy Council's Schedule B, and had taken the bloom off the higher branches of mathematics and physical science, French, German, Latin and Greek. . . . If he had only learned a little less, how infinitely better he might have taught a little more![33]

This is all very well; I doubt, however, if the criticism aided the securing of a sufficient number of properly trained teachers, a project which could only be effectively carried out by the state, and which the state was reluctantly initiating.[34] The state had set up a system for training pupil-teachers in 1846; between that date and 1856, when the course was revised and standardized, it certainly contained too many subjects; many of them, however, were optional, and they varied from school to school and from year to year. Dickens was not quite fair because, in the first place, he lumped all the subjects together as if they were all required in one training-school, or in one year; in the second place, there was no question that the trained teachers were superior to those who were not trained. "As a class, they are marked, both men and women," reported the investigating commissioners in 1861, "by a quickness of eye and ear,

[33]*Hard Times*, chap. II, p. 254.
[34]Birchenough, *History of Elementary Education in England and Wales*, p. 377.

a quiet energy, a facility of command, and a patient self-control, which, with rare exceptions, are not observed in the private instructors of the poor."[35]

Perhaps Dickens was being humorous. With this book, however, he appears to have lost his hilarious ridicule, which he never fully regained. This depiction of Mr. M'Choakumchild's school is satirical; it is too bitter to sparkle or amuse. The fundamental philosophy of Mr. M'Choakumchild's system was, as we have observed, to teach the boys and girls nothing but facts: "Facts alone are wanted in life. . . . Nothing else will ever be of any use to them. . . . This is the principle on which I bring up these children."[36] The children were very much like "little pitchers" arranged in rows before him, and it was the task of this "inflexible, dry, and dictatorial voice" to pour facts into them until they were full to the brim. The home environment of the five little Gradgrinds aided this process, to their ultimate misfortune. Their father was that "man of realities," Mr. Gradgrind, who, as Oscar Wilde remarked in another connection, "knew the price of everything, and the value of nothing." It is also apparent that the state inspector agrees with both M'Choakumchild and Gradgrind on the fundamental purpose of their system—the storing of the mind with facts.

Dickens then proceeds to devastate the abuse of the so-called "object lessons" which had deteriorated by this time into mere definitions given out by the teacher, to be memorized by the pupils with little or no reference to the objects themselves. As soon as Mr. Gradgrind had explained the underlying principles of his system, he proceeded to conduct an oral examination of the class. He chose "to discuss" a horse and began by questioning Sissy Jupe:

"Girl number twenty," said Mr. Gradgrind, . . . "What is your father?"
"He belongs to the horse-riding, if you please, Sir."
. . . "Very well, then. He is a veterinary surgeon, a farrier, and horse-breaker. Give me your definition of a horse."
(Sissy Jupe thrown into the greatest alarm by this demand.)
"Girl number twenty unable to define a horse!" said Mr. Gradgrind. . . . Girl number twenty possessed of no facts, in reference to one of the commonest of animals! Some boy's definition of a horse. Bitzer, yours." . . .
"Quadruped. Graminivorous. Forty teeth, namely twenty-four grinders, four eye-teeth, and twelve incisive. Sheds coat in the spring; in marshy

[35]Education Commission, 1861, Report, *Parliamentary Papers*, XXI, 1861, I, 150. In one district, the grading for a group of 470 trained teachers was 24 per cent good, 49 per cent fair, and 27 per cent inferior; whereas for a group of 216 untrained teachers it was 3 per cent good, 39 per cent fair, and 58 per cent inferior.
[36]*Hard Times*, Bk. I, chap. I, p. 247.

countries, sheds hoofs, too. Hoofs hard, but requiring to be shod with iron. Age known by marks in mouth." Thus (and much more) Bitzer.

"Now girl number twenty," said Mr. Gradgrind. "You know what a horse is."[37]

Sissy Jupe, born of circus folk, is thus intellectually enlightened through Bitzer's definition to a comprehension of "what a horse is." The withering sarcasm of Swift could scarcely have cut deeper. Shades of the Mayos and Pestalozzi!

As soon as Mr. Gradgrind had finished this illuminating discussion, the third man, whom I take to be a state inspector of schools, stepped forward. "Very well," said this gentleman, briskly smiling and folding his arms, "That's a horse." But the discussion went further, for Sissy Jupe had the temerity to affirm that she would like to have the floor of a room covered with a carpet having pretty designs of flowers on it:

. . . "Why would you?"

"If you please, Sir, I am very fond of flowers," returned the girl.

"And is that why you would put tables and chairs upon them, and have people walking over them with heavy boots?"

"It wouldn't hurt them, Sir. They wouldn't crush and wither, if you please, Sir. They would be the pictures of what was very pretty and pleasant, and I would fancy——"

"Ay, ay, ay! But you mustn't fancy," cried the gentleman, quite elated by coming so happily to his point. "That's it! You are never to fancy."[38]

This quotation, judging from Dickens's own extant notes in the Forster Collection, London, England, and a letter of Cole to Wills dated June 17, 1854, in the Morgan Library, New York, provides some evidence by its reference to floral designs on carpets that the delineation of the inspector was based in part on this same Henry Cole, who was Superintendent of the (London) Department of Practical Art. There is another passage, however, in a letter to W. H. Wills, dated January 25, 1854, in the Huntington Library, San Marino, California, which infers that the satire is directed against the state schools and the state training of teachers: "I want (for the story I am trying to hammer out) the Educational Board's series of questions for the examination of *teachers* in schools. Will you get it?" In any case, Sissy Jupe must not have pictures of horses on wallpaper, no foreign birds and butterflies painted on

---

[37]*Ibid.*, Bk. I, chap. II, pp. 249–51. There is a similar definition in Mrs. Barbauld (1743–1825), *Evenings at Home*, pp. 158 f.

[38]*Hard Times*, Bk. I, chap. II, p. 253. See Fielding, "Charles Dickens and the Department of Practical Art," 270–7. Cf. Manning, "Charles Dickens and the Oswego System."

crockery—*that* is fancy and not fact! Anything that might stimulate the imagination of the children in this school was relentlessly crushed out; no fairies dwelt in the test-tubes as they were to do for Madame Curie when she was a little girl.

Dickens is careful to point out that even though Sissy Jupe had been brought up in a circus, she had, at least, been able to enjoy her childhood there. She had enjoyed the companionship and love of her father. She had played with their dog, Merrylegs. She had let her imagination roam as she read to her father from her storybooks. Young as she was, she had noted how often he forgot his cares as he wondered whether the sultan would let the beautiful maiden finish her story or whether he would have her head chopped off before it had ended. The children of Mr. Gradgrind, on the other hand, had never been permitted to indulge in such fanciful pleasures: "No little Gradgrind had ever seen a face in the moon. . . . No little Gradgrind had ever associated a cow in a field with that famous cow with the crumpled horn who tossed the dog who worried the cat who killed the rat who ate the malt, or with that yet more famous cow who swallowed Tom Thumb: it had never heard of those celebrities, and had only been introduced to a cow as a graminivorous ruminating quadruped with several stomachs."[39] Instead, each little Gradgrind had his little cabinet of specimens all neatly arranged and labelled, and the earliest recollection of each little Gradgrind was that of a lecture-room with blackboard and white chalk.

What were the results of such a system of education? Did it enable a child to develop his personality, and to live a happy and useful life in a complex society? There was no hesitancy in Dickens's answer. He makes it clear in the disgrace of Thomas Gradgrind, who becomes a most despicable thief; in the jaded and starved imagination of Louisa Gradgrind, who when submitting herself to the arranged marriage with Bounderby, thirty years her senior, bitterly remarks to her father: "What are my heart's experiences? . . . You have been so careful of me, that I have never had a child's heart . . . , never dreamed a child's dream . . . , never had a child's belief or a child's fear."[40] Ironically, Gradgrind is elated to hear this testimony to the success of his system. The pen of Dickens is dropping vitriol here. Later, when Louisa's marriage has slowly but surely dissolved, both she and her father taste the bitterness of his "success." After she has fled from her lover in despair, Gradgrind hears her say: "This night, my husband being away, he has been with me, declaring himself my lover. . . . I do not know that I am sorry, I

[39]*Hard Times*, Bk. I, chap. III, pp. 256 f.
[40]*Ibid.*, Bk. I, chap. xv, p. 357.

do not know that I am ashamed, I do not know that I am degraded in my own esteem. All that I know is that your philosophy and your teaching will not save me."[41] This was Dickens's answer. These were the results, as he saw them, of Mr. Gradgrind's system.

But the heart of Sissy Jupe did not wane or wither. If she was unable to retain a mass of facts in her memory—and was therefore such a disappointment to Gradgrind—love and gratitude had accomplished that which Gradgrind had left undone. An atmosphere favourable to such a development could have been secured, it would seem, just as well in a schoolroom as in a circus.

Such was the scorn Dickens heaped on the education administered by the state in England, in 1854, as depicted in *Hard Times*. In *Bleak House*, however, he was just as severe in his condemnation of the neglect of the state in matters of education as he had previously been of its efforts to render some assistance. Jo, the crossing-sweeper, is ordered by the constable "to move on," but when the street-urchin naïvely asks to what place he is "to move on," the constable himself is nonplussed.[42] Even Snagsby, the law-stationer, admits the justice of the boy's question. Dickens goes on to say that the "great lights of the parliamentary sky" fail to give any answer either. Jo is eventually brought to court to testify concerning the death of Mr. Krook:

> Name, Jo. Nothing else that he knows on. Don't know that everybody has two names. Never heerd of sich a think. Don't know that Jo is short for a longer name. Thinks it long enough for *him*. *He* don't find no fault with it. Spell it? No. *He* can't spell it. No father, no mother, no friends. Never been to school. What's home? Knows a broom's a broom, and knows it's wicked to tell a lie. Don't recollect who told him about the broom, or about the lie, but knows both. Can't exactly say what'll be done to him arter he's dead if he tells a lie to the gentlemen here, but believes it'll be something wery bad to punish him, and serve him right—and so he'll tell the truth. . . .
> "We can't take *that* in a Court of Justice, gentlemen. It's terrible depravity. Put the boy aside."[43]

True to form, the Rev. Mr. Chadband, the snivelling hypocrite, affirms that Jo is in a state of bondage, darkness, and sin. At that, there must have been something akin to true barbarism about a boy to whom civilized life appeared so bewildering. There is little doubt that the descrip-

[41]*Ibid.*, Bk. II, chap. XII, p. 485.
[42]Sweepers of all ages, all types, and of both sexes, preferred this "work" because of the smallness of the capital outlay—twopence or threepence for a broom —the opportunity for begging, and an eventual, known clientele. See Mayhew, *London Labour and the London Poor*, II, 527–73.
[43]*Bleak House*, I, chap. XI, p. 177.

tion was a true one, as the case of George Ruby, testifying at the Guildhall on January 8, 1850, would bear out.[44]

At first glance, there would appear to be something inconsistent in Dickens's condemnation of the state both for its neglect and for its aid in the matter of education. Obviously, only some adequate state intervention, some national scheme of social welfare, including the provision of food, clothing, shelter, and education could solve the problem presented by Jo. The suffering figure of the crossing-sweeper for whom Dickens pleaded with more pathos than humour, and, if I dare say it, with more sympathy than intelligent analysis, not only represents the hard lot of the poor in general, but is also a symbolic embodiment of Dickens's own sufferings at the blacking-warehouse. The schools Dickens had attended could not, as we know, be described as "cram schools," but a man with his vivid sensory perceptions, his tremendous creative power, and his intuitive sympathy with children was bound to be repelled by the mechanical instruction which was so heartily approved by the state inspector at Gradgrind's model school. To Dickens, the neglect of Jo and the subjection of the pupils at Gradgrind's were both intolerable, but he probably had no well-thought-out administrative scheme to offer as an alternative. It was his compassion for neglected waifs like Jo and subjugated children like Gradgrind's charges that prompted him to depict their plight in his novels. That was his contribution—and it was an essential and incomparable contribution—to their welfare.

To realize how genuine was his love for children, and how acute was his understanding of them, one has only to turn to the memories of his daughter. Mamey tells how her father played with them, sympathized with their troubles, wrote special prayers for them, and gave special prizes for punctuality, industry, and neatness. She describes how he taught them to act little plays, or dressed as a magician on Twelfth Night to give them a conjuring entertainment, or permitted them to teach him to dance the polka. Her father sang comic songs, such as the one about the old man who had caught cold and rheumatism, and whose sneezes, coughs, and gesticulations he admirably imitated. His daughter relates how his eyes filled with tears at her happiness on receiving a watch on her birthday, how his sympathy was kindled anew as he tended them in sickness, and how, on New Year's Eve, he would assemble them all at the door, watch in hand, looking out over the moonlit snow, to await the chimes of the New Year.[45]

---

[44]Suddaby, "Little Jo," pp. 246–50; the actual trial was reported in *Household Narrative of Current Events*, Jan., 1850, p. 7.

[45]"Charles Dickens at Home." See also chap. VIII below.

With all this evidence of Dickens's views on education, we are now in a position to attempt a final estimate of the extent, if any, to which they were influenced by Froebel's theories. The erroneous attribution of the article "Infant Gardens" to Dickens carried with it the implication that Dickens was an authority on Froebel and a conscious expositor of his principles. Dickens, as has been shown, was not familiar with Froebel's philosophy before 1854, and we were unable to find in "Mrs. Lirriper's Lodgings" or "Mrs. Lirriper's Legacy" ideas that Dickens could not have received from English educational theorists. But what about the novels written after 1854? We will need to recall the delineations found in *Little Dorrit* (1855–7), *Great Expectations* (1860–1), *Our Mutual Friend* (1864–5), and the unfinished *Edwin Drood* (1870). In the first of these, there is nothing Froebelian about Mr. Cripples's Academy, or about Mrs. General with her designs on Dorrit's fortune. *Great Expectations* contained the account of Miss Wopsle's school: Miss Wopsle spent most of the time sleeping; her assistant was down-at-heel Biddy who had been "brought up by hand"; and the textbooks consisted of one ragged spelling-book and three tattered Bibles. There appears to be no more Froebelian philosophy in this than in Mr. Wopsle's mauling and grotesque dramatic performances. In *Our Mutual Friend*, the mechanical Bradley Headstone could scarcely be considered a disciple of Froebel; nor could the dreary abstract grammar lesson in which the buxom Miss Peecher drilled little Mary Anne be considered in accord with Froebelian tradition; while the lessons meted out to infant and prostitute alike in the "miserable loft" where Charley Hexam got his first schooling were about as far away from Froebel's philosophy as one could get. In the fourth novel subsequent to 1854, *Edwin Drood*, we are delighted to make the acquaintance of the light-hearted Miss Twinkleton, smartening up her curls, or livening up her eyes after dusk; to enjoy the clandestine festivities in the girls' bedrooms as vacation draws near; and even to sympathize with Mrs. Tisher's chronic sigh and weak back; yet we fail to observe any exposition of the ideas of Froebel in all this.

Dickens's short stories that were written after 1854 do not reveal any trace of Froebelian influence either. In "Mugby Junction," the extra Christmas number for *All the Year Round* (1866), Phoebe, crippled and bed-ridden since infancy, teaches a few children to read, and to sing little tunes to the words of the multiplication table. In "Doctor Marigold's Prescription" (1865), the Cheap Jack, or peddler, Doctor Marigold, endeavours to teach a foundling girl to read, and eventually sends her to be educated at a deaf-and-dumb school. The exquisite fantasy, "Holiday Romance" (1868), in which the tables are turned, and the "grown-up people are obliged to obey the children, and are never allowed to sit up for supper, except on holidays," portrays the Misses Drowvey and Grimmer, a pair of grotesque schoolmistresses in Mrs. Lemon's Preparatory School "for grown-ups," concerning whom a debate rages among the pupils as to which is the greatest beast! In "George Silverman's Explanation" which was written for the *Atlantic Monthly* in the same year, 1868, George Silverman, after being furnished with disinfectant, food, and clothing, attends a Foundation School and is duly exposed to the charity sermons of the hypocritical Brother Hawkyard.

In short, in all this portrayal of schools, pupils, and pedagagues in Dickens's fiction subsequent to 1854, there appears to be little or no exposition of the educational philosophy of Froebel. In fact, in an article written the year before his death, Dickens satirized the whole Rousseau-Pestalozzi-Froebelian tradition in his sardonic denunciation of that irrepressible, didactic, tutorial maniac, Mr. Barlow.[46]

Suppose we take a glance backward to the schools depicted in Dickens's fiction before 1854, to those schools of which he approved: Mr. Marton's in *The Old Curiosity Shop* (1840–1), and Doctor Strong's in *David Copperfield* (1849–50). We find that Dickens's delineations of good schools will not bear critical examination in the light of Froebelian principles. There are no short journeys, or long walks, to study land masses; there is none of Froebel's stress on the commitment of prayers and hymns to memory; progressive studies of schoolroom objects, leading to a study of the family as the centre of man's activity, and eventually leading to a study of the local community, are not even mentioned;[47] no suggestions appear in regard to Froebel's net-drawing as a means of expression. Again, Dickens laid no emphasis on manual activities in his fiction, whereas Froebel thought they should form part of the daily curriculum. Moreover, in the schools Dickens praised in his fiction, there are no indications of creative activity, or of the philosophic synthesis of humanity and nature through divine law.[48] Indeed, a resemblance between Mr. Marton and the practical, non-mystical John Pounds was suggested earlier in this book, and Doctor Strong's awkward gait, slovenly

[46]See chap. VII below.

[47]The fact that Dickens was separated from his wife for twelve years detracts from Booth's stress on Dickens's sense of family (*Charles Dickens und seine Werke*, p. 16 f.). Frieser's attempt to make capital out of conditions in the great English public schools little supports his own summary and Hughes's conclusion, which he quotes, for Froebel was mainly concerned with pre-school children (Frieser, *Die Schulen bei Dickens*, p. 134).

[48]For a complete list of Froebel's practices see *Die Menschenerziehung*, sec. 87, or *The Student's Froebel*, ed. Herford, I, 39–57; II, 21–94.

attire, and philological propensities suggest the redoubtable Dr. Samuel Johnson rather than the genial Froebel.

The lack of manual activities among the scholars in Dickens's fiction, however, should not be interpreted as an indication that Dickens was opposed to manual activities *per se*. In his many articles, as we shall see in chapter VII, Dickens approved of the provision of domestic activities for the inmates of the home for homeless women at Shepherd's Bush, of the work activities of the half-time scholars at the Stepney Union, the repairs made to their clothing by the pupils of the ragged school at Saffron Hill, and the work permitted the inmates of the jail at Kingston, Canada. Yet this idea may well have been one of practicality rather than of Froebelian philosophy. All that has been said concerning Dickens and Froebel is not to gainsay, either, that Froebel, Pestalozzi, and Rousseau on the continent, and the Edgeworths, Wilderspin, Stow, Owen, and the Mayos in Britain were at one with Dickens in their respect for childhood as a stage of value in itself, in their sympathy with children, and in their realization of the usefulness of games in the teaching of very young children.

Having reached this conclusion about the influence of Froebel, we should turn to a closer consideration of what Dickens envisioned in the way of a state system of education. It has been asserted by some of Dickens's most ardent admirers that he "favoured," or "saw the need" of, state education, or that he was "one of the first great advocates of a national system of schools."[49] Although these statements are couched in guarded language, the general impression likely to be received by an uncritical reader is that Dickens saw clearly that a nation-wide state system of education for all was the solution for the chief problems of education in his day, and the definite end for which he worked. In the light of the various inferences given in his novels, such statements as the following are also apt to be quite misleading: "Dickens was one of the first Englishmen to see the need of normal schools to train teachers, and to advocate the abolition of uninspected private schools and the establishment of national schools. He taught these ideals in the preface to *Nicholas Nickleby*, issued in 1839."[50] We will pass over the question of the training of teachers for the moment, and consider first what Dickens had to say about education by the state in the Preface to *Nicholas Nickleby*. He mentions the state's disregard of education in one sentence:

[49]See, respectively, Birchenough, *History of Elementary Education in England and Wales*, p. 57; Hughes, *Dickens as an Educator*, pp. 7, ix.
[50]Hughes, *Dickens as an Educator*, p. 7.

"Of the monstrous neglect of education in England and the disregard of it by the state as a means of forming good or bad citizens, and miserable or happy men, private schools long afforded a notable example"; and then goes on, in the rest of the paragraph, to speak of the unfitness of school teachers. There is nothing about the efficacy or the formation of a national system of state education. No positive suggestions are given in the Preface or in the novel as to possible methods of state supervision or administration; there are no suggestions as to the necessary machinery or organization. Moreover, passages from Dickens's *American Notes*[51] about the charitable institutions of Massachusetts, the House of Industry, the Boylston School for Boys, or the jail at Kingston, Canada, give at best but feeble support to the notion of state education. In these passages Dickens is thinking solely of handicapped, neglected, or delinquent children. His speeches, as we shall see,[52] do express a desire for the wider diffusion of education, but they also express his decided opposition to education dominated by a religious group. Dickens must be given credit, surely, for knowing that any state system of education in England would inevitably be closely allied with the English state church, and in any case his acquaintance with the educational administrator, Kay-Shuttleworth, and the columns of *The Household Narrative of Current Events* would have made him fully aware of it.

From January, 1850, to December, 1855, this monthly supplement, *The Household Narrative of Current Events*, was published in conjunction with *Household Words*—a weekly periodical which Dickens conducted from March, 1850, to May, 1859. This supplement (reporting the news under such headings as "Parliament and Politics," "Law and Crime," "Accident and Disaster," "Foreign Events," "Social, Sanitary, and Municipal Progress," etc.) had only a very short life of a scant six years, but its editorial commentary under the heading of "The Three Kingdoms" had an even shorter one, and was discontinued in February, 1853. Accounts of educational controversy and proposed legislation concerning education were carried in its news columns as a matter of course, but it is interesting to note also the amount of space given to educational comment in the editorial columns. It has been said that "its editorial commentary, under the title of 'The Three Kingdoms,' frequently argued the necessity of a State system of education."[53] This remark was made in an annotated bibliography, and so, naturally, was

[51]See *American Notes*, chap. III, pp. 31, 34, 37–40; and chap. XV, pp. 239 ff.
[52]See chap. VI below.
[53]Collins, *Dickens's Periodicals*, p. 6. (On several of the pages in *The Household Narrative of Current Events* which were cited in support of the statement quoted above, I was unable to discover more than a passing reference to education.)

not demonstrated further. An acceptance of this statement at face value, however, involves the knotty problem as to who actually wrote these commentaries, or, indeed, who actually assumed editorial responsibility for the complete supplement. It has been said that Dickens's own father handled the *Household Narrative*,[54] but he could not have done so for very long, because he died on March 31, 1851. It has also been said that Dickens's father-in-law, George Hogarth, was the editor,[55] and it is clear from several extant letters that Hogarth had a good deal to do with it. On the other hand it is certain that Dickens's associate editor, Wills, had agreed at some time to take "the labouring oar" in editing the supplement.[56] Hence Dickens's part in this particular publication is difficult of identification.

When discussing Dickens's contributions to newspapers and periodicals in a later chapter of this book, I have excluded any reference to the editorial comments in the *Household Narrative*, because of their anonymity and because of the uncertainty of Dickens's participation in the supplement. But here, the claim that through this anonymous editorial commentary Dickens argued for a state system of schools is pertinent. The style of the commentary is by no means uniform, and bears the mark of several hands. A remark such as "education is the only safeguard against crime" is certainly one which Dickens may well have made, but the references which follow to such classical writers as Livy, Horace, Homer, and Thucydides smack of a more erudite pen.[57] Dickens would probably have agreed with the statement that "The poor must be taught as well as fed; and to a sound system of universal education we must look for our only effective antidote to crime and bigotry."[58] On the occasion of W. J. Fox's proposal of a bill (subsequently defeated) in the House of Commons for the promotion of secular education, the *Household Narrative* commented: "All that it [Fox's bill] asks to do is to educate such waifs as neither Churchman nor Dissenter can draw into their respective folds."[59] It appears that Dickens had no carefully thought-out administrative plan for a state system of schools—and neither did the *Household Narrative*, which preferred to support schemes suggested by others—but Dickens would have supported Fox in any attempt to provide state care for neglected waifs, and would certainly have given a hearty amen to the *Narrative*'s comment on Fox's proposal.

[54]Johnson, *Charles Dickens*, II, 707.
[55]Eckel, *The First Editions of the Writings of Charles Dickens*, p. 216.
[56]Lehmann, *Charles Dickens as Editor*, pp. 24, 65, 115, 148, 165, 173, 177.
[57]April, 1851, p. 97.
[58]Oct., 1850, p. 219.
[59]Feb., 1850, p. 26.

It is apparent also that there is no clear or definite statement in Dickens's fiction that he had formulated in his mind a national state system of free, compulsory education. True, he attacked private schools. But when he wanted to present a good school, it was still a private school such as Doctor Strong's or Mr. Marton's. And he had nothing to offer in his fiction as a replacement for a wretched school such as Dotheboys Hall. He merely broke it up. Nor did he offer in *Bleak House* any solution save benevolent charity for the evil symbolized in Jo. If a state system of education were Dickens's goal, is it not strange that he did not set forth his views in more certain terms? J. S. Mill made himself clear: "Is it not almost a self-evident axiom that the state should require and compel the education, up to a certain standard, of every human being who is born a citizen?" Ruskin did the same: "The first duty of the state is to see that every child born therein shall be well housed, clothed, fed, and educated till it attains years of discretion."[60] During an era when men such as Brougham, Russell, and Kay-Shuttleworth were straining every nerve to secure some sort of state system of education, or to place a school in every parish, it seems strange, if Dickens had thought the problem through to a nation-wide state system, that he did not give his whole-hearted support to the plan of having the state pay grants, supply inspectors, and train teachers, no matter what the weaknesses of the plan in its initial stages; instead, as we have seen, he pilloried state inspection and state training of teachers in *Hard Times* and in *Our Mutual Friend*.

As to Dickens's complaint in the Preface to *Nicholas Nickleby* about the government's policy of laissez-faire, it must be borne in mind that this was the dominant economic and political theory of the day. Indeed, as has been pointed out,[61] it was in the field of education that the English government made some of its first departures from the theory—in the Health and Morals of Apprentices Act, 1802, and in the allocation of state grants to education, 1833—before Dickens had written a single sentence either in praise or condemnation of the schools of England. In the very year in which Dickens completed *Nicholas Nickleby*, 1839, the Committee of the Privy Council on Education was established. Six years before, Roebuck's bill had tried to establish compulsory education for all children between the ages of six and twelve, an infant school in every parish, evening schools for all children over fourteen years of age, and training schools for teachers. Between the years 1850–8, there was literally a stream of education measures proposed in the Commons.[62]

---

[60]*On Liberty*, chap. v, p. 129; and *The Stones of Venice*, App. VII, XI, 263.
[61]See Introduction to this book.
[62]Smith, *The Life and Work of Sir James Kay-Shuttleworth*, pp. 228–57.

In regard to the training of teachers, there are also some additional facts which need to be borne in mind. As was observed above, Hughes's statement that Dickens "was one of the first Englishmen to see the need of normal schools to train teachers" is rather misleading. The very first act of the Committee of the Privy Council in 1839 under the direction of Kay-Shuttleworth was an attempt to set up a state training college. A grant of 10,000 pounds sterling was set aside for this purpose, but the project did not get enough support and the grant found its way to the National and British school societies, so in 1840 Kay-Shuttleworth helped to set up a private training school at Battersea. In 1843 it, too, passed into the hands of the National society. Thus frustrated, Kay-Shuttleworth settled in 1846 for the pupil-teacher system of apprenticing pupils from the ages of thirteen to eighteen to a regular headmaster or mistress, and paying state grants to both master and apprentice.[63] There appears to be little doubt, then, that the chief educational official of the state was trying to train teachers; but he could scarcely have considered that Dickens appreciated his efforts. Consider, for example, Dickens's attack on the state training received by Bradley Headstone, and the withering scorn he heaped on the training of Mr. M'Choakumchild. Dickens apparently did not altogether take into account the heavy odds and difficulties involved in training teachers. My suggestion is that it was not the need for training teachers that Dickens saw, but rather the need for choosing men and women of finer quality to be trained.

It is probable that in this sense Dickens saw beyond Kay-Shuttleworth. Both men were opposed to clerical or religious control of education and the training of teachers. Kay-Shuttleworth did much to raise the status of teachers, but he had come to the conclusion that the profession was so ill paid that recruits could be secured only from the ranks of the labouring poor, and further, that only those who regarded teaching as a social or religious mission would remain in the work. In addition, he was faced with the immediate and practical problem of staffing the schools. Kay-Shuttleworth's problem is pointed up by the comments of the Education Commission of 1861 on the low talents and inferior social prestige necessary to qualify for teaching, and the jibe, in very bad taste, that teachers secured their meagre culture at public expense.[64] Nevertheless, Dickens's view also finds expression in the same report: the principal of the York Training College testified that there was too much "retailing of facts," and added that "the master has been crammed himself, and so he crams

[63]See *ibid.*, pp. 82–4, 91–4, 104–21, 164, 172–4.
[64]Education Commission, 1861, Report, *Parliamentary Papers*, XXI, 1861, I, 160–3.

his pupils."[65] Dickens was aware that cheap men drive out dear. In order to attract satisfactory men into the profession, both the unsympathetic and the inefficient—the "teachers of good intentions"—would have to be debarred or got rid of. Thus, I repeat, it was not so much the need of training that Dickens saw as the need for people of high character and wide capacity, and the further necessity of giving them a more liberal training. The inferior calibre of many already in the profession, and the mechanical nature of the training that was given, discouraged suitable personnel from entering the profession in the first place, and from remaining in it afterwards.

[65]*Ibid.*, pp. 135–6.

CHAPTER VI

Dickens's Speeches on Education

"A reader will rise from the perusal of a book," observed Charles Dickens in a speech at Hartford, Connecticut, on February 7, 1842, "with some defined and tangible idea of the writer's moral creed and broad purposes . . . , and it is probable enough that he may like to have this idea confirmed from the author's lips." The relation between Dickens's private beliefs about education and the ideas emanating from his fiction is precisely what we want to know. In the same speech, he summarized his moral creed in three parts: he had faith in beautiful things; he held all meanness, such as falsehood, cruelty, and oppression, in contempt; and refused to accept social status as a criterion of moral judgment. A few days before, in Boston, he had said that he wanted to contribute to human happiness, and was inclined to think that virtue shows herself in "rags" as well as in "fine linen," and that she "dwells rather oftener in alleys and by-ways than she does in courts and palaces."[1] Some years later, in an apparent reference to the world of literature, he affirmed: "In my sphere of action I have tried to understand the heavier social grievances, and to help to set them right." He believed that "public progress is far behind our private progress"; and that since "the drowsy twaddle" in the House of Commons revealed "little adequate expression [or] even understanding of the general mind," he considered it his duty to speak for the people to effect a "great peaceful constitutional change."[2] We thus have Dickens's own "moral creed and broad purposes" publicly expressed from his own lips. Is his fiction a confirmation or denial? His championship of Oliver Twist; the virtue of Jo and Little Nell; his attacks on the laws of divorce and the delays of chancery; his ridicule of elections at Eatanswill, and of my Lord Verisopht, are a few examples, among many, that give the answer.

His speeches also confirm other ideas expressed throughout his fiction. For example, in a speech at London, March 12, 1856, he made a withering attack on smugness, on show, and on toadying to distinguished indi-

[1]Shepherd, ed., *Speeches*, pp. 64 f., 57–62.
[2]Speech at Drury Lane Theatre, June 27, 1855 (*ibid.*, pp. 164–71). Cf. *The Letters of Charles Greville*, ed. Johnston, p. 236.

viduals. He castigated the "desire for show," "the long inquiry," and "its preposterous pretence"; he condemned the "smug, traditional, conventional party, bent upon . . . its own annual puffery at costly dinner-tables and upon a course of expensive toadying" instead of on the fulfilment of its primary obligation to relieve distress.[3] In an earlier London speech on May 10, 1851, he had expressed his conviction that sanitary reform must precede even educational or religious reform. Building up a case against centralization and delays, he stressed the need for adequate knowledge and earnest sympathy. A few hours' teaching, he pointed out, can do little against a loathsome environment. He pleaded for the relief of distress and suffering, reminding his listeners that vaccination had been opposed "because it imparted part of the bovine nature of a cow to humans"; and, similarly, that the use of chloroform had been opposed because it "contravened divine infliction of pain."[4] On February 9, 1858, he asked his audience in the name of Charles Lamb's dream children—the children they loved, had lost, wished they had, or had been themselves—for aid to a hospital for sick children which had only thirty beds for the whole of the vast London metropolis. The patients were so tiny that the adult nurses looked like "reclaimed giantesses, and the kind medical practitioner like an amiable ogre"; and if a visitor glanced around, he could see "how the little tired, flushed cheek has toppled over half the brute creation on its way into the ark; or how one little dimpled arm has mowed down . . . the whole tin soldiery of Europe."[5] Is there any person rash enough to claim that Dickens, in his fiction, failed to make an equally strong appeal for sick and neglected children, to stress cleanliness, and to attack smugness? His depiction of frail Paul Dombey and neglected Copperfield, his attacks on unsanitary workhouses and schoolrooms in *Oliver Twist* and *Nicholas Nickleby*, and on Podsnappery in *Our Mutual Friend* stand as evidence.

It is, however, educational theory and practice with which we are concerned. On these matters we find that Dickens made some very forthright condemnations in his speeches. There is extant an address of his which sets forth in no uncertain terms seven specific types of schools which he did not like: a type of private-venture school; a certain group of ladies' schools; schools where endowments had been "perverted"; utilitarian schools; charity schools; denominational schools where the

---

[3]Shepherd, ed., *Speeches*, pp. 177–9.
[4]In London, June 5, 1867, and June 27, 1855 (*ibid.*, pp. 128 f., 264–7). Cf. *The Letters of Charles Greville*, ed. Johnston, pp. 264–7.
[5]Shepherd, ed., *Speeches*, p. 192.

catechism was dinned into the pupils by rote; and of course, the cheap and distant Yorkshire schools.[6]

The private-venture schools Dickens had in mind were proprietary schools of the sort he had experienced as a boy when in attendance at Jones's academy, and which he regarded as a "pernicious humbug." The proprietors, all too often, were ignorant and bad-tempered men whose sole aim was to make money out of the pupils, and who always gave all the prizes to the boy who had four younger brothers who might later come to the school and increase its revenue. Dickens remarked that he "never could understand the wholesomeness of the moral preached by the abject appearance and degraded condition of the teachers who plainly said to us by their looks every day of their lives, 'Boys never be learned; . . . be warned . . . in time, by our sunken cheeks, by our pimply noses, by our meagre diet, by our acid beer, and by our extraordinary suits of clothes. . . .' "

Dickens also called on his boyhood experience to describe the sort of ladies' schools that displeased him. The young ladies from the school that joined his school for dancing on Wednesdays always seemed to be in the twin condition of wearing "new stays" and of being "in disgrace." "Memory," he said, "always depicts the youthful enthraller of my first affection as for ever standing against a wall in a curious machine of wood which confined her innocent feet in the first dancing position, while those arms which should have encircled my jacket . . . were pinioned behind her by an instrument of torture called a backboard, fixed in the manner of a double direction post."

Dickens then turned to the endowed schools which had been founded by "worthy scholars and good men long since deceased" for the advancement of learning and for the sound education of those who were both willing and able to profit from such institutions. Some of these schools, he said, had had their endowments "monstrously perverted from their original purpose" and were being "struggled for and fought over with the most indecent pertinacity." Bentham's utilitarianism and Manchester materialism came in for equally severe disapprobation. Dickens did not like those utilitarian schools where, as he observed, "the bright childish imagination is utterly discouraged, and where those bright childish faces . . . are gloomily and grimly scared out of countenance; where I have never seen among the pupils, whether boys or girls, anything but little parrots and small calculating machines."

[6]Address to Fourth Anniversary Dinner of the Warehousemen and Clerks' schools, Nov. 5, 1857, in Shepherd, ed., *Speeches*, pp. 181–4.

He came down even harder on the charity schools for the indignities they inflicted on children. The pupils, dressed "in leather breeches and with mortified straw baskets for bonnets . . . file along the streets in long melancholy rows under the escort of that surprising British monster—a beadle, whose system of instruction, I am afraid, . . . is given in a grave report of a trustworthy school inspector to the effect that a boy in great repute at school for his learning, presented on his slate, as one of the ten commandments, the perplexing prohibition, 'Thou shalt not commit doldrum.' " Certain of the denominational schools, those which had as their chief aim the indoctrination of the young with catechism and church dogma, did not fare any better at Dickens's hands. "I don't like those schools," he observed, "even though the instruction given in them be gratuitous, where those sweet little voices which ought to be heard speaking in very different accents, anathematise, by rote, any human being who does not hold what is taught there."

Dickens's statement on the cheap Yorkshire schools is mild compared with the damning he gave them in *Nicholas Nickleby*, but its matter-of-fact tone is no less convincing. There is no mistaking his views: "I do not like, and I did not like some years ago, cheap distant schools, where neglected children pine from year to year, under an amount of neglect, want, and youthful misery far too sad even to be glanced at in this cheerful assembly."

There is no disparity therefore between the educational theory and practice condemned in Dickens's speeches and those condemned in his novels. A cursory review makes this clear; the infamous Salem House in *David Copperfield* was a private school; Miss Pinch's eldest pupil had "arrived at *such* a pitch of whalebone and education" in *Martin Chuzzlewit* as not to be outdone by Mrs. Wackles who attended to "punishment, fasting, and other tortures and terrors" in her Seminary in *The Old Curiosity Shop*; Uriah Heep attended a foundation school; Sissy Jupe had about as difficult a time at Mr. Gradgrind's school as did little Paul Dombey in Doctor Blimber's Academy; the charity school in *Dombey and Son* was where the quondam Grinder was "huffed and cuffed" in his preposterous outfit; it was there, too, that children were stuffed with "all the proper names of all the tribes of Judah" after the manner of the church school—the "miserable loft"—attended by Charley Hexam in *Our Mutual Friend*; and Dotheboys Hall needs no introduction as a cheap Yorkshire school.

What did Dickens have to say in his speeches in a positive way about schools he *did* like, and what educational theory and practice was he prepared to support? It was at this point that he became rather vague in his speeches, as in his novels. In the speech from which we have been quoting he cited the Warehousemen and Clerks' schools as examples of schools he liked. It should be noted carefully that these were schools that had been established by members of an industrial group for orphan children of men who had been in their particular trade, and that they were administered by members of this group. Dickens advocated religious (but not sectarian) instruction, and a homelike atmosphere—a school was, in fact, to be a home. Dickens was in deadly earnest here; he entreated his audience "not to suppose that my fancy and unfortunate habit of fiction has anything to do with the picture I have just presented to you. It is sober matter of fact." It is important to notice that Dickens did not suggest that there should be a state system of education, or give any inkling that he had any such thoughts in his own mind.[7] Indeed, he insisted that only the children of those members who had contributed the threepence a week should be permitted to benefit.[8]

Similarly, when he appealed at the Adelphi Theatre in London, May 11, 1864, for funds to support a school according to his own standards, the school was for a special needy group—children of distressed actors, actresses, or dramatic writers. This was an attempt to found a new set of schools—the Shakespeare Schools—not to secure support for an old foundation, and the appeal was made only six years before Dickens's death. If a nation-wide system of state schools was his aim, what opportunities he was missing! How he was dissipating his resources! He insisted that the school be self-supporting, but he expected the public to provide donations for forty foundation scholars who were to receive "a sound, liberal, comprehensive education." Moreover, in the same speech, he launched into a brief eulogy of "public" schools such as Eton, describing them as "socially liberal," free from "servility to mere rank," and careful cultivators of a "free, manly, independent spirit."[9]

It should be observed that Dickens approved of schools which were designed for the unfortunate children of actors, warehousemen, and clerks. Another example of this interest was the speech he made on

[7]Cf. statement by Hughes, *Dickens as an Educator*, p. ix, that Dickens was "one of the first great advocates of a national system of schools," and see discussion of this contention in chap. v above.

[8]A capital of 14,000 pounds sterling had been set up for the school, which was located at Newcross; thirty-nine pupils were on the roll at this time (Shepherd, ed., *Speeches*, pp. 184 f.).

[9]*Ibid.*, p. 234. The fact that the Provost of Eton had approved the scheme for the Shakespeare Schools may have prompted Dickens's eulogy, but note that the Baroness Burdett-Coutts had sent Dickens's eldest son, Charles, to Eton, and that Dickens sent three of his other sons to a school at Boulogne where they were taught by an old Eton master.

behalf of the orphan and unfortunate children of the Commercial Travellers' schools. Appropriately enough, perhaps, he discussed travelling rather than education on that occasion.[10] It would seem sound to make the general assertion that Dickens, in his speeches, did not appeal for state control of all education or indeed for universal education as we understand it, but rather for homes and schools for orphan and unfortunate children, and, as we shall see in a moment, for the Mechanics' Institutes. Consider the number of unfortunates he championed in his novels. And on whose behalf did he write articles? For whom did he want schools in his contributions to papers and periodicals such as *Household Words*? "A Paradise at Tooting," "A Sleep to Startle Us," "Crime and Education," "The Finishing Schoolmaster," "Stores for the First of April," provide part of the answer, as we shall see in the next chapter.

There is another observation about Dickens's speeches that is of even more significance for the portrayal of schools in his fiction. It is simply this: Dickens was very much in earnest in his appeal for the hospital for sick children, yet he could not refrain from depicting the nurses and doctors as giantesses and ogres—characters from a land of fairy tale. The appeal he made, both in his fiction and his speeches and articles, to human sympathy, imagination, dignity, and sense of fun, simultaneously, has often been missed, especially by pedagogical critics[11] straining for abstruse educational principles. Here is an example of his imaginative fun in an appeal he made for funds at the Anniversary Festival of the Hospital for Sick Children on February 9, 1858. He loved children, he championed their cause, and he favoured what we now call child study, but he knew (he was the father of ten children) what happens when children won't go to bed: "We know how they prop their eyelids open with their forefingers when they *will* sit up; how, when they become fractious, they say aloud that they don't like us, and our nose is too long, and why don't we go? And we are perfectly well acquainted with those kicking bundles which are carried off at last protesting." He was also well aware that theory was often one thing, and practice too often quite another:

An eminent eye-witness told me that he was one of a company of learned pundits who assembled at the house of a very distinguished philosopher of the last generation to hear him expound his stringent views concerning

---

[10]In London, Dec. 30, 1854 (Shepherd, ed., *Speeches*, pp. 156 f.).

[11]See Hughes, *Dickens as an Educator*, or Frieser, *Die Schulen bei Dickens*, or Booth, *Charles Dickens und seine Werke*. Throughout all three monographs there is nowhere the slightest suggestion that Dickens at times is being imaginatively ludicrous in his delineations of school life.

infant education and early mental development, and he told me that while the philosopher did this in very beautiful and lucid language, the philosopher's little boy, for his part, edified the assembled sages by dabbling up to the elbows in an apple pie which had been provided for the entertainment, having previously anointed his hair with syrup, combed it with his fork, and brushed it with his spoon.[12]

After this speech the members of the audience reached for their pocket-handkerchiefs with one hand and for their pocket-books with the other.

The nineteenth-century agitation to extend educational opportunities for the very young had its complement in attempts to widen them for adults as well. By mid-century, almost every industrial town had its Mechanics' Institute or the equivalent. In 1850, there were between six hundred and seven hundred such institutes, with a membership somewhere between ninety thousand and one hundred and ten thousand.[13] The aim appeared to be to give the workmen a grounding in scientific principles so that they could apply the knowledge in their work and thus increase their skill. For some thirteen years, Dickens was president of the Mechanics' Institute at Chatham, and served for brief periods as president of similar institutions at Birmingham and Reading. On no less than six occasions he gave public readings from his works to raise funds for the Chatham Institute; and he gave readings for the same purpose at Birmingham in 1853; at Reading, Bradford, and Sherborne in 1854; at Folkestone, Peterborough, and Sheffield in 1855; and at Bristol and Edinburgh in 1858.

Dickens gave considerable time and energy to the movement in other ways: he presided at various foundings or opening sessions; officiated at prize-giving sessions; and made public speeches in support of specific institutes.[14] It was his custom to review the resources and achievements of the respective institutions, the fees levied, the number of volumes in the library, the courses offered, the membership reached, the buildings and rooms acquired, and the number of affiliated educational institutions.

In at least ten of his speeches he chose to discourse on "education" at some length, and a brief account of his views may be given here. At Manchester, October 5, 1843, he suggested that self-education gave a man self-respect. It gave him strength in adversity and companionship

[12]Shepherd, ed., *Speeches*, pp. 168 f.

[13]True, in most places, the institutes eventually declined; but the London Institute was the origin of Birkbeck College, and those at Huddersfield, Leeds, and Bradford eventually developed into technical institutions. See Hammond and Hammond, *The Bleak Age*, pp. 162–70; Adamson, *English Education*, pp. 154–6; Curtis, *History of Education in Great Britain*, pp. 300–4. J. W. Hudson is the real historian of the institutes: see his *History of Adult Education*.

[14]See Collins, "Dickens and Adult Education," pp. 115–27.

in his work; it enabled him to achieve kindness and tolerance and to accept responsibility in his daily life. His influence was extended beyond his home to mankind at large. A little knowledge, far from being a dangerous thing, had brought unspeakable blessings to men of low estate and limited means, such as Crabbe, Franklin, and Burns.[15] At Liverpool on February 26, 1844, Dickens again praised the principle of self-education which gives every man the right to aspire to wisdom for the conquest of ignorance and prejudice. On that occasion he also commended the formation of a girls' school.[16] At Birmingham, on February 28, 1844, he lauded the usefulness of an institution which, by providing education, induced honesty and goodness, corrected evil, and prevented the workers from becoming mere machines.[17] At Leeds, on December 1, 1847, he again stressed the need to continue education throughout life, and asserted that whenever education had been said to fail, it was not true education, but usually "preposterous spelling book lessons to the meanest purpose."[18]

At Glasgow, on December 28, 1847, he returned once more to these themes: everyone, he insisted, had the right to improve himself; mere reading and writing were not education; education lay, rather, in the cultivation of the requisites for earning a living, and in the acquisition of virtue "to which all knowledge tends."[19] Again at Birmingham, on January 6, 1853, he praised the accomplishments already achieved by the local institute's various educational "threads"—courses in grammar, a course for girls in designing, polytechnic courses, deaf and dumb classes, its two colleges, and its proposed Literary and Scientific Institution.[20] Still again at Birmingham, in December of the same year, when giving a public reading of *A Christmas Carol* on behalf of the Birmingham and Midland Institute, he supported the right of the worker to educate himself; to have an institution to which all working men go, to which they all contribute, in the management of which they all may share, and which truly educates the imagination as well as the reason.[21] In his presentation of the prizes at Manchester on December 3, 1858, Dickens dwelt at length on the working-class status of the recipients; pertinently, he pointed out that they were faced with

> Those twin gaolers of the daring heart
> Low birth and iron fortune.[22]

[15]Shepherd, ed., *Speeches*, pp. 74–81.
[16]*Ibid.*, pp. 83–6.   [17]*Ibid.*, pp. 92–5.
[18]*Ibid.*, pp. 102–6.   [19]*Ibid.*, pp. 111–14.
[20]*Ibid.*, pp. 143–6.   [21]*Ibid.*, p. 152.
[22]Lines spoken by Claude Melnotte in Bulwer-Lytton's *The Lady of Lyons.*

He described the sacrifices of the brother from Chorley; the youthful plasterer from Bury; the chain-maker; the iron-moulder;[23] and the mule-frame piecer who could not read at eighteen years but became the best French scholar in his district by the time he was thirty. Dickens asked that their training for machines should not be concentrated on to the exclusion of the child's fairy tale, the adult's grace and ornament, the human fancy and imagination.[24] It is not without significance that at Birmingham, more than ten years later (September 27, 1869), he publicly quoted Bulwer-Lytton's lines again, and lauded the introduction of penny evening classes. It was here, too, that he stated his oft-quoted maxim that success resulted from "the quality of attention," and re-affirmed his widely quoted political faith—no faith in those who govern, but unlimited faith in those being governed.[25] Finally, on January 6, 1870, only five months before his death, when he was presiding at the prize-giving of the Birmingham and Midland Institute of which he was president, he enlarged on this last statement, quoting Henry Thomas Buckle[26] to the effect that whenever law-givers have been successful, they have merely given legal sanction to the wishes of the people whose servants they actually are.[27]

It would appear from these speeches that Dickens saw the value of a little knowledge in the dispersion of ignorance and prejudice; that he saw the cultural value of self-education in stimulating the imagination and cultivating virtue. Since Dickens was typically Victorian to the extent that he envisaged society as being composed of various classes, it is not surprising that he argued for the extension of education to more and more people on the grounds that an uneducated class constituted a danger to the rest of society. In a society with less rigid class distinction these grounds have less appearance of validity. Yet his recognition that formal schooling alone is not an adequate preparation for complete living, and that education should therefore be extended into adult life, is readily accepted as being as valid today as in the nineteenth century. Why were these institutions for adult education so near his heart? The reason was that they were intended for the labouring poor, in whom he had faith in spite of their "low birth and iron fortune." These workers, the neglected tenders of machines, needed a "little knowledge" and a "little culture" most, and yet they were required to make the greatest sacrifices for the most meagre educational attainment. Ragged schools

[23]See Introduction to this book.
[24]Shepherd, ed., *Speeches*, pp. 216–20.
[25]*Ibid.*, pp. 302–9.
[26]Author of a *History of Civilization in England*.
[27]Shepherd, ed., *Speeches*, p. 313.

and Mechanics' Institutes both furthered Dickens's desire to extend the meagre education of the poor.

Whatever Dickens was trying to say in his speeches on behalf of the Mechanics' Institutes, it is apparent that there was no mention of state schools, or a state system of schools. Indeed, the fact that he gave public readings to raise funds for the Mechanics' Institutes is evidence of too great a dependence on patronage and charity.[28] When the institutes decided to allow girls to attend their classes, and books were needed for them, Dickens had recourse to the time-worn method of a fancy bazaar under royal patronage.[29] He himself, of course, preferred self-help to patronage. His heart went out to the workmen who had made such great sacrifices in order to profit by the classes at the Mechanics' Institutes, but he failed to see that, all too often, they did not have sufficient knowledge of even the rudiments of learning to benefit from the education and culture that were offered; that the white-collar workers would eventually force out these horny-handed workmen from the institutes; that only a small fraction of any social group would continue to make the tremendous sacrifices that these institutions required of them; that trained teachers and personnel were needed; and that central organization and financial support from the state were essential requisites for the lasting success of the movement.

[28]For example, when he read *A Christmas Carol* at Birmingham in December, 1853, he raised about 400 pounds sterling for the Institute (*ibid.*, p. 152).

[29]*Ibid.*, pp. 113–14.

CHAPTER VII

Dickens's Articles Relating to Education

"No writer's name will be used . . . every paper will be published without any signature, and all will seem to express the general . . . purpose of the journal, which is the raising up of those who are down. . . ." In a letter to Mrs. Gaskell, January 30, 1850,[1] Dickens gave this as the policy of *Household Words* which he edited (with W. H. Wills as his associate) from March, 1850, to May, 1859. In the introductory number he expressed his aim as the displacing of those whose existence is a national disgrace, the bringing together of those of greater and lesser degree, and the fostering of tolerance and perseverance, and when announcing (in *Household Words*, May 28, 1859) the approaching publication of *All the Year Round* (the journal edited by Dickens from its inception until the time of his death), he added that it was necessary for the welfare of the community that "the graces of the imagination" should be fused with "the realities of life."[2] These two statements indicate a consistency of general purpose in both Dickens's articles and his fiction. "Long before this Journal [*Household Words*] came into existence," he avowed, "we systematically tried to turn Fiction to the good account of showing the preventible wretchedness and misery in which the mass of the people dwell, and . . . that reform of their habitations must precede all other reforms."[3]

To some people, Dickens's articles, in comparison with his fiction, make rather dull reading. Yet it may be observed that both dealt with much the same problems. We are reminded of the dreary Sundays of Arthur Clennam's childhood in *Little Dorrit* as we read of "the case of overstrained Sunday observance, and the denial of innocent popular reliefs from labour";[4] or of Stephen Blackpool in *Hard Times* by such a passage as: "The law of divorce is in such condition that from the tie

[1]Hogarth and Dickens, eds., *Letters*, p. 213. The fact that the articles were published anonymously has led to unfortunate errors—some articles that were not written by Dickens have been attributed to him. For instance, see chapter v above and Appendix C below for correction of the widely held view that Dickens wrote the article "Infant Gardens."

[2]Matz, ed., *Miscellaneous Papers* (hereafter cited as *Misc. P.*), I, 181–4.

[3]*Household Words* (hereafter cited as *H. W.*), Oct. 7, 1854 (*Misc. P.*, I, 485).

[4]*H. W.*, Oct. 11, 1856 (*Misc. P.*, II, 123).

of marriage there is no escape . . . except under proved circumstances . . . , and then only on payment of an enormous sum of money.
Ferocity, flight, felony, madness, none of these will break the chain,
without the enormous sum of money."[5] The callousness and indifference
of the upper classes in such articles as "The Amusements of the People"[6]
recall Mr. Dombey or Mr. Bounderby. The righteous indignation expressed in the novels at the exploitation of the poor comes out vehemently
again in "Trading in Death," where Dickens castigates the conduct of
the state funeral of the Duke of Wellington, when the public were de-
luded into buying tawdry souvenirs, indigestible refreshments, and even
positions on the route of the cortège.[7] Dickens's severity with the wil-
fully improvident comes out in "Betting-Shops," in which he remarks
that it would do apprentices who indulge in betting "a world of good"
to be "convicted before a magistrate, and shut up in the House of Correction, to pick a little oakum, and tip a little gruel into their silly
stomachs."[8] Mrs. Jellyby of *Bleak House*, who projected her energies to
the left bank of the Niger much to the detriment of her family responsibilities, epitomizes "The Niger Expedition"; the expedition, Dickens
thinks, is a waste of time, effort, and money; it involves a fruitless
squandering of human life; and in so far as it encourages indifference to
social savagery at home, it amounts simply to misplaced idealism.[9] "The
Poor Man and His Beer" brings the problem of poverty closer to home,
and not only reveals the sympathy for the poor which so often emanates
from Dickens's fiction, but also expresses that faith in self-help so often
observed in his speeches.[10] Finally, in "Railway Dreaming," when Dickens describes the small child who continuously waves his hand to the
passengers in the stream of carriages, not one of whom returns a single
responsive gesture, we are reminded of the many lonely children portrayed in his novels; and when Dickens confesses "I am not a lonely
man, though I was once a lonely boy," we realize how faithfully he portrayed life in his writings.[11]

Now that the general similarity between Dickens's fiction and non-
fiction, both as to aims and problems, has been observed, it is proposed
to examine in much greater detail the articles that specifically relate to
education.

[5]*H. W.*, Oct. 11, 1856 (*Misc. P.*, II, 122 f.).
[6]*H. W.*, March 30, 1850, April 13, 1850 (*Misc. P.*, I, 187–91, 192–9).
[7]*H. W.*, Nov. 27, 1852 (*Misc. P.*, I, 374–81).
[8]*H. W.*, June 26, 1852 (*Misc. P.*, I, 373).
[9]*The Examiner*, Aug. 19, 1848 (*Misc. P.*, I, 117–35).
[10]*All the Year Round*, April 30, 1859 (*Misc. P.*, II, 196–294).
[11]*H. W.*, May 10, 1856 (*Misc. P.*, II, 103–10).

We shall begin with three articles concerning pauper children which Dickens contributed to *The Examiner* during the editorship of John Forster. By January 20, 1849, the date on which Dickens contributed "The Paradise at Tooting,"[12] his novel on the same problem, *Oliver Twist*, had been published for over ten years. The article was concerned with the disgraceful conditions found at a farm conducted by a Mr. Drouet, at Tooting, Surrey, to whom certain boards of guardians had "apprenticed" pauper children at four shillings and sixpence per week. An epidemic resembling cholera had broken out among the children and a number of them had died. Inquiries set in motion by Coroner Wakely and by Dr. Granger of the Board of Health led Dickens to expose the wretchedly overcrowded conditions on the "farm." He revealed that the food was so unwholesome that the children furtively climbed over fences to "pick up scraps of sustenance from the tubs of hog-wash"; that their clothing by day and their covering by night were shamefully inadequate; that the rooms they lived in were cold, damp, dirty, and rotten; and that sick children were left four in a bed. A medical witness testified that the boys suffered from debility, boils, and an itch more aggravated than he had seen in thirty years of medical practice. The article quoted a surgeon of St. Pancras as reporting "that a great deal of severity, not to use a harsh term, had been exercised," and Dickens added that the boys were continually "knocked down, beaten, and brutally used." If they complained, they were placed "on short diet." On May 9, one of the guardians for Holborn, Mr. Winch, visited the farm, and on cutting about one hundred potatoes at different tables discovered that not a single one of them was fit to eat. "All this," Dickens wrote, "is distinctly in proof before the coroner's jury." A verdict of manslaughter was returned against Drouet by the coroner's jury, and the case was referred to the criminal court.

On January 27, 1849, Dickens contributed another article to *The Examiner*, entitled "The Tooting Farm."[13] He complained that attempts were being made to "soften" the points of evidence, he placed the blame squarely on the boards of guardians for sending the children to Tooting, and he demanded that the "farming out" of pauper children be abolished. Chartism was rife at the time, and besides stressing the obvious humanitarian aspects of the Drouet case, Dickens pointed out that the Chartist leaders then in prison had found their converts among the "discontented poor." The just settlement of this Tooting case, he said, would serve as an admirable educational opportunity to convince the masses that the

[12]*Misc. P.*, I, 150–7.
[13]*Ibid.*, pp. 157–60.

state had their interests at heart: "There are few poor working-men in the kingdom who *might* not find themselves next year, next month, next week, in the position of those fathers whose children were sent to Tooting; and there are probably very few working-men who have not thought 'this might be my child's case tomorrow.' "

A third article, "The Verdict for Drouet," appeared on April 21, 1849, after Drouet had been freed under a technicality of law.[14] No evidence could be produced to say that the child with whose death Drouet had been specifically charged—one child of the hundred and fifty who had died in the epidemic—would have recovered from the cholera if he had not suffered from Drouet's ill treatment. Dickens pointed out, however, that hunger, unwholesome food, cold, neglect, sore eyes, itch, insufficient clothing, and ill treatment had been sufficiently proved, and he felt that public opinion would be sufficiently aroused to wipe out the so-called farms: "No one doubts that the child-farming system is effectually broken up by this trial."

Seven years later, Dickens attacked another disgraceful consequence of the poor-law—the overcrowding of the casual ward of the workhouses. He had wandered into Whitechapel on a dark and miserably wet night. As he was passing a workhouse, he noticed what appeared to be "five bundles of rags" crouched on the muddy pavement in the meagre shelter of the workhouse wall. It turned out that the "bundles" were young women who had been refused entrance to the casual ward because preference had to be given to women with children. Dickens gave them money for food and lodging, and resolved to bring their plight to the attention of the public. He was so angry that he did not trust himself to write immediately, but as soon as he was calmer, he composed and published "A Nightly Scene in London."[15]

He was always disturbed by the relation between neglect, particularly the neglect of education, and crime. In "Pet Prisoners"[16] he pointed out that the government's "model prison" at Pentonville, London, had cost only seven thousand pounds less than the total educational grant for the year 1847. A prisoner was, he showed, better treated and fed than an inmate of a workhouse, or a lady boarder at a select school. Nevertheless, work done by five hundred prisoners during 1848 had resulted in a loss of over eight hundred pounds sterling. Dickens asked the pertinent ques-

[14]*Ibid.*, pp. 160–3.
[15]*H. W.*, Jan. 26, 1856 (*Misc. P.*, II, 87–91).
[16]*H. W.*, April 27, 1850 (*Misc. P.*, I, 239–53). Cf. "Crime and Education," a letter to the *Daily News*, Feb. 4, 1846 (*Misc. P.*, I, 25–9), where Dickens urges society to begin with neglected children "some distance from the police office" before the chaplain of the gaol "becomes their only schoolmaster."

tion why public money should not be spent *before* the neglected children of the streets, or those farmed out to the Drouets, became inmates of the prison: "Where is our Model House of Youthful Industry, . . . Model Ragged School, costing . . . from ninety to one hundred thousand pounds, and for its annual maintenance upwards of twenty thousand pounds a year?"

This was not the first time that Dickens had discussed this relation. In three short articles to the *Daily News*, March 9, 13, and 16, 1846,[17] he inveighed against the attempt to "educate" the public by allowing them to witness the disgusting spectacle of public hangings, and demonstrated its ineffectiveness. He quoted from Wakefield's "Facts Relating to the Punishment of Death" which showed that of one hundred and sixty felons sentenced to death, all but three had witnessed public executions. The prevention of the related problem of drunkenness, insisted Dickens in *The Examiner*, July 8, 1848, required the removal of "disgusting habitations" and bad working conditions; something would have to be done to relieve the "mental weariness and languor," to provide relaxation and fill the want for stimulus and excitement, and to abolish the main cause, "inclusive of all the rest, ignorance."[18] He was but continuing the theme, "Ignorance and Crime," begun in the same newspaper on April 22, 1848, which was a review of a government report on the persons taken into custody by the metropolitan police force during 1847 and an appendix that provided some comparisons with those apprehended during the years 1831 to 1847. Nine thousand of 25,000 women prisoners could not read or write at all; eleven thousand could do so very imperfectly. Thirteen thousand of 41,000 men prisoners could neither read nor write. Or to state the facts more impressively, out of 25,000 women and 41,000 men held as prisoners, only 14 women and 150 men could read and write well.[19]

So-called education such as the parroting of church catechism, the tracing of pot-hooks, the spelling-out of syllables about a pig, or using the New Testament as "a dog-eared spelling book" must be discarded, urged Dickens. In its place he requested education which was "immediately applicable to the duties and business of life, directly conducive to order, cleanliness, punctuality, and economy." Dickens sincerely believed that neglect of education led to crime and poverty: "Side by side with Crime, Disease, and Misery in England, Ignorance is always brooding, and is always certain to be found. The union of Night with Darkness is not more certain and indisputable."[20] Similarly, in "A December

[17]*Misc. P.*, I, 30–51.
[19]*Ibid.*, I, 108.
[18]*Ibid.*, I, 113–17.
[20]*Ibid.*, I, 109 f.

Vision" he used allegory to demonstrate the callousness of those who were indifferent to ignorance, injustice, and disease,[21] and in "The Finishing Schoolmaster" he examined a dozen letters of application for another John Ketch (a new hangman), lamenting that this, apparently, was the only schoolmaster the government felt itself obligated to provide![22]

It is refreshing to turn from such depressing accounts of ignorance and crime to a much brighter article describing positive and effective rehabilitation. It is of interest here because of the educational and psychological principles involved. Dickens not only stated them in the article in question, "Home For Homeless Women," but, with the financial aid of the Baroness Burdett-Coutts, put them into practice at Shepherd's Bush.[23] The article appeared in *Household Words* on April 23, 1853, and related the story of five and a half years of gallant effort to reclaim fifty-six girls in their late teens.[24] Officials were satisfied if they managed to rehabilitate about half these young women, representing poor needlewomen, seduced servants, poor girls from ragged schools, shoplifters, and such unfortunates; actually, about thirty of the fifty-six cases were salvaged.

The educational practice followed at the school is interesting. Two hours each day were spent in studying the rudiments of knowledge and the rest in acquiring skill in washing, housework, and the preparation of meals. Captain Macconnochie's system of marking was used as an incentive: good marks earned a monetary award, and the money so earned was saved for the girls so that they would have a small fund when they went to their first jobs. Certain times of the day—three hours

[21]*H. W.*, Dec. 14, 1850 (*Misc. P.*, I, 300–4).
[22]*H. W.*, May 17, 1851 (*Misc. P.*, I, 329–34).
[23]It is unfortunate that Miss Coutts's work for education is so little known. In 1848 she was instrumental in the founding of elementary schools for children adjacent to St. Stephen's Church, Westminster, and, in 1876, in the opening of the Chauncey Hare Townshend Free Schools in Rochester Street. She supported courses in domestic science, by means of prizes and annual addresses, at the Whitelands Training College which had been founded by Lord Ashburton. She aided a sewing school in the east end of London and an evening school for boys at Cooper's Gardens. Mainly through her efforts, the Westminster Technical School was built and equipped and presented to the London County Council. She generously gave her support to the Destitute Children's Dinner Society which provided tens of thousands of children with meals at a penny a meal. She aided in the founding of a home for poor girl art students and gave generously to the Birkbeck Literary and Scientific Institute. In much of her work, Charles Dickens, her friend for over thirty years, was her trusted adviser and almoner. See Osborne, ed., *Letters to Burdett-Coutts*; Johnson, ed., *Heart of Charles Dickens*; Fielding, "Miss Burdett-Coutts: Some Misconceptions"; also chap VIII below.
[24]*Misc. P.*, I, 395–410. See also Johnson, ed., *Heart of Charles Dickens*.

altogether—were set aside for recreation, and on Sundays everybody went to church. All the girls engaged in needlework, and as they sat sewing, someone read aloud to them (a practice recommended also by Ruskin).

The psychological methods that were used were quite advanced for the time. Some time after their admission, the girls were given an opportunity to recount their experiences (not to the superintendents, but to a visiting committee, so as to ensure free expression), and it was a curious circumstance that the poorest of the girls insisted that their connections were wealthy. The members of the committee learned that it was best not to ask leading questions of the girls or to express either approval or disapproval, but to be perfectly imperturbable and to repress stock religious expressions and comments. The girls were allowed to write to relatives, old teachers, or people who had been kind to them, and when they received letters they could read them first themselves and were not compelled to show them to the superintendent if they preferred not to, though it had never been found that they refused to do so.

It proved possible to maintain discipline by keeping the directions simple and as few in number as possible. A judicious use was made of commendation, and threats were never resorted to. Ready access to keys was thought to be too much of a temptation, but the girls developed a sense of responsibility by taking turns at acting as porteress. They could leave the school permanently if they wished, but were usually asked to take a day to reconsider their decision. It was noticed that restlessness increased considerably at holiday seasons and after six months' residence.

A case-history was kept on each girl, and some of these showed remarkable results. One girl, presumed to be eighteen, had been brought up at the notorious Drouet "farm"; after that she had been apprenticed to artificial flower-making but had run away because of ill treatment. After about a year at the school, she was re-established abroad. Another, convicted of thieving under stress of hunger, was successfully married and established. Still another, nineteen years old, who had been locked out by her dressmaker employer, was given hospital treatment in addition to training at the school, and was sent abroad. One girl from a ragged school, sentenced for breaking windows, was so disreputable on entering the school that her matted hair had to be completely shaved off; she broke windows, she said, "having nowheres as you can think of to go to," but insisted that it "be wrote down" that she had never gone wrong otherwise. Another girl aged sixteen who had been "lost" by her father when she was ten, answered some very searching questions without reserve, "and not at all in her own favour"; later she learned diligently all that was required of her. There were, however, failures and heartbreak, as may be gathered from Dickens's letters to Miss Coutts.

Another educational project dear to the heart of Dickens was that of the ragged schools. It is not surprising, therefore, to find him writing an article such as "A Sleep to Startle Us," in which he describes his acquaintance with such a school for slum children located in West Street, Saffron Hill.[25] It had been opened by a few nameless undenominational Christians who had resolved "to set up places of instruction" in the haunts of the poor. When Dickens first visited it, about ten years before he wrote his article, it was "pitifully struggling for life, under every disadvantage." It operated "in a sickening atmosphere, in the midst of taint and dirt and pestilence, with all the deadly sins let loose." Unfortunately, these public-spirited teachers, for all their zeal, had had no training. Dickens thus soberly recorded: "The pupils with an evil sharpness [had] found them out, got the better of them. . . . The place was stormed and carried, over and over again; the lights were blown out, the books strewn in the gutter, and the female scholars carried off triumphantly to their old wickedness."[26] But the teachers "stood it out," with the result that when Dickens visited the school the second time, about two years before he wrote his article, he could describe it as "quiet, orderly, full, lighted with gas, well white-washed, numerously attended, and thoroughly established." The founders of the ragged school had also started a dormitory when they became aware that many destitute scholars had no place to go after school hours. It was set up in "a wretched house," and Dickens was doubtful whether the pupils were better off there than in the streets, except that it gave them a shelter from the weather. By the time of his third visit, however, the dormitory had developed into an industrial school for men and boys, teaching the three R's, tailoring, and shoe-repairing. The pupils therefore not only learned useful trades, but were able to keep their clothes and shoes in repair. No pupil could receive shelter at night unless he was in regular attendance at the "school."

In a scene undimmed by time, Dickens gives an eye-witness account of a ciphering-lesson at this industrial school. The "teacher" was a moni-

[25]*H. W.*, March 13, 1852 (*Misc. P.*, I, 358–66). See also discussion on ragged schools in the Introduction to this book. For other articles on the subject appearing in *Household Words* by Morley and others, see Collins, *Dickens's Periodicals*, pp. 12–15.

[26]In contrast, there is extant a letter (dated Sept. 16, 1843, quoted in Johnson, ed., *Heart of Charles Dickens*, from the original in the possession of R. W. Barrett, Kenilworth, Illinois, U.S.A.) which describes a ragged school taught by capable men trained in "the Glasgow system." See Manning, "Charles Dickens and the 'Glasgow System,'" pp. 202–6.

tor, a young boy from the streets, and he had to compete with a group on the other side of the screen who were singing the multiplication table. His handwriting was legible, and he had written the problem on a broken slate. Walking to and fro before his "class," soothing his ego or "nerves" by spitting every thirty seconds, he launched into the lesson:

> Now then! Look here, all on you! Seven and five, how many?
> *Sharp Boy* (in no particular clothes). Twelve!
> *Pupil Teacher.* Twelve—and eight?
> *Dull Young Man* (with water on the brain). Forty-five!
> *Sharp Boy.* Twenty!
> *Pupil Teacher.* Twenty. You're right. And nine?
> *Dull Young Man* (after great consideration). Twenty-nine!
> *Pupil Teacher.* Twenty-nine it is. And nine?
> *Reckless Guesser.* Seventy-four!
> *Pupil Teacher* (drawing nine strokes). How can that be? Here's nine on 'em! Look! Twenty-nine, and one's thirty, and one's thirty-one, and one's thirty-two, and one's thirty-three, and one's thirty-four, and one's thirty-five, and one's thirty-six, and one's thirty-seven, and one's what?
> *Reckless Guesser.* Four and two pence farden!
> *Dull Young Man* (who has been absorbed in the demonstration). Thirty-eight!
> *Pupil Teacher* (restraining sharp boy's ardour). Of course it is! Thirty-eight pence. There they are! (writing 38 in slate-corner). Now what do you make of thirty-eight pence? Thirty-eight pence, how much? (Dull young man slowly considers and gives it up . . .). How much you? (to sleepy boy, who stares and says nothing). How much *you*?
> *Sharp Boy.* Three and two pence!
> *Pupil Teacher.* Three and two pence. How do I put down three and two pence?
> *Sharp Boy.* You puts down the two, and you carries the three.
> *Pupil Teacher.* Very good. Where do I carry the three?
> *Reckless Guesser.* T'other side the slate!
> ————and so on.

A description of the dormitory follows,[27] after which Dickens drives his point home to government and church: how the county rates could be diminished, prisons be relieved, loads of shame and guilt cleared out of the streets, and the results of the "devoted" multiplied, if the government would take steps (other than an annual grant of money, he doesn't say what steps) to "unshackle its preposterous Red Tape conditions" and

---

[27]The dormitory, which accommodated 167 boys and men, was clean, well ventilated, and properly supervised. Every pupil was given six ounces of bread to eat, and was allotted one of the shallow, wooden, box-like beds and a coarse blanket. Troughs were provided for bathing and for washing clothes. A hymn was always sung before bedtime, and an officer kept watch throughout the night. In the morning the whole dormitory was sluiced down with water.

look after the neglected children Dickens had seen in the ragged school, and the boys and men ("representatives of many thousands") in the dormitory school. Is it not possible for the religious groups, he asks, to forget their controversies for a short time, and do a little practical Christian charity?[28]

In none of these articles does Dickens press for a carefully planned universal system of state education; he wants the state, however, to assume responsibility for neglected and helpless children. To *The Examiner*, and to *Household Words*, he contributed a number of minor articles relating to education, stressing early training in "Gone to the Dogs," or describing briefly the "Edinburgh Apprentice School Association," or whimsically ridiculing the education of girls in "An Extraordinary Traveller,"[29] but he comes back to the same point again and again—state interference for a special class of children. In "Stores for the First of April" he indulges in a number of extravagant desires on which he expects "to be fooled." He would like a special parliamentary bill: "for taking into custody by the strong arm, of every *neglected or abandoned child* of either sex, found in the streets of any town in this kingdom; for the training and education of that child, in honest knowledge and honest labour; for the heavy punishment of the parents if they can by any means be found; or making it compulsory on them to contribute to the costs . . . ; for their summary and final deprivation of all rights as parents . . . ; and for the transfer of those rights to the State."[30] Obviously, Dickens is not thinking of a state-wide system of education for all children as we understand it today, but of a special class of neglected children that he wishes to become wards of the state.

On January 16, 1869, towards the close of his career, Dickens contributed an article to *All The Year Round* entitled "Mr. Barlow."[31] It

[28]Cf. Johnson, ed., *Heart of Charles Dickens*, pp. 50 ff.

[29]See, respectively, *H. W.*, March 10, 1855 (*Misc. P.*, II, 17–24); *The Examiner*, Dec. 30, 1848 (*Misc. P.*, I, 146–7); and *H. W.*, April 20, 1850 (*Misc. P.*, I, 227).

[30]*H. W.*, March 7, 1857 (*Misc. P.*, II, 139). The italics have been added. Cf. "The compulsory industrial education of neglected children, and the severe punishment of neglectful and unnatural parents, are reforms to which we must come, doubt it who may" (*H. W.*, April 5, 1851, p. 42, under "Chips"); or *ibid.*, Sept. 11, 1852, p. 598.

[31]All the articles were published anonymously, but Kitton examined an "office set" of the journal in the possession of W. H. Howe, in which, against every article, the author's name had been inscribed by a member of the printing staff. All the articles in the discussion that follows have been checked against Kitton's findings.

During 1860, the journal contained a series of articles written by Dickens, entitled "The Uncommercial Traveller." At the end of the year, seventeen of these articles were published as a separate volume under the same title; eleven more sketches were added in the edition of 1866; and eight more added in the edition

was obviously a satire on *Sandford and Merton* (1783–9) by Thomas Day, who was, it will be recalled, an eccentric friend of R. L. Edgeworth. Both men were disciples of Rousseau: Edgeworth reared one of his sons on Rousseau's principles, and Day brought up a pair of orphan girls along the same lines, with the intention of making one of them his wife. In neither case could the education be called successful. Nevertheless, Rousseau's naturalistic methods for the inculcation of truth and virtue were favoured by Thomas Day in his pedagogical novel: incidental instruction was made as pleasurable and as interesting as possible, and was only given when children showed a desire or need for learning; girls (Miss Simmons, for example) received a little geometry, much domestic training, and, for leisure moments, music. It was part of their training, as it was of the boys' also, to be inured to physical hardship.[32]

Dickens says that he read *Sandford and Merton* at such an early age that he felt as though he had been born under the superintendence of "the instructive monomaniac, Mr. Barlow," who, in Day's novel, was tutor to Master Harry Sandford and was given the job of re-educating the pampered lad, Master Tommy Merton. It is obvious from Dickens's article that he despised the whole point of view implicit in the novel. He complained that this tutor of young minds "improved all sorts of occasions, from the consumption of a plate of cherries to the contemplation of a starlight night." Without the influence of Mr. Barlow, it seems, "youth wore buckles and powder, conducted himself with insupportable levity at the theatre, [and] had no idea of facing a mad bull single-handed." Dickens did not think this conduct was so "reprehensible," as it slightly reflected his own character, and indeed he thought it was Mr. Barlow's destiny "to go down to posterity as childhood's experience of a bore."

The charges Dickens levels at the tutor are devastating. He condemns him for his complete insensibility to humour, which casts dark gloom over normally happy childhood. He condemns him for his "adamantine inadaptability" to amusement and imaginative fancy and for his obsession with science. It would be typical of Mr. Barlow to trespass on the fanciful kingdom of the Arabian Nights, and to subject it to scientific scrutiny with the aid of "that hypocritical young prig Harry." Harry, indeed, is so detestable that if he were reported to be "studious in the South," Dickens would flee to the "extremest North" so as to be idle and

---

of 1875. The article "Mr. Barlow," published in *All The Year Round*, Jan. 16, 1869, was one of the articles included in the 1875 collection and in most subsequent editions.

[32]Critical works include: Scott, *The Exemplary Mr. Day*; and the scholarly treatise by Haar, "Education in the Eighteenth Century English Novel."

avoid Harry's presence. Because of Barlow, Dickens affirms in mock confession, "I forbore enlightenment in my youth and became, as they say in melodrama, 'the wreck you now behold.' " For in Barlow's hands, knowledge is not just power—it is power to bore.

Dickens's final condemnation of the "infamous" tutor is that Barlow still walks the world in various disguises, trying to make backward pupils of us all, even in our maturity. Illustrated lectures (what Dickens calls "pictorial entertainment on rollers") should be shunned, for Barlow is sure to be there "in the dark with a long wand in his hand"; he is liable to be the speaker at any public assemblage where a bottle of water and a notebook are in evidence; he injects moral homilies into light entertainment for the edification of juveniles; and may even be disguised as a pretty lady in a burlesque show, who ruins the fun of the evening by trilling exhortations to virtue. The worst of it is that the Barlows, who "get up abstruse subjects with infinite pains," discharge them as if they had always been authorities on the subjects in question, having imbibed them with their mother's milk. Dickens's "closing article of impeachment" is that Mr. Barlow is everywhere, and that he *will* preach. There is no getting rid of him.

If Dickens disapproved of the incidental and naturalistic pedagogical methods of Rousseau as delineated by Mr. Day in the character Barlow, he felt quite differently about a practice which was once quite common in England, that of attending school half time. This system was still in operation at the pauper schools of the Stepney Union at Limehouse when Dickens wrote his article "The Short-Timers."[33] Dickens praised their activities, which he witnessed: physical exercises and drill, the playing of musical instruments, and the rigging of sails on a "decked mimic ship" with a "mainmast seventy feet high." He considered the system a very good one. His own conviction was that the attention of children begins to wander after a certain period of continuous study, and his conviction was strengthened by the experience of the Stepney schools, where it was claimed that eighteen hours of book-learning had proved more profitable than thirty-six. Moreover, the cost was less—only fourpence halfpenny a week per child—and that was an important consideration for poor parents. The children, both boys and girls, showed that they could cook, mend, write from copy and dictation, cipher, and also play musical instruments. In a writing competition with the full-time pupils of a first-

[33]June 20, 1863, in *The Uncommercial Traveller*. The number of pupils attending school half time slowly diminished. Curtis, *History of Education in Great Britain*, p. 247, gives a typical set of figures for the city of Leeds: in 1860 there were 1,264; thirty years later, 846; forty years later, only 61; in 1902, 44; and by 1915, a mere 5. The half-time system was finally abolished in July, 1922.

class national school, the pupils of the Stepney Union were superior. The boys were in great demand by captains of merchant shipping, and were esteemed in the navy. During a period of three years, ninety-eight of them had entered regimental bands. The girls made excellent domestic servants. The physical health of the students was remarkable because, Dickens says, sanitation was just as carefully regulated as everything else. The moral health of the students, who were never subjected to corporal punishment, was exemplified in their high standard of truthfulness. The students seemed to appreciate the benefits of their training, for they used to return for visits after they had made their way in the world. It is significant that Dickens opened and closed his article with the appeal that pauper children be taken off the streets and similarly trained, either by other unions or by the state. In his opinion, the Stepney board of guardians, aided by "a most admirable master," had set a worthy example.

A paper presented by Edwin Chadwick to the British Association at its Oxford meeting in 1860 gave some support to the view that the limits of attention did not extend beyond one-half the usual time which children of the common day-schools spent in the classroom.[34] Dickens was warm in his acknowledgment of this paper. But he was on slippery ground; by his own admission the Stepney Union had "a most admirable master," and that fact may well have accounted for a great deal of the pupils' excellence. Of course Dickens did not attribute the excellence of the schools entirely to the half-time system. He recognized that there were other factors. He said that the Stepney schools always had been excellent, and cited good sanitation, the lack of corporal punishment, and "the good influences of music on the whole body of children." But the title and opening paragraph of the article implied that the "half-time" practice was the school's salient feature, whereas Kay-Shuttleworth, who was in a position to know, insisted that the half-timers in the popular schools held the full-time pupils back, created difficulties in teaching and organization, and, in any group of six to ten schools, where the half-timers amounted to not less than one-third and to not more than one-half the total number of scholars, tended to gravitate towards the lower part of the school.[35] *The Minutes of the Committee of Council on Education,* 1844, reported that the half-time girls under thirteen were listless and heavy-eyed; stained with the blue dye from their half day in the textile

---

[34]Chadwick's paper was entitled "On the Physiological as well as the Psychological Limits to Mental Labour." Another paper, given two years later by G. R. Fisher, demonstrated that boys of average weights had highest intelligence!
[35]Kay-Shuttleworth, *Memorandum on Popular Education,* p. 57.

mills, they seemed to have "no business there," and "not to belong."[36] On the other hand, a factory inspector testifying before the Commission to Inquire into the Present State of Popular Education in England in 1861, reported that "the half-time system, so far from having proved a failure, has been eminently successful"; he added the qualification, however, that the half-timers had to be in receipt of good wages and attending a "good and efficient school."[37]

In addition to the two papers, "Mr. Barlow" and "The Short-Timers," the one on the theory and the other on the practice of education, the many other articles in *The Uncommercial Traveller* contributed much to adult education and the forming of public opinion. Like Horace in the ancient world, and Addison and Steele in the reign of Queen Anne, Dickens has given us a unique picture of the life of his time. Just as Addison and Steele described human foibles and frailties in *The Spectator* of their day, so Dickens, in *The Uncommercial Traveller*, through ridicule and laughter, sentiment and satire, sought to mould public opinion for the eradication of the social abuses of his time. Here, he describes life in a workhouse,[38] or religious endeavour on Sunday evenings in the theatres;[39] there, as he sardonically exposes the traps set by underworld parasites for unwary sailors on shore leave, he pleads for marine regulations and sailors' rest-homes.[40] The scalding of his throat with "thickened" brown water, the sight of "brown pimples and pickled cucumber," and the chilling of his face and feet in draughty eating-houses provoke him to urge an improvement in English restaurants.[41] He scourges the army for compelling soldiers to "live in worse than swinish foulness" and for the unnecessary suffering endured by troops on a voyage back from India.[42] Now, recalling his own boyhood experiences, he ridicules the Sunday "purification" and "scrubbing" of children in general which sentenced them to be "steamed like a potato" and to snuff the odours of the dead in the church vaults for two hours weekly, or to be poked in the ribs by adults with umbrellas for daring to have visions of marbles or other playthings.[43] Then he acquaints the public with the order and comfort on Mormon emigration ships,[44] or spreads a delicate charm as he depicts an old couple gathering hay in a cemetery and a charity

---

[36]*Minutes of the Committee of Council on Education*, 1844, II, 280, as quoted in Gardiner, *English Girlhood at School*, p. 478.

[37]Education Commission, 1861, Report, *Parliamentary Papers*, XXI, 1861, I, pp. 201 f.

[38]"Wapping Workhouse."   [39]"Two Views of a Cheap Theatre."

[40]"Poor Mercantile Jack."   [41]"Refreshments for Travellers."

[42]"The Great Tasmania's Cargo."   [43]"City of London Churches."

[44]"Bound for the Great Salt Lake."

couple courting in a church,[45] or invokes the sleepy atmosphere of a stage-coaching town stranded in the age of railways.[46] Next, with a more practical bent, he draws attention to an admirable new eating-house for labouring people where wholesome food is provided at reasonable prices;[47] but almost immediately he whisks the public off to France,[48] or to life among primitive peoples (which he considers to be no more ludicrous than the Commons, or Chancery),[49] or back again to view life in the English alms-houses or to investigate the state of Mechanics' Institutes.[50] But he inevitably returns to strike sledge-hammer blows on behalf of inarticulate workers and neglected children. He exposes the dire straits to which labouring people in east London are reduced by unemployment, and cites the children's hospital as the only help for the children of the district.[51]

In his pamphlet, "Sunday under Three Heads,"[52] he speaks again for the inarticulate poor, lashing out at the puritanical Victorian Sunday which was a genteel and comfortable day for the rich, but an ugly and unbearable interlude for the poor:

Long rows of charity children cleanly dressed, preceded by a portly beadle, and a withered schoolmaster, are returning to their welcome dinner. . . . The powdered footmen glide along the aisle, place the richly-bound prayer-books on the pew desks . . . and hurry away, leaving the fashionable members of the congregation to inspect each other through their glasses, and to dazzle and glitter in the eyes of the few shabby people in the free seats. . . . The clergyman enters the reading desk—a young man of noble family and elegant bearing, notorious at Cambridge for his knowledge of horse-flesh and dancers, and celebrated at Eton for his hopeless stupidity. The service commences. Mark the soft voice in which he reads. . . .

At St. Giles's, in vulgar contrast: "Women with scarcely the articles of apparel which common decency requires, with forms bloated by disease, and faces rendered hideous by habitual drunkenness—men reeling and staggering along—children in rags and filth—whole streets of squalid and miserable appearance, whose inhabitants are lounging in the public road, fighting, screaming, and swearing—these are common objects. . . ." Why were the Victorians shocked? Because the poor spent money on liquor instead of on necessaries? Or was it because the poor and the

---

[45]"The City of the Absent."   [46]"An Old Stage-Coaching House."
[47]"The Boiled Beef of New England."   [48]"In the French-Flemish Country."
[49]"Medicine Men of Civilisation."
[50]"Titbull's Alms-Houses," and "Dullborough Town."
[51]"A Small Star in the East."
[52]First published June, 1836, by Chapman and Hall under the pseudonym Timothy Sparks. In *Reprinted Pieces*, pp. 328–48. (In the Nonesuch edition it is included in *Sketches by Boz*, pp. 493–525.)

places they lived in were so dirty? Dickens implied that whether the poor did or did not take action on these matters, they would still be proverty-stricken, and nothing could make their wretched hovels really satisfactory. It never seemed to have occurred to the legislators or pious churchmen who opposed a freer Sabbath that it might have been better to open the gates of the green parks and gardens on Sundays and to close the doors of the gin-shops; or to have occurred to the chapel officials who had won such splendid victories at the Cornwall pit-heads that ritual, stained glass, organ music, and ceremonial pomp might well bring some sense of beauty and culture into drab lives engrossed in the harsh and bitter struggle for daily sustenance. As a respectability, like autumnal shadows, settled down over what was formerly a disturbing noncon-formity, special seats and pew rents emerged again; industry and frugal-ity produced solid comforts; and the fruits of wealth brought the happy thought that poverty resulted exclusively from idleness and wickedness.

In another article, Dickens illustrated once again the neglected "slice" of childhood for whose education he wanted the state to accept respon-sibility. Quickening his pace as he turned down a street or court near Temple Bar which the police reported "no man dared turn down," he

overturned a wretched little creature, who, clutching at the rags of a pair of trousers with one of its claws, and at its ragged hair with the other, pattered with bare feet over the muddy stones. I stopped to raise and succour this poor weeping wretch, and fifty like it, but of both sexes, were about me in a moment, begging, tumbling, fighting, clamouring, yelling, shivering in their nakedness and hunger. The piece of money I had put into the claw of the child I had overturned was clawed out of it, and was again clawed out of that wolfish gripe, and again out of that, and soon I had no notion in what part of the obscene scuffle in the mud, of rags legs and arms and dirt, the money might be.[53]

Dickens is "astounded" that such a great nation as England, which con-siders itself in such an advanced and "polished state" of civilization, and which proudly boasts of its far-flung power, condones such public neglect in the very streets of its capital.

There are passages in his *American Notes* which are pertinent here.[54] Of Boston he writes: "I sincerely believe that the public institutions and charities of this capital of Massachusetts are as nearly perfect as the most considerate wisdom, benevolence, and humanity can make them." He is pleased that no uniform is worn, and notes that these charitable institutions are either supported or assisted by the state. He quotes at

[53]"On An Amateur Beat" in *The Uncommercial Traveller*.
[54]*American Notes*, chap. III, pp. 31, 34, 37–40; and chap. xv, pp. 239 ff.

great length Doctor Howe's report on blind Laura Bridgman, and describes his visit to the House of Industry, the home for the aged, and the Boylston schools for boys (one for neglected, another for delinquent boys). Similarly, at Hartford, he visits homes for the deaf and the insane. On his visit to the province of Canada he refers to the College of Upper Canada, where "a sound education in every department of polite learning can be had at a very moderate expense," speaks of the laying of a corner-stone for a new college at Toronto, and notes an admirable jail in Kingston where the inmates were taught various trades; for example, the girls were taught sewing. All these observations show the great interest which Dickens took in educational institutions whether at home or across the Atlantic; his belief in broader opportunities for education; his recognition that in North America much progress had been achieved by state action in the training of neglected and handicapped children and in the reclaiming of delinquents.

In this discussion of Dickens's articles on education I have limited my presentation to those articles which as far as I have been able to ascertain were exclusively the products of Dickens's own pen.[55] And in order to keep to Dickens's views as closely as possible I have also omitted a number of articles on education on which Dickens is known to have collaborated with Wills, Morley, or others. Dickens's views were well known to his staff, and he was a very careful editor; from this it could be inferred that he gave at least nominal approval to whatever articles were published in the journals which he "conducted"; but there is always the possibility that certain articles, for one reason or another, escaped his careful scrutiny, or that the full import of certain passages written by another hand was not fully realized in the rush to meet deadlines for copy.

It is clear from this examination that the views on education expressed by Dickens in his articles were in accordance with the principles he had proclaimed, and were consistent with the views expressed in his novels. He was intent on the conquest of ignorance, for he saw it as the formidable ally of poverty, unrest, crime, and disease, as the destroyer of children, and as the main source of dangerous elements in society. Education was not to be a mechanical, sanctimonious grind. It should help children and young people to cope with the realities of life. It should stimulate the imagination and widen the sympathies.

The efforts Dickens made to investigate conditions at first hand are very impressive, and his strengthening of the forces for enlightenment appears beyond calculation.

[55]See pp. 172–3 n. 31, and App. C, pp. 220–1.

CHAPTER VIII

Dickens's Private Views on Education
as Evidenced in His Letters

There is always the possibility that the views expressed in a writer's fiction may not be those that the writer himself holds. Evidence presented in the two preceding chapters, however, clearly demonstrated a harmony of general aim in Dickens's fiction, public speeches, and published articles. Similar problems were discussed, and in educational matters, similar points of view were maintained. Sceptics could well argue, however, that a dissembler, concealing his real thoughts and feelings under a disguise of prepared public addresses and published materials, might hold private views which differed profoundly from those which he chose to express publicly; and, further, that his private views would only be revealed during disarming and unpremeditated private correspondence with personal friends. It is imperative, therefore, to present evidence concerning Dickens's personal views on education as revealed in his letters.[1]

Dickens's general philosophy and purposes, as expressed in private correspondence, do not reveal any inconsistency with those expressed in his speeches and articles. For example, we read: "While you teach in your walk of life . . . trust me that in mine, I will pursue cruelty and oppression . . . so long as I have the energy of thought and the power of giving it utterance."[2] This letter, written April 8, 1841, to Rev. Thomas Robinson,[3] reveals that Dickens's championship of the needy, neglected, unfortunate, helpless, and oppressed was more than a matter of duty; it was a matter of conviction. The refusal to accept wealth or social status as a criterion of worth that is so often expressed in his speeches and

---

[1]Many of Dickens's letters to various persons have been published privately in several small and scattered collections. One of the earliest and largest collections was that published by his sister-in-law and eldest daughter. The most recent and most complete collection, edited by Walter Dexter *et al.*, is unfortunately very rare. A new and fuller set is now being compiled and edited under the auspices of the Pilgrim Trust. The tentative date for the publication of the first volume is 1960.

[2]Hogarth and Dickens, eds., *Letters*, p. 43.

[3]Dexter, ed., *Letters*, I, 314.

articles is reiterated in a letter to John Scott, editor of the *Morning Advertiser*, March 22, 1841: "There is no character I detest and abhor so much as a man who presumes on his prosperity. I feel its baseness so strongly that if I supposed that my children could at any future time believe me to have been a creature of that kind I should be wretched."[4] His public expressions of his political creed find their counterpart a few months before his death in a letter to John Henry Chamberlain: "My faith in the people governing is, on the whole, infinitesimal; my faith in The People governed is, on the whole, illimitable."[5] Dickens's letter to T. Ross and John Kenny in regard to the silencing of Sunday bands,[6] enclosing a donation of ten pounds, is evidence enough that he was not writing with tongue in cheek, or merely for entertainment, when he lashed out against the puritanical Victorian Sunday, in his pamphlet entitled "Sunday under Three Heads." Exposure of conditions in workhouses and appeals on behalf of the sick recur constantly in his private papers, as in his publications and public utterances. "My knowledge of the general condition of the sick poor," he wrote to Ernest Hart in February, 1866, "is not of yesterday. . . . Few anomalies in England are so horrible to me as the unchecked existence of so many shameful sick wards for paupers, side by side with the . . . conventional wonder that the poor should creep into corners and die."[7]

Dickens's letters reveal not only his championship of the poor but also the necessity of educating them. Even a casual perusal of the volumes containing his letters would show that he was well aware of the fact that indifference and apathy would have to be overcome before the liberal education of the people could begin. Writing to Sir Austen Layard, M.P.,[8] who earlier in the year had spoken on administrative reform at Drury Lane Theatre, Dickens observed on April 10, 1855: "Until the people can be got up from the lethargy, which is an awful symptom of the advanced state of their disease, I know of nothing that can be done—beyond keeping their wrongs continually before them."[9]

[4]*Ibid.*, I, 308.

[5]Dated Nov. 17, 1869, in *ibid.*, III, 751. Since the Reform Bill of 1832 increased the vote by less than one-half, and even after 1867 only about one in ten of the population had a vote, and since the Lords still dominated the cabinet, Dickens had no faith in what still appeared to be an aristocratic government. The gap between the government and the people seemed all the wider because there was no secret ballot, and until the 1870's, the aristocracy still retained substantial privileges in the civil service, the army, and the judiciary.

[6]May 19, 1856, Dexter, ed., *Letters*, II, 774. See also chap. VII above.

[7]Dexter, ed., *Letters*, III, 462 f.

[8]Ley, *The Dickens Circle*, pp. 170, 262.

[9]Hogarth and Dickens, eds., *Letters*, p. 367; Dexter, ed., *Letters*, II, 651 f.

In a letter to W. C. Macready, October 4, 1855, he acknowledged his realization that the ballot would not fulfil its intended purpose unless the people who used it were well informed: "We appear to me to have proved the failure of representative institutions without an educated and an advanced people to support them. What with teaching people to 'keep their stations', . . . to be a good child, or to go to the beer shop, to go a-poaching and go to the devil; what with having no such thing as a middle class . . . ; what with flunkyism, toadyism . . . , I do reluctantly believe that the English people are habitually consenting parties to the miserable imbecility into which we have fallen, *and never will help themselves out of it*."[10] A similar indictment of apathy was made against the administrators of workhouses in regard to the "schooling" they provided the inmates. "Do they teach trades in workhouses," Dickens exclaimed in a letter to W. H. Wills, "and try to fit *their* people for society? Come with me to Tothill Fields Bridewell, and I will show you what a workhouse girl is. Or look to my 'Walk in a Workhouse'[11] and to the glance at the youths I saw in one place positively kept like wolves."[12] The importance which Dickens attached to education is expressed further in a letter to Charles Knight, who had launched a successful scheme of Book Clubs for all Readers: "If I can be of the feeblest use in advancing a project so intimately connected with an end on which my heart is set—the liberal education of the people—I shall be sincerely glad."[13]

His disapproval of the practice of cramming children with church catechism, his belief in non-denominational teaching in day-schools, and his insistence that missionary work abroad should not be carried on at the expense of the exploited, neglected, and unfortunate at home, are no less fervently stated in Dickens's personal letters than in his public utterances. He believed that in dealing with the petty offences peculiar to children, offences so common that they are almost a part of the stage of life known as childhood, it is wrong to make so much mention of the "Almighty," to impress children "with fear of death," or to threaten them with the dire prophecy that three-quarters of us are going to perdition.[14] In his treatment of Jo, the crossing-sweeper, and of Mrs.

[10]Hogarth and Dickens, eds., *Letters*, p. 379; Dexter, ed., *Letters*, II, 695.

[11]*Household Words*, May 25, 1850.

[12]March 10, 1853, Hogarth and Dickens, eds., *Letters*, p. 286; Dexter, ed., *Letters*, II, 453; Lehmann, *Charles Dickens as an Editor*, p. 100.

[13]June 4, 1844, Hogarth and Dickens, eds., *Letters*, p. 112; Dexter, ed., *Letters*, I, 606.

[14]To Mrs. Godfrey, July 25, 1839, Dexter, ed., *Letters*, I, 221.

Jellyby, he was charged with being unjust to foreign missions. There are several letters in reply to this charge in which Dickens affirms that the balance should be in favour of home missions, "as being the stronger and more pressing of the two."[15] As always, Dickens linked religion with instruction of the poor, and linked the lack of it with ignorance and crime. He became exasperated with those persons who indulged in doctrinal squabbles at the expense of charitable practice. A letter dated September 16, 1843, to Macvey Napier, editor of the *Edinburgh Review*, admirably sums up Dickens's stand:

> Would it meet the purposes of the *Review* to come out strongly against any system of education based exclusively on the principles of the Established Church? If it would, I should like to show why such a thing as the Church Catechism is wholly inapplicable to the state of ignorance which now prevails; and why no system but one, so general in great religious principles as to include all creeds, can meet the wants and understandings of the dangerous classes of society. This is the only broad ground I could hold consistently with what I feel and think on the subject. But I could give, in taking it, a description of certain voluntary places of instruction, called "the Ragged Schools," now existing in London, and of the schools in jails, and of the ignorance presented in such places, which would make a very striking paper, especially if they were put in strong comparison with the effort . . . to maintain exclusive Church instruction. I could show these people in a state so miserable and so neglected, that their very nature rebels against the simplest religion, and that to convey to them the faintest outline of any system of distinction between right and wrong is in itself a giant's task before which mysteries and squabbles for forms *must* give way. Would this be too much for the *Review*?[16]

There was further discussion about the date of submission, but since no such article, to my knowledge, has ever come to light, the inference is that it *was* too much for the *Review*.

In reply to an anonymous correspondent who also had found some comments in *Household Words* along these lines too much for him, Dickens reiterated that benevolent societies had been spending large sums abroad for many years "when there was no such thing as a ragged school in England." He insisted that England could undertake no better task than "the bestowal of its wealth and energy on the making of good Christians at home, and on the utter removal of neglected and untaught childhood from its streets, before it wanders elsewhere." By this means Dickens hoped that all English travellers abroad would prove to be

---

[15]Hogarth and Dickens, eds., *Letters*, pp. 264, 269 f.; Dexter, ed., *Letters*, II, 401 (and cf. I, 541 f.).

[16]Hogarth and Dickens, eds., *Letters*, pp. 98 f.; Dexter, ed., *Letters*, I, 540.

"exemplary, practical missionaries, instead of undoers of what the best professed missionaries can do."[17]

The issues discussed in the novels spill over into the letters. Dickens's scorn of the Benthamite calculus and the tendency to regard human beings as so many statistical units is not by any means confined to his portrayal of Mr. Gradgrind and his school in *Hard Times*, where utility and education joined forces to stifle emotion and imagination. Writing to Charles Knight on January 30, 1855, Dickens inveighs against the objectivity that would clothe a soldier in the Crimea on the basis of the average temperature and leave him to freeze to death in the bitter Crimean night; or that would quote four miles as the average distance between urban sites in England to the labourer who is forced to travel twelve miles to and from work each day.[18] References concerning his visit to the Yorkshire schools and to the progress of the novel *Nicholas Nickleby* recur in Dickens's letters (and the fragments of a diary) from 1838 to 1839.[19] His letters to Forster often discuss and explain the future course of a plot, as witness the misfortunes he planned for Paul Dombey at Doctor Blimber's Academy: "As the boy begins to grow up, I shall show him [Mr. Dombey] quite impatient for his getting on, and urging his masters to set him great tasks. . . . The death of the boy is a death blow, of course, to all the father's schemes. . . . The rejected daughter . . . will come out better than any son at last." Or he makes a memorandum to instruct Hablôt K. Browne to "make the next youngest boy three or four years older than he [Paul]." Or he confesses to Mrs. Howitt: "I was a great writer at eight years old or so . . . and worked many childish experiences and many young struggles into *Copperfield*."[20] The connection of the visits to Yorkshire with the exposure of the Yorkshire schools in *Nickleby*, and the confirmation that David Copperfield's experiences at school had some autobiographical foundation are perhaps obvious; the reference to *Dombey and Son* is intended to make the point that the death of little Paul turns on the necessities of the plot rather than on any designated pedagogical principle.

Throughout his letters, Dickens gives occasional glimpses of the educational theory and practice of which he approved or disapproved. Writing from Baltimore, he observes that the United States had reached

[17]July 9, 1852, Hogarth and Dickens, eds., *Letters*, pp. 269 f. (possibly to Rev. H. Christopherson).

[18]Hogarth and Dickens, eds., *Letters*, p. 329; Dexter, ed., *Letters*, II, 619 (date corrected to 1855).

[19]Dexter, ed., *Letters*, I, 147, 154, 157, 193.

[20]July 25, 1846, *ibid.*, I, 770 f.; Dec., 1846, *ibid.*, I, 824 f.; Sept. 7, 1859, *ibid.*, III, 122.

his expectations only in its concern and provision for the education and care of poor children.[21] We learn from a letter to Dr. Samuel Gridley Howe of Boston that Dickens is sending seventeen hundred pounds to provide 250 copies of *The Old Curiosity Shop* in Braille for the benefit of blind people.[22] There are a few isolated remarks about public schools: that they are showing greater liberality in their policies of admission (two actors' sons had been admitted—Kean's to Eton and Macready's to Rugby); that certain foundation scholars should win their way into the public schools rather than be maintained indiscriminately by the Artists' Benevolent Society; and, finally, that he would like Wills to "hit the Charterhouse again hard" because of "Thackeray's distorted praise of it."[23] Some of these glimpses express his support of adult education through the Mechanics' Institutes and similar organizations. Writing to Macready, after having given a public reading from his novels at Manchester, he praises the provision made at the London Exhibition of Art for the comfort of "the common people." In a letter to Mr. Arthur Ryland of the Midland Mechanics' Institute, Birmingham, he urges a concerted attempt to secure representatives of all classes of society in the institutes, remarking: "I have never yet seen with these eyes of mine a mechanic in any recognised position on the platform of a Mechanics' Institution." In another letter, about a request for him to speak at Birmingham on the advantages of education, Dickens reveals that it is the practical usefulness of these institutions, and the perseverance and determination of their members to study, in which he is interested.[24]

Not only did Dickens speak well of institutions for adult education in his letters, but also of two elementary institutions for boys. One of these was the school at Boulogne, France, to which he sent four of his sons. In 1855, while the eldest son Charley was getting business experience at Birmingham and in the City, and the second son, Walter Landor, was being coached at Wimbledon for the India examination, the next three boys, in order of birth, were all attending this school at the same time. It had been recommended to Dickens by John Delane, editor of *The Times*.[25] To Dickens, the school was apparently satisfactory in all respects. This is evident not only from the fact that he continued to send

[21]Hogarth and Dickens, eds., *Letters*, p. 60; Dexter, ed., *Letters*, I, 413.

[22]Dexter, ed., *Letters*, III, 648, 655.

[23]Hogarth and Dickens, eds., *Letters*, p. 461, and Dexter, ed., *Letters*, III, 50 f.; Hogarth and Dickens, eds., *Letters*, p. 625; and Dexter, ed., *Letters*, III, 525; Dexter, ed., *Letters*, II, 693, and Lehmann, *Charles Dickens as an Editor*, p. 177.

[24]Hogarth and Dickens, eds., *Letters*, pp. 433, 328, and Dexter, ed., *Letters*, II, 867, 536; Hogarth and Dickens, eds., *Letters*, p. 726, and cf. Dexter, ed., *Letters*, III, 743.

[25]Hogarth and Dickens, eds., *Letters*, p. 284; Dexter, ed., *Letters*, II, 486.

one son after another there but also from a letter to Mrs. Watson, five years later, in which he explained that all the boys in attendance were English, and that the teaching (by Rev. M. Gibson, an old Eton master, and Rev. J. Bewsher, a Protestant clergyman of the town) was "unusually sound and good." The Eton master was awarded high praise for maintaining an absence of pedantry on his part and an absence of servility on the part of his charges. "The boys," Dickens noted, "combined an ease and frankness with a modesty and sense of responsibility that was really above all praise."[26] (When another boy, Alfred, was transferred to Wimbledon, and another was placed under the tutorship of Mr. Barrow at Southsea, both new masters wrote Dickens commending the results of the Boulogne training.) Dickens also commended the school in a letter to E. F. Piggott, describing the happiness of three of his sons then in attendance, telling about the period of vacations (two months in the summer), the entrance fee of three guineas, and the annual charge of forty pounds per annum for each boy; he made quite a point of the honourable tactics of the proprietors in regard to "extras."[27]

The other school Dickens praised was located at Bruce Castle; in a letter to Macready he described it as a school that recognized education to be "a broad system of moral and intellectual philosophy." The school offered the usual course, including study of the great books in Greek and Latin, and owned a library of five or six thousand volumes managed by the boys themselves. In addition to these facilities for sound study, and this inducement to self-reliance and self-exertion, there were, according to the prospectus, ample means for recreation.[28]

It is apparent from Dickens's letters that even as he was working hard at the writing of *The Old Curiosity Shop*, *Barnaby Rudge*, and *Martin Chuzzlewit*, he gave unstintingly of his time and support to the provision of free instruction and clean living quarters for a number of the poor, homeless, and neglected children from the slums of London. His letters to the Baroness Burdett-Coutts tell of these activities as he spent evening after evening visiting the ragged schools, offering advice, questioning the waifs in attendance, investigating possibilities of securing better and larger premises, reporting progress to Miss Coutts, and obtaining the details she needed in order to render her financial support where it was likely to prove most effective. It was in some of these schools that Dickens made the acquaintance of the devoted but incompetent people,

[26]Sept. 14, 1860, Hogarth and Dickens, eds., *Letters*, pp. 501 f.
[27]Dexter, ed., *Letters*, II, 730 f.
[28]Hogarth and Dickens, eds., *Letters*, pp. 142 f.; Dexter, ed., *Letters*, I, 694 f.; and Morgan MSS, Aug. 17, 1845.

those "teachers of good intentions" whom he deplored in his novels. He mentions, for example, a Miss Payne, who made the whole project "such a scramble," and who, though deadly in earnest, was "bitterly in want of sound teaching" herself. Not all the teachers in the ragged schools were incompetent, however, for in a letter to Miss Coutts in 1843 Dickens gives high praise to the teachers of a school in Field Lane which he visited with Stanfield, a noted artist; he attributes their competence to the training they received in the "Glasgow system" of instruction.[29] Dickens's account of the procedure—its simple and practical moral instruction, its avoidance of creeds and catechisms, the simultaneous responses (in answer to questions) by all the children at once, the moral courage of the teachers, the singing of hymns, and so on—points to the training school for teachers founded by David Stow in Glasgow, Scotland.[30] Obviously, Dickens preferred teachers who had received this type of training to those who had been trained in England along the lines advocated by Kay-Shuttleworth—such as Bradley Headstone, and the stilted training he was said to have received in *Our Mutual Friend*.

It may well be that another project to which Dickens devoted many years of his life—the establishment and supervision of a rehabilitation centre for homeless women, Urania Cottage, Shepherd's Bush—grew out of his interest in, and work among the ragged schools of London. As his numerous letters to Miss Coutts reveal, a number of girls from the ragged schools were chosen as potential cases for admission to this institution.[31] In October, November, and December of 1847 Dickens outlined in his letters his general ideas as to how these women were to be rehabilitated: the whole educational scheme was to be based on kindness, cheerfulness, and trustfulness; strict order, punctuality, and neatness were to be rigorously demanded; each case was to be treated individually according to the background and disposition of the girl; good habits were to be established by means of a daily routine; as much variety as proved feasible was to be introduced; no sanctimonious person was to be engaged to frighten or berate the girls but rather they were to be "tempted" to virtuous living.[32] Dickens thought it better not to allow the girls to wander around London, for fear that their old friends would

[29]Johnson, ed., *Heart of Charles Dickens*, pp. 50, 173, 176. See also Morgan MSS, Oct. 13, 1843; Sept. 4, 1843; Sept. 5, 1843.
[30]See chap. VII above. Cf. "A Sleep to Startle Us," discussed in chap. VIII above.
[31]Johnson, ed., *Heart of Charles Dickens*, pp. 100, 171–4, 187, 191; see also Morgan MSS for Sept. 4, 1843, where Dickens remarks that girls from the ragged schools were quite numerous.
[32]Johnson, ed., *Heart of Charles Dickens*, pp. 95–110; Dexter, ed., *Letters*, II, 56–9; Osborne, ed., *Letters*, pp. 92–8.

entice them back to their old way of life. He engaged John P. Hullah, a competent musician who had been a pupil at the Royal Academy of Music at the same time as Dickens's sister Fanny, to teach singing at the "home." The girls were encouraged to look forward to possible marriage and emigration abroad.[33] Approximately five hundred letters from Dickens to Miss Coutts, now in the Pierpont Morgan Library, New York, testify to Dickens's continued connection with the affairs of the "home," to his painstaking care in its operation, to his investigation of individual cases of misconduct, and to his firmness in dealing with several inmates who proved incorrigible. He visited the home at regular intervals and kept a strict check on its expenses; he reported regularly to Miss Coutts who generously underwrote all its finances; he designed forms for keeping records of each case and devised a system of rewards for good conduct based on Captain Macconnochie's system of marking.[34] While pursuing a strenuous literary career, he did all this extra work out of sheer interest in, and concern for, the education and rehabilitation of the destitute and unfortunate.[35]

Although Dickens was critical of incompetent teachers and condemned the mechanical nature of much of the training they received in English training schools, he was, nevertheless, insistent that their labours were most worthy and should receive adequate compensation. One of his letters admirably illustrates his point of view on this question:

It appears to me that the non-payment of the teachers, in the case you so well set forth, is a point of vital weakness in the case. They have as good a right to be paid for their labour as the Working Man has to be paid for his; and they are not, in their degree, really better paid than he is. I must say that if technical education be of such importance to these recipients as they feel it to be, they are not truly independent (to my thinking) when they take it for nothing from men who can very indifferently afford to give it. And even if they were all men of fortune who could well afford it, the principle would be no less objectionable.[36]

Plowman explains that at that time no government grants were made for the promotion of technical education, "and in order to provide it on the cheap, teachers and others were asked to give gratuitous instruction in

---

[33]Johnson, ed., *Heart of Charles Dickens*, p. 95.

[34]Johnson, ed., *Heart of Charles Dickens*, pp. 78, 102 f., 122 f.; Dexter, ed., *Letters*, I, 749–54.

[35]Cf. discussion of "A Home for Homeless Women," chap. VIII above; see also chap. VII above.

[36]Nov. 25, 1869, to J. A. Langford, Birmingham antiquary and journalist, quoted in Plowman, *In the Days of Victoria*, p. 315. There is a short excerpt from this letter in Dexter, ed., *Letters*, III, 753. I am indebted to W. J. Carlton for this reference. (Original since traced to Rare Book Dept., Philadelphia Free Library.)

their leisure time for the benefit of the other working-classes. This was abhorrent to Dickens, who always laid it down that the labourer was worthy of his hire, and he was the last man to be a party to robbing Peter to pay Paul."

A communication to Edmund Yates, April 28, 1858, testifies to the sense of humour that Dickens showed even over serious matters, such as appeals for charity: "Benevolent men get behind the piers of the gates, lying in wait for my going out; . . . I see their pot-bellied shadows projected on the gravel. Benevolent bullies drive up in hansom cabs. . . . Benevolent area-sneaks get lost in the kitchens, and are found to impede the circulation of the knife-cleaning machine."[37] Dickens's sense of humour, and the exaggeration and caricature which emanated from it, must be taken carefully into account in any appraisal or interpretation of his work. A few examples chosen from his personal correspondence will make this clear. In the old stage-coaching days, he expects "to be spilt before . . . [he can] pay a turnpike"; he is so ill that he has been forced to abstain from porter for "four and twenty mortal hours";[38] on sailing for America, his cabin is so small that "neither of the portmanteaus would go into it. There!";[39] his bed is a "muffin beaten flat" (p. 55); Stanfield so entangles himself in laughing that he has to be pounded on the back with the baggage to bring him round (p. 80); Collins's long, straggly whiskers jut out "like a partially unravelled bird's nest" (p. 88). When Dickens is busy, he curses the postman's knock from the bottom of his heart for disturbing him, but when he sees the handwriting of a friend on the letter, he silently blesses the postman, asks him in, treats him to a glass of whiskey, inquires about his family's health, and opens the letter "with a moist and oystery twinkle" in his eye (p. 101). When Dickens is on a reading tour in the United Kingdom, he writes from Liverpool of rolling around "knee-deep in cheques" (p. 454); in Leeds, his man is so crushed in the crowds that he spends some time upside down "with his head amongst the people's boots" (p. 464); and in Dublin, his ailing agent, Smith, who has been seated in slippers and jacket, waiting for his bath, suddenly becomes quite well when he sees the receipts of the tour, and sits down "on the bag of silver" to write a letter (p. 460). Shortly before Dickens goes on a trip to Europe, he receives from the Count D'Orsay the gift of a purse, for whose contents, apparently, the whole of Europe yearns; and he apostrophizes: "You see this notch, boy? Five

[37]Hogarth and Dickens, eds., *Letters*, p. 449.
[38]Dexter, ed., *Letters*, I, 39, 127.
[39]Hogarth and Dickens, eds., *Letters*, p. 54. The rest of the examples in the paragraph are from this edition, and the page references are given in the text.

hundred francs were laid low on that day for post horses. Where this gap is, a waiter charged your father treble the correct amount—and got it. . . . Take it boy. Thy father has nothing else to give" (pp. 128–9). He exaggerates the hardships of a journey on which he was "upside down most of the trip" and was one of a party of "thirteen individuals with one comb and a pocket handkerchief" (p. 346).

The fact that Dickens's humour reaches into all aspects of his work is of course extremely important in the interpretation of his treatment of education. In a letter to Mrs. Watson, for instance, he had a veritable picnic himself in describing the excursion of a hundred school pupils to the Great Exhibition of 1851. The children nonchalantly clung to prancing horses or passed among their legs, calmly wandered in and out the wheels of carriages, drew patterns in spittle on everything in sight, and distended themselves with the inevitable cake and ginger-beer. One of the smaller ones became lost: "He was found by the police at night, going round and round the turnpike, which he still supposed to be part of the Exhibition. . . . When his mother came in the morning, he asked when it would be over? It was a great Exhibition, he said, but he thought it long!"[40] In similar vein, Dickens wrote a letter to Mrs. Cowden Clarke in connection with the very serious problem of nominating boys and girls to charitable foundations. Dickens had used both his own votes and those of the Baroness Burdett-Coutts for deserving youngsters on numerous other occasions,[41] but in writing to Mrs. Cowden Clarke he indulged in his ludicrous style: "I am very sorry that my Orphan Working School vote is promised on behalf of an unfortunate young orphan, who, after being canvassed for, polled for, written for, quarrelled for, fought for, called for, and done all kinds of things for, by ladies who wouldn't go away and wouldn't be satisfied with anything anybody said or did for them, was floored at the last election, and comes up to the scratch next morning, for the next election, fresher than ever. I devoutly wish that he may get in, and be lost sight of for evermore."[42]

It is precisely at this point (the ludicrous exaggerative style of Dickens) that many critics go astray. It may well be that the unfortunate young orphan was *not* shuttlecocked back and forth to the extent which Dickens implied, yet there is no doubt that Dickens's vote was in fact already pledged. It is unfair, in failing to make allowance for Dickens's humour and exaggeration, to charge him with falsification of facts.

[40]July 11, 1851, Hogarth and Dickens, eds., *Letters*, p. 251.
[41]Cf. letter to Wills, Feb. 8, 1853: ". . . Give Mr. Brownlow a call. . . . He was interested in a child's election for the St. Ann's School. I got Miss Coutts' votes— also enclosed." (Lehmann, *Charles Dickens as an Editor*, p. 98)
[42]May 5, 1849, Dexter, ed., *Letters*, II, 151.

There is, moreover—and this point applies especially to literature—truth of *impression* as well as truth of *fact* to be considered. On the one hand, a presentation of facts may not succeed in conveying the truth, because facts are often cold and unmoving; on the other hand, attempts to make facts impressive may result in distortion. But Dickens's letters show that he was well aware of this danger: "I have no sympathy with any misstatement of fact, or hesitation in withdrawing it." And he comments further: "I wouldn't be unfair, if I knew it, to any human being. I should hate myself if I were."[43] He continually admonishes his associate editor, W. H. Wills, to "brighten" *Household Words*, but he warns him also that the journal must be accurate as well: "I wish to be within the facts." In another letter to Wills he reiterates: "Nothing can be so damaging to *Household Words* as carelessness about facts. It is as hideous as dulness." Similarly, he carefully explains to Wills, on another occasion, that there are two Chancery cases that he does not wish to record, not because there is any doubt that justice has been done, but because it only chanced to be done, and it seems to him "that the real philosophy of the facts is altogether missed in the narrative."[44]

It is obvious that the canvassers for charities did not impede the circulation of the knife-cleaning machine, that the portmanteaus would have gone into the cabin, and that Stanfield would have recovered from his laughing without being pounded on the back with his luggage; *of course* Dickens's man did not have his head, for very long, at least, among people's boots; and *of course* the children at the fair did not really run such mortal risks as Dickens implied. On the other hand, there is little doubt of the truth underlying these statements: Dickens was canvassed relentlessly by agents for numerous charities; the ship's cabin was indeed very small; Stanfield really did double up with laughter; there *was* a great crush to get tickets for the readings; and the hundred youngsters at the Great Exhibition behaved as any group of normal, dirty, indulged, mischievous children on holiday would. Dickens's amusing way of expressing himself, therefore, even when he is in deadly earnest, necessitates that any interpretation of his work for education—or anything else for that matter—make allowance for his rollicking manner of communication.

Ordinarily, one would not expect to find expositions of educational theory and practice in a man's personal correspondence, except, perhaps, in the letters of a professional educationist. Dickens was a novelist

[43]Osborne, ed., *Letters*, pp. 149 f.
[44]Lehmann, *Charles Dickens as an Editor*, pp. 114 f., 102, 220. Cf. Dexter, ed., *Letters*, II, 454 f., 480–2, 660, 794.

and a journalist. Yet, besides the lengthy discussions with Miss Coutts about the ragged schools, the home at Shepherd's Bush, the provision of education or vocational training for individual waifs, and so on, Dickens's letters contain many other references to the education of his own children. The difficulty of tracing the care and thought which Dickens devoted to the education of his large family is complicated by two factors: one is that the family alternated their residence between England and the continent, chiefly in Italy, Switzerland, and Paris; the other, as if to bedevil the investigator, is Dickens's bewildering habit of ascribing various nicknames to the children at varying times. For instance, Edward, the youngest, was variously known as "the Plorn," the Plornishghenter," "Plornish," and "the Plornish Maroon." Others were known as Chickenstalker, Sampson Brass, Skittles, and so on. Moreover, there appears to be no satisfactory way of ascertaining exactly what curriculum was followed when two of the boys were sent to Germany to round out their education; or when tutors were employed during periods of residence abroad, say in Paris; or when various governesses travelled with the Dickens family to Italy or elsewhere.

From the letters it is clearly evident, however, that Charles Dickens believed that childhood was a period of life to be enjoyed, and he gave time and thought to the provision of enjoyment for his own children. If he became somewhat cool towards his children as they approached their teens, there is no doubt that he was very warm towards them in their infancy and childhood. In this regard, his many little gifts and remembrances to the "noble Plorn" may be noted. Born in March, 1852, Plorn was cherished the more because a little girl, Dora, born in 1850, had died in infancy. Promising to look for a box of bon-bons for the "noble and fascinating" Plornish, the doting father sends "a thousand kisses." "I am grieved to hear about the Plorn's black eye," he wrote on another occasion, when he expected the eye to be in "the green and purple state" on his return. "Kiss the noble Plorn a dozen times for me." "My best love to the noble Plornish. If he be quite reconciled to the postponement of his trousers, I should like to behold his first appearance in them. But if not . . . it would be a pity to disappoint and try him."[45] As to further provisions for the enjoyment of childhood, the gracious tributes paid by Dickens's daughter to her father, and her memories of him, were mentioned in chapter v. The letters add other instances: "I enclose a short note for each of the boys. Give Harry ten shillings pocket money, and

[45]To Georgina, Feb. 16, 1855, Feb. 8 and March 14, 1856, and Sept. 26, 1858, Hogarth and Dickens, eds., *Letters*, pp. 359, 392 f., 465 f.

Plorn six."[46] Such injunctions as this to his daughter Mamey were common.

He often took the children on hikes, or "down the river gypsying." On June 24, 1851, for example, he secured Rev. D. Hawtrey's permission to take Charley and three other boys on such an expedition, promising to get them back "in good condition." Dickens and his friend Beard appeared at Slough with two huge hampers from the firm of Fortnum and Mason in the luggage van. When the first hamper came out Dickens was conscious of the boys' "dancing behind the guard"; at the second, "they all stood wildly on one leg." The champagne made the boys oblivious of the rain which came down quite heavily, and Dickens had to abandon any idea of "getting them to their dames with any sort of sense that they were damp."[47] There is an elusive childhood charm in many of the father's notes to his children as the following shows: ". . . It is expected at school that when Walter puts on his jacket all the Miss Kings will fall in love with him to desperation." Practical lessons in kind-heartedness were given the children also, as when he wrote to his daughter to ascertain "kindly and sensibly," whether their old servant Anna "is pinched in the articles of necessary clothing, bedding or the like."[48] Dickens went to astonishing pains to entertain his children with conjuring tricks, performing his magic with great gusto at Christmas and Twelfth Night parties.[49] At home or abroad there were the inevitable bon-bons and crackers; the games of battledore and bagatelle; the father's comic songs of "Lord Bateman" and "Guy Fawkes"; and the wonderful suppers followed by dances or amateur theatricals.[50] Henry, Dickens's sixth son, has further testified to his father's mimic gift, and to his habit of taking long walks with his children and the dogs.[51]

In the education and training of his children, however, Dickens also stressed discipline, reliability, neatness, and the acceptance of responsibility. We have seen that, in writing to his friends about the two schools he approved of (the one at Boulogne and the one at Bruce Castle), Dickens praised the masters' attempts to develop these very characteristics. Henry also testified to his father's enforcement of neatness and discipline. According to Henry, the boys were taught to keep their chests

[46]To Mamey, Feb. 1, 1863, *ibid.*, p. 553.

[47]Dexter, ed., *Letters*, II, 320; Hogarth and Dickens, eds., *Letters*, pp. 249 f. (July 11, 1851, to Mrs. Watson).

[48]Hogarth and Dickens, eds., *Letters*, pp. 192, 662 (Jan. 23, 1868, to Mamey).

[49]This legerdemain began in earnest about Christmas, 1843. See Dexter, ed., *Letters*, I, 556 f. (Jan. 3, 1844, to Macready), and chap. v above.

[50]*Ibid.*, I, 651, 663 f., 670; II, 663.   [51]*Memories of My Father*, p. 14.

of drawers in the neatest manner possible, and to recognize that pegs were meant for specific purposes. Daily parade and inspection were held, sometimes to the antagonism of the boys. But Henry adds significantly: "We gave no open utterances . . . that we dare not do."[52] Dickens described his second son Walter as a very good boy; yet Walter spent at least one Sunday in solitary confinement in a bathroom, on a diet of bread and water, for "terminating a dispute with the nurse by throwing a chair in her direction."[53] Again, when Frank was nearing sixteen, Dickens wrote the boy's tutor requesting that the boy be given more freedom to go about alone in order to develop more self-reliance.[54]

From remarks dropped here and there by Gladys Storey, it appears that Dickens's daughters were subjected to the same discipline in neatness and orderliness as their brothers, and encouraged to assume responsibility. A letter from Dickens in September, 1858, shows Mamey's acceptance of considerable responsibility: she was instructed to use the extra pound sterling added to the housekeeping cheque to assist a poor railway man, giving him ten shillings one week, and if necessary, ten shillings the next. After he was separated from his wife in 1858, Dickens wrote: "My eldest daughter, Mary, keeps house with a state and gravity becoming that high position; wherein she is ably assisted by her sister Katey. . . . Two big dogs . . . are their principal attendants."[55]

For all Dickens's inveighing against the teaching of catechism in schools by rote, it should not be inferred that he neglected the religious and moral instruction of his children. Henry testified to his father's deep religious convictions.[56] Dickens might write a history of England for his boys to keep away "any Conservative or High Church notions" but he also wrote a life of Christ for them as well. As was his custom when he sent his boys out into the world to earn their own living, he presented Plorn with a New Testament (and a box of cigars from Aunt Georgina) when the sixteen-year-old boy set sail on the *Sussex* for Australia, never to return. In the letter which he gave Plorn on parting Dickens enjoined his son not to take "mean advantage of anyone," to say his prayers, and to read his Testament.[57] The many clergymen who were asked to tutor Dickens's children are noteworthy. Clergymen were in charge at the Boulogne school, for example, and in the winter of 1856, Rev. James

[52]*Ibid.*, pp. 25 f.   [53]Hogarth and Dickens, eds., *Letters*, p. 296.
[54]Dexter, ed., *Letters*, III, 123.
[55]Hogarth and Dickens, eds., *Letters*, pp. 463, 451 (July 7, 1858, to M. De Cerjat).
[56]*Memories of My Father*, p. 28.
[57]Hogarth and Dickens, eds., *Letters*, pp. 697 f. (Sept. 26, 1868), and 706. (Cf. pp. 722, 742.)

White assisted with the education of the girls at 49 Champs Elysées. When searching for a schoolmaster for Plorn, an inquiry from his father to Rev. W. Brookfield asked whether "any such . . . good and reliable man in this wise" has "ever come in your way."[58] As a result, while the eleven-year-old boy was temporarily at Brighton, his father wrote to Rev. W. C. Sawyer, Tunbridge Wells, to say that he was bringing him his son from Wimbledon for further education.[59] Another clergyman, Rev. John Taylor, also assisted with Plorn's education.

It is significant also that Dickens's correspondence reveals that he permitted his children to have some say in the choice of the type of education they pursued, and that he took into account their individual handicaps, preferences, and mental abilities. In discussing with Miss Coutts the education of his oldest son Charley, for instance, Dickens wrote: "My object is to make him a good man and a wise one; and to place him in the best position I can help him to, for the exercise of his abilities and acquirements."[60] This letter was quickly followed by another telling of a long discussion between father and son as to whether Charley wished to become a soldier or a merchant. Arrrangements were then made for him to leave Eton and to set out for Germany.[61] In 1858, when Edward (Plorn) was at Wimbledon, he found the school there too "confusingly large" for him and requested his father to send him to a smaller school. This was done in accordance with the boy's wishes. In May, 1867, when Plorn was just past fifteen years, his father requested that his education be given a more practical bent; and that Latin be dropped in favour of more time for natural philosophy and history; he also mentioned the possibility of sending the boy to Australia. Plorn was then asked to make some choice about manual training and studies in chemistry. It would seem, from a letter dated January, 1868, that for a very brief period he attended the Agricultural College at Cirencester. It was suggested further that he was to spend a few months with a sheep farmer after Christmas.[62]

[58]*Ibid.*, pp. 383, 559 f. (May 17, 1863).

[59]Dexter, ed., *Letters*, III, 370 f. (Nov. 6, 1863).

[60]Johnson, ed., *Heart of Charles Dickens*, p. 69 (Morgan MSS, Sept. 10, 1845).

[61]Hogarth and Dickens, eds., *Letters*, p. 278. Eventually, Charley was apprenticed to a London broker, and about September, 1855, began to work for Baring's at fifty pounds a year. Under the auspices of Baring, he made a trip to China to make business connections, arriving back home early in 1861. About seven years later, he took Morley's place on the staff of his father's periodical, *All the Year Round*, in which his father left him a share. (See Dexter, ed., *Letters*, II, 492, 483; Hogarth and Dickens, eds., *Letters*, pp. 283, 327, 496 f., 515; and Morgan MSS, Sept. 7, 1849, Dec. 6, 1849, Sept. 6, 1850.)

[62]Hogarth and Dickens, eds., *Letters*, pp. 559 f.; Dexter, ed., *Letters*, III, 501, 526, 537, 595.

Dickens's third son, Frank, had ideas of becoming a doctor. His father sent him back to Boulogne, in September, 1859, however, to keep up his French and German, while making up his mind. Eventually, Frank went to Germany to round out his education. In a letter to his father from Hamburg, the lad then confessed: "I have given up all thoughts of being a doctor. My stammering is the cause, all professions are barred against me. The only thing I should like to be is a gentleman farmer."[63] The same regard for his boys' wishes prompted Dickens to entreat the proprietors of the school at Boulogne, where his fifth son Sydney was in attendance, to ascertain if they could whether or no Sydney, then eleven years of age, really had a call for the sea.[64] Evidently everyone agreed that he had, for in the middle of September, 1860, we learn from a letter to Mrs. Watson that "Sydney has just passed his examinations as a naval cadet and come home, all eyes and gold buttons."[65] Actually, the boy was only thirteen years old; he had to stand on a portmanteau in the cabin to wash himself.[66] Nevertheless by March 16, 1862, he was on his way to Bermuda on H.M.S. *Orlando* as a midshipman.[67]

The amount of choice afforded the fourth son, Alfred ("Skittles"), is not, however, quite as clear. When he was only eleven years of age or so, Dickens wrote to William J. Eastwick requesting a cadetship for either Alfred or Frank, and this idea was pursued. A letter to Mr. Gibson, proprietor of the Boulogne School, acquainted him with the fact that Alfred was about to be sent to Wimbledon (where his brother Walter had been sent before him) to prepare for the cadet examinations. Alfred, however, was not forced to enter upon a military life. For about two years, he worked in "a large China House in the City," and then in May, 1865, he sailed for Melbourne, Australia, to seek his fortune in the sheep-farming business.[68]

The amount of choice given Henry is not entirely clear either. He

[63]Hogarth and Dickens, eds., *Letters*, p. 481; see also pp. 502, 543. Frank (Francis Jeffrey) was destined to be neither a country squire nor an urban office worker but a capable mounted officer. In 1875, after nine years' service in India with the Bengal Police, during which time he was promoted to the rank of captain, he secured a commission with the Canadian North-West Mounted Police. (Dexter, ed., *Letters*, III, 288, 340, 371, 378; Storey, *Dickens and Daughter*, p. 174; and records of R.C.M.P., Ottawa, Canada.)

[64]Dexter, ed., *Letters*, III, 69.

[65]Hogarth and Dickens, eds., *Letters*, p. 502.

[66]Dexter, ed., *Letters*, III, 280.

[67]See also Hogarth and Dickens, eds., *Letters*, pp. 543, 504 f., 522. (His captain certified him as "a highly intelligent and promising young officer." Sydney died at sea, 1872.)

[68]See Dexter, ed., *Letters*, II, 817; III, 103, 421.

followed his brothers to Boulogne. But in March, 1860, Dickens wrote to Rev. J. Bewsher explaining that he was withdrawing Harry in order that he might be at home as a companion for his younger brother Edward, and that he might attend the Rochester Grammar School.[69] Thus the general plan which Dickens had followed in the education of his sons appears to have changed somewhat at this point. Henry received a sound English grammar school training, and in due course entered Trinity Hall, Cambridge, in October, 1868. A letter, dated the middle of October reminded the boy that his father had had no such financial aid as two hundred and fifty pounds sterling per year when he was a boy, and urged the son to capitalize on his "past expensive education."[70] He did, to become Sir Henry Fielding Dickens, K.C.

Dickens, moreover, did not neglect the development of his children's imaginative faculties. He criticized the education that the English government was attempting, under the direction of Kay-Shuttleworth, to provide the common people. He satirized, in his novels, the mechanical nature of the training given to the teachers and the excessive amount of learning by rote required of the children, to the detriment of their imagination and understanding. M'Choakumchild, Gradgrind, and Bradley Headstone were all as lacking in imagination as Sissy Jupe was overflowing in this faculty. It is scarcely surprising, therefore, to find Dickens writing in a letter to Miss Coutts: "It would be a great thing for us, if more who are powerfully concerned with Education, thought as you do, of the imaginative faculty."[71] He is able to recommend to her in the same note the three best publishers of children's books and "a charming collection of stories called *The Child's Fairy Library*." Dickens's letters reveal his efforts to provide his own children with books, to teach them singing, dancing, and acting. We read of him taking a party of children to the theatre, and there are direct references to the vocal and pianoforte accomplishments of Mamey and Katey, and also to dancing the polka.[72] Elsewhere, Mamey is said to have possessed talent in floral arrangement, and her father compliments her on her excellent manner of writing little stories.[73] Later, we are informed that Katey has made some more capital portraits,[74] and we know from Miss Storey that she had studied art at Bedford College. To all this may be added the numerous entertainments Dickens planned for festive occasions.

The letters do not provide conclusive evidence on just what part Aunt

[69]*Ibid.*, III, 153.

[70]*Ibid.*, III, 673.

[71]*Ibid.*, II, 231.

[72]*Ibid.*, II, 370; I, 670.

[73]*Ibid.*, II, 795 (also Morgan MSS, Feb. 18, 1853); III, 41.

[74]*Ibid.*, III, 760.

Georgina played in this imaginative education of the girls. As their close and constant companion, however, she no doubt wielded considerable influence. From remarks dropped here and there throughout the letters it is evident that she did much more than merely teach her nieces the rudiments of learning: she often read to them, participated in their dramatic presentations, and judiciously guided them in their selection of clothes and party dresses; she made it her business to chaperon Mamey and Katey to balls and to set the stage at home for the display of their artistic and musical talents in the drawing room; and helped them to acquire the deft social poise needed to put their shy guests at ease. It is certain that Dickens never entrusted his daughters to such ridiculous schools for girls as appear in his novels. They were afforded competent tutors at home (Manin for example), and permitted more freedom than the boys. And while they were forced to accept domestic responsibility at an early age, they were given the compensation of much foreign travel, dramatics, and conversation. For Dickens believed that one result of sound education for girls, as for boys, should be the development of the imagination, good taste, and propriety; education for girls should capitalize on the feminine love of colour, brightness, and refinement. Dickens had observed "a love of colour and brightness to be a portion of a generous and fine nature."[75]

The accounts given in the letters of the educational opportunities Dickens afforded his children might be interpreted as revealing a stress on the development of personality rather than on the acquisition of academic knowledge. However, it should not be inferred that this latter acquisition was neglected. At home or abroad, Dickens provided his children with competent tutors. He was extremely proud of Charley's knowledge of the classics when he took him up to Eton, and of Henry's scholastic honours at Cambridge. Moreover, French was practically a second language to most of the boys, German a third to Charles and Edward at least, and Italian was not neglected in the case of either the sons or the daughters.

Dare we apply a pragmatic test of results? Dickens himself hoped that the boys would remember that they "had a kind father" and would do their duty, but above all that they would recognize that "nothing is to be attained without striving."[76] Three boys, one in India, one at sea, one in the North-West Mounted, died in early manhood, in the best Victorian tradition, rendering honourable and faithful service. Two other sons, after careers in England and Australia respectively, fell back some-

[75]*Ibid.*, II, 842 f.
[76]*Ibid.*, III, 668; Morgan MSS, Oct. 7, 1862, to Letitia.

what on their father's fame by giving public lectures on his life and works. The youngest was not very successful in Australia—but that again raises a very pertinent question as to what constitutes success. It is significant, however, that Henry, the son to whom Dickens afforded a sound English grammar school and university education, and who was therefore not sent out early into the world, had his feet set firmly on the lower rungs of the ladder of professional success.

Finally, it may well be observed that however indulgent and playful Dickens might have been with his children in their early childhood, he sternly—if not a little harshly—forced the hard realities of life and work on all of them, save one, in early adolescence. He sent Charley to Germany for further education at fifteen and the lad was in business by eighteen; he sent another son, Walter, to India at sixteen; Frank was urged to seek his fortune at sixteen also, and was put to work in his father's office at eighteen; Alfred was sent to Australia by the time he was twenty; Sydney was a naval cadet at thirteen, and on a voyage to Bermuda at fifteen; Henry alone received a sound academic education; while the youngest, Edward ("the Plorn"), received neither sound schooling nor a sound business training. Dickens himself, it must be admitted, had some misgivings,[77] and his parting from Plorn was sorrowful. Dickens was then in his middle fifties, and there is little doubt that he greatly loved the boy. He knew that he might never (and he did not) see Plorn again; yet he let him go. Moreover, just as he had sent Walter off to India in 1857, he sent Plorn away to Australia, which was then the ends of the earth. Are we to blame his domestic situation, broken since 1858? Was Aunt Georgina to blame? Dickens never hinted so. Are we to accept the verdict of Dickens's younger daughter Katey (Mrs. Perugini) that, after her mother's separation from their home, her father "did not care a damn what happened to any of us"?[78] If the latter, then the sailor son, apparently felt the repercussions also. This thesis would not hold, however, for Henry, the only son of the seven (and the only child of the nine children surviving infancy) on whom Dickens lavished an expensive education. What are we to conclude then from these early partings? The practice probably stemmed, in part, from a double legacy —the misfortunes of Dickens's own childhood, and the grim Victorian way. But it more likely resulted from Dickens's belief in independence and "self-help," and a conviction that adolescents should early accept responsibility for their own welfare.

[77]Dexter, ed., *Letters*, III, 669.
[78]Storey, *Dickens and Daughter*, p. 94; but cf. Johnson, ed., *Heart of Charles Dickens*, p. 344.

CHAPTER IX

The Contribution of Dickens to Education

Looking back, critically, from this vantage point over the general picture of English education in the nineteenth century, it becomes apparent that the work Dickens did for education might have proved abortive but for the general confusion and educational ferment in Dickensian England. These industrial and social disturbances inevitably intensified educational needs and simultaneously precipitated educational legislation. At the time of Dickens's death in 1870, controversy was still raging around the question as to where the responsibility for educating the masses lay. Many Victorians found it difficult to decide whether this responsibility belonged to the family, the community, the church, or the state; discussion endeavoured to resolve such knotty problems as the feasibility of schools for an *élite* group, for religious groups, or for everyone, and to resolve the social implications of the earlier provision of education according to class. Yet, as we have seen, the state had nevertheless been gradually assuming more and more responsibility, and although the educational facilities for the poor were still inadequate at the time of Dickens's death, it was in that year that the Forster Act—a major provision for the education of the masses—was ultimately passed by the British House of Commons. It is doubtful whether this acceptance of responsibility for education by the state could have been achieved without intensifying the clashes of fundamental philosophy, without the flaring of denominational rivalries, and without shifting the aim from that of educating an *élite* group to that of educating all children. Thus, one of the greatest educational advancements of the nineteenth century would appear to be the greater and greater assumption by the state of the responsibility for providing administrative machinery by means of which education was extended to more and more children and its costs more equitably distributed. Dickens, as this study has shown, was neither a pioneer nor a revolutionary in this movement; but he certainly gave it additional momentum.

Looking back, in addition, over Dickens's own schooling and youthful experiences, it is well to remind ourselves that Dickens's early years were such that he acquired a heart-felt sympathy for the unhappy lot of the neglected and the poor. If he did not actually experience the physical pain, he gained a knowledge of the wretchedness which children may experience at the hands of brutal schoolmasters. The sterling kindness and sound scholarship of Mr. Giles, which was later put in sharp contrast to the petty tyranny of Mr. Jones, imprinted on his mind the importance of a generous teaching personality. During his days in the offices of the law he became acquainted with the insolence of office and the pettiness of authority. Through his father's debts, the fickleness of Maria Beadnell, and the snobbery of her family, he learned the bitter taste of humiliation. Throughout his four years of newspaper life he observed politicians arousing public passions for personal advantage, and learned that public opinion is aroused by appeals to the emotions, through pathos, laughter, and imagination. Through his early reading in the little room upstairs, his days at the Museum, and the hours he spent at the theatre, he caught an appreciation of the educational and recreative value of imaginative pursuits. It is well to remind ourselves, further, that the article "Our School," which purported to give an account of Dickens's early school-days in retrospect, proves, on close analysis, to be a curious mixture of fact and fancy, and, that when Dickens seeks to give a truthful impression, the line between the two, like that between laughter and tears, becomes almost imperceptible.

If, however, as we have seen in the earlier chapters of this book, movements were on foot in England to initiate a state system of free and compulsory education long before Dickens had written a single line, and if he was neither a pioneer nor a revolutionary in this movement, then what were his specific contributions to the advancement of education?

At the outset it may be said that Dickens contributed a unique picture of the elementary schools of his day, making public exposure of the intolerable abuses which were current or the vestiges of them which remained. He provided an *exposé* of the callous exploitation of children in the isolated schools of Yorkshire which Dotheboys Hall epitomized. The brutal corporal punishment inflicted in too many private schools was depicted in the school of Mr. Creakle. The evils of cramming in many of the schools were recognized in the presentation of Doctor Blimber's Academy. The drudgery of the lessons as a result of the system of the Revised Code which forced children to memorize too many useless facts instead of permitting them to develop character and imagination was recognizable in the system of Mr. Gradgrind and Mr. M'Choakumchild. The stigma attached to the wearing of charity-school uniforms, the humiliating obsequiousness demanded in the charity schools, and the humbug teachers who conducted classes in some of the church schools were all starkly revealed. In the education of girls, the hodge-podge, emptiness, superficiality, and snobbishness of the curriculum in the fashionable boarding- and day-schools were exposed, as well as the degrading, humiliating, and rigorous treatment meted out to those girls who were forced to attend the semi-charitable schools; and provision for the education of poor girls was seen to be practically non-existent. Dickens exposed the low status which society accorded governesses, and the humiliation they experienced from the condescension of their superiors. He made plain the searing line drawn in too many schools between rich and poor girls as he depicted the snobbishness of Miss Monflathers. He held up to public ridicule the artificiality of some of the preposterous teachers in the girls' schools, their perverse manner of dress, and their insistence that their young charges endure tortures such as those occasioned by the use of the backboard and the wearing of stays. Dickens exposed the nefarious treatment accorded pauper children in the workhouses and on such "workhouse farms" as that operated by Drouet. Again and again in his articles and novels Dickens held up to public view the disgraceful neglect of the homeless urchins who roamed the city streets, and the dire results of a belief in the cruel doctrine of the depravity of children.

Of course, there are some qualifications to be made. In "The Half-Timers" Dickens recognized the success of the administrative methods practised by the officials of the Stepney Union; he was very disappointed when the majority of ragged schools were not considered eligible for state aid; and, yet again, he was most practical in the administrative guidance he gave to the Home for Homeless Women at Urania Cottage. Nevertheless, the fact remains that he gave little of what might be termed broad administrative guidance on a grand scale. Although he carped at the specific shortcomings of church schools, charity schools, foundation schools, and private and state-assisted schools, at the boorish arrogance of the privileged classes in their failure to provide care and education for the neglected children of the streets, nowhere did he suggest wide and far-reaching measures, other than benevolent charity, for the accomplishment of such purposes. Seldom, for example, did he adequately consider the political aspects of such matters as local rates or government grants-in-aid. Perhaps it was just as well. Whenever Dickens moved outside his experience or milieu, his sparkling genius remained behind; only where he returned to his own forte did the flames on the hearth begin to dance gleefully, the andirons smile, kettles sing merrily, children cry out, and fretful pedagogues rant and fume.

Thus, in the fields of educational administration and theory, Dickens appears to have had only a partial grasp of the situation. In his withering attack on the governmental system of inspection and the training of teachers, for example, he did not always appear to be thoroughly acquainted with the total situation. He opposed the dominance of any particular religious denomination in the educational system. He gave sympathetic support to any plan which helped to relieve suffering and to provide some schooling for the poor. Yet it is difficult to find conclusive evidence in his novels that he envisioned a state system of free compulsory education for all: for instance, he offered no solution to the problem of caring for unwanted children such as Jo or Smike; he gave no substitute in *Nicholas Nickleby* for Dotheboys Hall. When he wished to depict a good school, it was still a private school—but with a finer personality as teacher. Indeed, Dickens demonstrated in his novels that it was not necessary to have a state system to produce good masters such as Doctor Strong or Mr. Marton.

On the other hand, there *is* a plea in Dickens's writings for state *intervention*. This plea is scarcely perceptible in his novels or in his speeches, but a demand for state intervention is quite clear in his articles. Nevertheless, it should be noted, further, that Dickens asks state intervention for a *special class* of children—not a state system for *all* children. Two very practical demonstrations of what might be accomplished in this regard were described, one in which Dickens was early interested, and the other for which, with the aid of Miss Coutts's benevolence, he made himself directly responsible—ragged schools, and the home at Shepherd's Bush. But these two projects owed little to the state. Both stemmed from private benevolence. Isolated instances of successful intervention by the state may be found in *American Notes*, and in Dickens's description of the half-time system practised at the Stepney Union in London, but in these cases, also, the intervention by the state is for a special class of children—the neglected, handicapped, and delinquent. Dickens argued vehemently for state help in specific needy cases—unsuccessfully for state grants to all ragged schools, for example. The monthly supplement to *Household Words* described and supported the various legislative schemes of others for state intervention in education and was vitriolic against the inhibiting effects of religious contention in educational matters. Yet Dickens turned down an opportunity to run for parliamentary office himself, he has few good words for government anywhere, and he attacked intervention by the state in respect of its efforts to train teachers as well as its neglect of its educational responsibilities. It has been sometimes said that he was not very practical. But no administrator was more practical than Dickens in his planning and supervision of Urania Cottage or in his organization of individual ragged schools. Nevertheless, he must have often appeared to lack historical perspective, wide administrative sagacity, and the political acumen necessary to weigh all the factors involved. Often he seemed more of a Santa Claus than a John Dewey or a Kay-Shuttleworth.

Readers who are specially interested in pedagogy will no doubt notice omissions in Dickens's account. Attention has already been drawn to the fact that he portrayed little of the life in the English grammar schools or public schools. There is the excursion into Doctor Blimber's Academy and a comment or two in *Bleak House* and elsewhere, but Dickens took few extensive journeys into this field. Moreover, it appears that he did not portray a really satisfying schoolmaster. As the medieval sculptors skilfully fashioned fantastic gargoyles for the cathedrals, in like manner Dickens fashioned many of his schoolmasters as fantastic and grotesque devils. Mr. Marton and Doctor Strong, Phoebe and Esther Summerson do not serve to redress the balance, for to many readers they are not fully satisfying. Besides, we never seem to get an adequate insight into the methods of the good teachers. Except for the lessons given by the pupil-teacher in "A Sleep to Startle Us," Phoebe in "Mugby Junction," Miss Peecher in *Our Mutual Friend*, Fagin in *Oliver Twist*, and Major Jackman in "Mrs. Lirriper's Legacy"—and these are also inadequate—no demonstration of sound teaching method in a good school is to be found. Moreover, there is no closely reasoned presentation of educational philosophy, but perhaps one could hardly expect it in Dickens.

Dickens's contribution was emotional rather than intellectual. There was little analytical sagacity about much of his discussion. Dotheboys Halls should be abolished. But what should be put in their place? Jo should be cared for. But how? As we have noted, Dickens gave no concrete method other than benevolent charity. True, he thought the state should care for the neglected and delinquent. He provides, however, no comprehensive plan for any large state scheme of social betterment or comprehensive educational system. It is always the charitable distribution of gifts, rather than the administrative distribution of justice. Dickens believed, as did Shelley, that emotion is the spur to action, and the motive force of the will. Thus, it was for warm hearts that he pleaded rather than for cool heads in the treatment of the poor in general and in the provision for their education in particular. Yorkshire schools, for example, had been exposed in one sense to the public view before, in the trial of Shaw, but Dickens put an emotional appeal into his *exposé* in *Nicholas Nickleby*. He did the same for pauper children in his article

"The Paradise at Tooting," and for neglected children in "A Sleep to Startle Us." Hence, Dickens contributed to the improvement of educational conditions in the nineteenth century through the emotional impact of his literary genius—an impact sufficient to arouse indignation hot enough to eradicate cheap distant schools, and to start humanitarian impulses warm enough to curtail the brutalities of men such as Creakle and Drouet.

Moreover, Dickens interpreted to adults the point of view of children. He requested for the children their rightful place in any school system. He put children first; appealed for a happy school life; pleaded for the development of their imagination, care for their health, kind treatment of their feelings; and encouraged confidence in their essential right to live as children. It seems reasonable to conclude that Dickens knew little about educational theory. Yet anything that placed children first and extended a sympathetic helping hand to guide them along pleasanter pathways always drew his interest, sympathy, and support. He was led by his sympathy for children to visit schools that lessened the rigour and brutality as then practised by teachers, and to encourage anything that tended to make children happier. Although he by no means consistently expounded the philosophy of Froebel, nevertheless with Froebel, Pestalozzi, Wilderspin, Stow, and other educational reformers, he considered children to be the pivotal point in any educational system. By popularizing this new spirit of education based on child study, milder discipline, and the rights of childhood, and by demanding the development of character and imaginative minds rather than the amassing of unintelligible facts, Dickens contributed much towards the development of a more enlightened adult attitude to children. His artistic genius led him to make Paul Dombey and Little Nell suffer in his novels so that children might live happily in the world. He had a sympathetic, generous heart which vibrated responsively to the hearts of children—to David Copperfield in his loneliness, to Miss Edwards in her mute appeal, to the young ladies of Miss Twinkleton's school in their happiness at vacation time, to the staunch-hearted Traddles, to Smike, and many others in real life. He desired with all his heart to bring happiness into children's lives, especially their schooldays. In so desiring perhaps he was nearer the truth of what needed to be done than some people seem to think.

Strangely enough, the surrendering of first place to the children imparted a new dignity to the position and influence of the teachers. Dickens ridiculed the teachers in his books in order that parents might secure teachers of a higher quality in life. Dickens wanted not only a higher calibre of education for the poor but also a higher calibre of teacher to direct it. As we have noted, when he wanted to depict a good school, it was still a private school with a finer personality such as Doctor Strong to direct it. Hence, another contribution of Dickens to education, especially through his portrayal of private schools, was the emphasis he placed on the potentiality, for good or evil, of the teacher. Dickens demonstrated that teachers needed not only careful training but also needed to be persons of highly select character in the first place. For teachers such as Headstone and M'Choakumchild, Dickens showed the desirability of less mechanical training, of wider vision and more intellectual freedom. For the teachers of girls, Dickens pleaded for less snobbishness, less artificiality. He appealed to the teachers themselves to give the Steerforths and the Uriah Heeps better training in character, to give the physically handicapped such as Marigold's deaf-mute special instruction, and to provide the Bitzers with more variety and wider imaginative pursuits. In depicting Mr. Wopsle he pleaded that teachers give greater consideration to highly intelligent children. Through his delineation of teachers such as Doctor Strong, Mr. Marton, and Phoebe, and laymen such as Major Jackman and even the unethical Fagin, Dickens implied a new spirit of instruction which would recognize the child's point of view, and be cognizant of childhood's depth of humiliation, imagination, and emotional feeling. All this could only be demanded from teachers of high calibre, carefully selected and adequately trained.

It was Dickens's vibrant humanitarian impulses which interested him in the improvement of education. Undoubtedly, his thousands of letters along with his practical generosity, his nominations of so many orphans to educational institutions, his personal direction of the financial resources of Miss Coutts into educational channels, his letters and speeches in support of Mechanics' Institutes, specific schools, and the reform of sanitary conditions within schools, had definite educational influence. How much it is difficult to estimate with precision. But there can be little doubt that the influence of his private correspondence and his public writing was positive, that it was in the direction which educational legislation eventually took, and that it was quite extensive. In these matters it is well to recall a statement made by Aristotle more than twenty-three hundred years ago, in the *Nichomachean Ethics*: "We must be content if we can attain to so much precision in our statement as the subject will permit. . . ."

The greatest contribution of Charles Dickens to the advancement of educational theory and practice appears to have been his aid in the formation of public opinion through the power of his artistic genius, which he was willing to place at the disposal of educational reform.

Although Dickens's influence on public opinion may not be objectively measured, the influence is clear enough. Few educational treatises reach the wide circulation accorded best-selling novels. Dickens's novels were best-sellers, widely circulated and widely read. How the sales went up! Before the fifteenth instalment of *Pickwick* was published, the sales had risen from four hundred to forty thousand! His novels were read in debtor's prison, in police courts, in lodging-houses, in theatre pits, at Greenwich Fair, in the cattle market at Smithfield, at the pubs, the pawn-brokers', in cheap eating-houses, on the new trains, and in Victorian parlours or spacious drawing-rooms. The circle of his public was widened still further by the Victorian practice of one person's reading aloud to an assembled family, or private or public group. Other authors, in associating Dickens's works with the lives of the characters in their own novels, show how far-reaching Dickens's influence was. In *Cranford* Elizabeth Gaskell includes the reading of Dickens among rural pastimes. Harry East of *Tom Brown's Schooldays* is shown chuckling over *Pickwick Papers*; Lord Kew in *The Newcomes* enjoys *Oliver Twist* as he recovers from a duel. Rough miners are depicted as sitting round a campfire while the youngest of their number reads them *The Old Curiosity Shop*; they are camped among the pines at the foot-hills of the Sierras, but as they follow the journey of Little Nell they wander in imagination through English meadows.[1]

These literary evidences of Dickens's familiarity were reflected in real life. Explorers in the neighbourhood of the Lake of the Woods, Ontario, named lakes after Dickens's characters.[2] Stout gentlemen smoked Pickwick cigars; cats and dogs were called Jingle; and according to George A. Sala, schoolboys burst out laughing in the middle of long sermons as they thought of amusing incidents in Dickens, only to suffer the humiliation of being removed by the beadle.[3] Undergraduates at the universities prided themselves on their detailed knowledge of Dickens's writings; Sir Walter Besant recounts how he won a prize given by one of his seniors at Cambridge for an examination of thirty questions on *Pickwick Papers*.[4] Such incidents could be multiplied.[5] In her study of the books of the nineteenth century, Amy Cruse noted that Mrs. Wood, the great-niece of Fanny Burney, recalled with amusement the surprise of a young man who discovered "Pickwick and Weller" cut in the stone of the Egyptian

[1]Bret Harte, in a poem entitled "Dickens in Camp."
[2]A. P. Coleman, "Sixth Report of a Bureau of Mines" in *Glimpses of Charles Dickens*, p. 46.
[3]*Life and Adventures*, I, 75.
[4]*Autobiography*, pp. 95–101.
[5]See Ford, *Dickens and His Readers*, pp. 79–98.

pyramids where he naturally expected to find hieroglyphics; and she remembered that Fanny Kemble began a letter to a friend with " 'Consekens is' as Mr. Sam Weller says."[6]

Schools are universal and novels depict life; thus, if, in imagination, we are able to transpose school life as it is delineated in a novel to the scene of the school life in our own experience, we may recognize similar motives, emotions, and aspirations among our daily companions. In this way, many a youth of Dickensian England recognized and went to school with Dickens's characters. As Amy Cruse noted, Francis Burmand referred to his nursery governess as a Cornelia Blimber, he "acted Paul Dombey to the life," and on first entering a school he felt like "one of Squeers' poor little devils"; George Richmond spoke of walking "the walks of Fagin"; a little girl wandered around Brighton to find where little Paul Dombey was "brought on."[7] Sala created puppets representing Dickens's boys and schoolmasters, or "murdered" his sister "Nancy" in the back bedroom.[8]

Dickens, as we have seen, acquainted the public through his articles with very practical demonstrations of what had been done and what could be done for the neglected, handicapped, and delinquent, both by benevolence and by the state, in North America, at Shepherd's Bush, in the ragged schools of London, and at the Stepney Union. Thus his numerous articles on social problems tended to make public opinion more sensitive to the problem of education, to the influence of environment, and to the inhibiting effects of religious contention. His genius enabled him to create in his novels a group of fussy old teachers, for example, and to place them in a series of fantastic situations and incidents in the girls' schools; he then created a number of highly charged emotional contingencies, relieved of tension by fancy or drollery, which aroused public interest in girls' education and appealed to common sense. His indication that girls should receive an education of a calibre equal to that for boys served to attract public attention by its very novelty.

Dickens was fundamentally right in his idea that the maximum amount of efficiency and efficacy in education (or in life) is secured when there is mutual understanding, co-operation, and sympathy between the public, parents, masters, and pupils. The educational conditions in Dickensian England permitted cruelty to children, starved their bodies, stuffed their minds with useless facts, crushed their imaginative development, or left them to grow up in the gutter. Dickens demanded

---

[6]Cruse, *The Victorians and Their Books*, chap. VIII.
[7]*Ibid.*
[8]*Life and Adventures*, I, 75.

that these conditions be changed; he did not know exactly how or to what they should be changed; but the hilarious laughter with which he demanded a change, in his novels, short stories, speeches, articles, and letters, was his way of moulding public opinion to that end. Like Shaw at a later date, he coated his appeal with the honey of laughter and slipped the draught past the public palate unawares. He welded comedy, fantasy, emotion, and realism into an effective weapon for arousing public opinion. Dickens's preposterous teachers, his caricatures of men like Squeers and Creakle, depicted with such realistic detail, first magnetized the English public, then rocked it with hilarious laughter; even the cadaverous Miss Blimbers and flinty Pipchins must have broken into a wry smile; and because the line between joy and sorrow is so thin, the public was often moved to tears as well—moved to the point where it was ready to support far-reaching educational reforms.

APPENDIX A

A Reference List of Schoolmasters, Schoolmistresses, Ushers, Tutors, and Governesses Found in the Works of Dickens

BAPS, Mr. A dancing-master at Doctor Blimber's Establishment. He was a very quiet, sedate person of slow and careful speech. (*Dombey and Son*, chap. XXIV.)

BIDDY. The young girl, who was a distant relative of Miss Wopsle, and who helped with the instruction in the so-called evening school. ". . . Her hair always wanted brushing, her hands always wanted washing, and her shoes always wanted mending and pulling up at the heel. On Sundays, she went to church elaborated." (*Great Expectations*, chaps. V, X, XV.)

BILLSMETHI, Signor. A dancing-master. ("The Dancing Academy," *Sketches by Boz*.)

BLIMBER, CORNELIA. Daughter of Doctor Blimber, and teacher at her father's boarding-school for boys. "She kept her hair short and crisp, and wore spectacles." (*Dombey and Son*, chaps. XI, XII, XIV, XLI, LX.)

BLIMBER, Doctor. The pompous and portly proprietor of a boys' private school at Brighton which was attended by Paul Dombey and Mr. Toots. Dressed in a suit of black, with strings at the knees and stockings below, he had a shiny head, a deep voice, and a double chin. (*Dombey and Son*, chaps. XI, XII, XIX, XXIV, XLI, LX.)

BLINKINS, Mr. A short-sighted, doubled-up Latin master, who walked with a crutch, and was always stuffing onions into his ears for deafness, or applying a screwed-up pocket handkerchief to his face. ("Our School," *Reprinted Pieces*.)

BROBITY, Miss. Mistress of a school in Cloisterham, and wife of Mr. Sapsea. (*Edwin Drood*, chap. IV.)

CHEESEMAN, OLD. A former pupil and "holiday-stopper" who became second Latin master, and who, eventually, came into a great deal of property. Later, he and his wife treat the boys to an annual feed, continue to visit the school, and to take home the "holiday stoppers" during vacations. ("The Schoolboy's Story," *Reprinted Pieces*.)

CHIEF, The. Headmaster described in "Our School" who was always drawing a pair of pantaloons tight with one hand and applying a "bloated mahogany ruler" with the other. ("Our School," *Reprinted Pieces*.)

CREAKLE, Mr. Headmaster at Salem House, where David Copperfield attended school. This "tartar" had a fiery face, a little nose, small eyes, and a large chin. He always spoke in a whisper which seemed to make his fiery face more angry and his thick veins thicker. "He had a delight in cutting at the boys, which was like the satisfaction of a craving appetite." (*David Copperfield*, chaps. V, VII, IX, LXI.)

CREEBLE, Miss. Mr. Booley met Miss Creeble (of The Misses Creeble's Boarding and Day Establishment for Young Ladies, Kennington Oval) with her young ladies in the New Zealand Bush. "Miss Creeble having very unsettled opinions on the subject of gunpowder, was afraid that it entered into the composition of the fire before the tent, and that something would presently blow up or go off. . . . [The pupils] took notice of the trees, as the Kaikatea, the Kauri, the Ruta, the Pukatea, the Hinau, and the Tanaka—names which Miss Creeble had a bland relish in pronouncing." (*Household Words*, April 20, 1850. *Miscellaneous Papers*, I, 227.)

CRIPPLES, Mr. Proprietor of Mr. Cripples's Academy. (*Little Dorrit*, chap. IX.)

CRISPARKLE, Rev. SEPTIMUS. A private tutor, noted for his understanding and Christian influence, in whose home Neville Landless was continuing his education. (*Edwin Drood*, chaps. II, VI, VIII, X, XII, XIV, XVII, XXI, XXIII.)

CRUMPTON, Miss AMELIA, and CRUMPTON, Miss MARIA. Precise maiden ladies, who conducted a "finishing establishment for young ladies," known as Minerva House. The two sisters were tall, upright, skinny, and rather yellow in appearance. "They were very precise, had the strictest possible ideas of propriety, wore false hair, and always smelt very strongly of lavender." ("Sentiment," *Sketches by Boz*.)

DADSON, Mr. Writing-master at Minerva House, who was depicted as wearing a white waistcoat, black shorts and stockings, and was said to display a leg large enough for two writing-masters. ("Sentiment," *Sketches by Boz*.)

DONNY, Miss. Proprietress of a boarding-school for girls, located at Reading and named Greenleaf. Esther Summerson spent six happy years at this school, as a sort of pupil-teacher, at Mr. Jarndyce's expense. Little more is told about Miss Donny, but it is inferred that she was a likable person. (*Bleak House*, chap. III.)

DROWVEY, Miss. A schoolmistress in partnership with Miss Grimmer, in the "make-believe" story of two little boys. There is divided opinion among the pupils as to which of the two teachers "is the greatest beast." (*Holiday Romance*.)

ENGLISH MASTER. Usher described in "Our School," "who smuggled the little boys through their rudimentary books" and played an old trombone, part of which was lost. ("Our School," *Reprinted Pieces*.)

FAGIN. A crafty instructor of systematic thieving, who kept a school for thieves in London. He would dress as an old gentleman and fill his pockets with valuables in order that the boys might practice removing them. (*Oliver Twist*, chaps. VIII, IX, XII, XIII, XV, etc.)

FEEDER, B.A., Mr. Assistant in Doctor Blimber's private school for boys. Later he became the Doctor's son-in-law, and succeeded him as headmaster. He is described as "a kind of human barrel organ" because his lessons were repeated over and over again. (*Dombey and Son*, chaps. XI, XII, XIV, XLI, LX.)

GENERAL, Mrs. A governess, forty-five years of age, a widow, engaged by Mr. Dorrit to "form the mind" and manners of his daughters. She had designs on Mr. Dorrit's fortune. "In person, Mrs. General, including her skirts, which had a lot to do with it, was of a dignified and imposing appearance; ample, rustling, gravely voluminous, always upright behind the properties." (*Little Dorrit*, II, chaps. I–V, VIII, XI, XV, XIX.)

GRIMMER, Miss. See *Drowvey* above.

GWYNN, Miss. Writing and ciphering governess at Westgate House, an "Establishment for Young Ladies" located at Bury St. Edmunds. (*Pickwick Papers*, chap. XVI.)

HEADSTONE, BRADLEY. Master of the boys' section of a school on the borders of Kent and Surrey. He was a pauper-lad who had been trained as a teacher according "to pattern," and was a sort of mechanical phonograph record. (*Our Mutual Friend*, chap. XVIII.)

HIGDEN, BETTY. The aged but active Betty Higden kept a "Minding-School" at Brentford. With the receipts from this, and aided by the mangle used in washing, she was able to keep out of the poorhouse. (*Our Mutual Friend*, I, chap. XV; II, chaps. IX, X, XIV.)

LANE, Miss. A governess in the family of Mr. Borum. (*Nicholas Nickleby*, chap. XXIV.)

LATIN GRAMMAR MASTER. A character in Master Robin Redforth's romance, who is master of the *The Scorpion*, an enemy vessel, captured by Captain Boldheart and his schooner *Beauty*. The Latin grammar master is turned adrift in an open boat, with two oars, a compass, a small cask of water, a bottle of rum, a piece of pork, a bag of biscuits, and a Latin grammar. Ultimately, he is hanged. (*Holiday Romance.*)

LEMON, Mrs. The "make-believe" proprietress of a preparatory school, supposed to admit only grown-up people; she is the creation of seven-year-old Nettie Ashford, who depicts a wonderful country where "grown-up people are obliged to obey the children, and are never allowed to sit up to supper, except on their birthdays." (*Holiday Romance.*)

M'CHOAKUMCHILD, Mr. A teacher in Mr. Gradgrind's model school, which captured childhood and held it prisoner, "dragging it into its gloomy statistical den by the hair." Facts! Facts! Facts! These were uppermost in his mind. There were no fairies in the test-tubes for his children, like those in which, in her childhood days, Madame Curie and her father delighted. (*Hard Times*, chaps. I, II, III, IX, XIV.)

MAJOR, The. Major Jackman, a boarder at Mrs. Lirriper's lodging-house, who instructs little Jemmy in primary number-work. ("Mrs. Lirriper's Legacy" and "Mrs. Lirriper's Lodgings," *Christmas Stories*, 1863–4.)

MARIGOLD, Doctor. A Cheap Jack who adopts a deaf and dumb child and teaches her himself. Later, he sends her to a school for the deaf to be further educated. (*Doctor Marigold*, 1865.)

MARTON, Mr. The mild, kindly, old schoolmaster who befriended little Nell and her grandfather on their wanderings. (*The Old Curiosity Shop*, chaps. XXIV, XXV, XXVI, XLV, LII–LIV, LXXI, LXXIII.)

MELL, Mr. CHARLES. An assistant master at Salem House, the school of Mr. Creakle. Depicted as a gaunt, sallow-faced young man, with sunken cheeks and dry, rusty hair, he, in the end, becomes Doctor Mell, headmaster of a Salem House in Australia. He was discharged by Creakle because it was revealed that Mrs. Mell, his mother, lived on the charity of an alms-house. (*David Copperfield*, chaps. V, VI, VII, XLIII.)

MONFLATHERS, Miss. Mistress of a Boarding and Day Establishment for girls. The large house had a high wall and a large garden gate, with a small grating through which every visitor was carefully scrutinized; nothing that resembled a man was allowed to pass this gate, not even the milkman. Miss Monflathers is introduced carrying a parasol of lilac silk, and "supported by two smiling teachers." (*The Old Curiosity Shop*, chap. XXXI.)

NETTINGALL, Misses. Mistresses of a girls' boarding school, attended by Miss Shepherd, who is a little girl with a "round face and curly flaxen hair"; she was an early boyhood sweetheart of David Copperfield, whom she met at dancing-school. (*David Copperfield*, chap. XVIII.)

NICKLEBY, NICHOLAS. Usher at Dotheboys Hall, in Yorkshire, the school of Mr. Wackford Squeers. Nickleby is a young man of impetuous temper, who, stung by the brutality of Squeers to all the boys in general, and to Smike in particular, thrashes the master soundly, and then leaves for London. He is about nineteen, slight, handsome, and intelligent, the hero of the story which bears his name; his history is recounted in the book. (*Nicholas Nickleby*, esp. chaps. III–IX.)

OUR SCHOOLMASTER. A broken-down, reduced, old master, instructor in a workhouse school. ("Our Parish," *Sketches by Boz.*)

PECKSNIFF, SETH. Proprietor of a school for architects near Salisbury, who never designed or built even a dog-kennel. "His genius lay in ensnaring parents and guardians and pocketing premiums." (*Martin Chuzzlewit*, chaps. II–VI and *passim.*)

PEECHER, Miss EMMA. Mistress of the girls' department in the school of Mr. Bradley Headstone. "Small, shining, neat, methodical, and buxom was Miss Peecher; cherry cheeked and tuneful of voice." (*Our Mutual Friend*, chap. XVIII.)

PHOEBE. Daughter of Lamps. Having been crippled by a fall in her infancy, she supports herself by making lace and teaching little children. ("Mugby Junction," *Christmas Stories*, 1865.)

PINCH, Miss RUTH. Tom Pinch's sister, and private governess in a brass-founder's family at Camberwell, where she is condescendingly visited by Pecksniff. Sweet-faced, pretty, with a slight and short figure, she is depicted instructing little girls whose figures are prematurely stiffened with whalebone and pride. (*Martin Chuzzlewit*, chaps. IX, XLVI.)

PIPCHIN, Mrs. The proprietress of a sort of nursery school for little children, at Brighton. "This celebrated Mrs. Pipchin was a marvellous ill-favoured, ill-conditioned old lady." (*Dombey and Son*, Chaps. VIII, XI, XII, XIV, XVI, XLIII, XLIV, XLVII, LI, LIX.)

PIPER, Professor. A member of a deputation which waited on the Honourable Elijah Pogram to request "the honour of your company at a little le-Vee, sir, in the ladies' ordinary at eight o'clock in the National Hotel." (*Martin Chuzzlewit*, chap. XXXIV.)

POCKET, MATTHEW. A tutor, a relative of Miss Havisham, who resided at Hammersmith and acted as tutor to Pip (Philip Pirrip). He had been educated at Harrow and Cambridge but had made an unfortunate marriage and was reduced to "the calling of a grinder." (*Great Expectations*, chaps. XXII, XXIII, XXIV, XXXIII, XXXIX.)

PUPFORD, Miss. Mistress of an establishment for six young ladies, an assistant, cook, and housemaid, all of whom complete "the educational and domestic staff of her Lilliputian College." It is difficult to imagine Miss Pupford ". . . without mittens, and without a front, and without a bit of gold wire among her front teeth, and without little dabs of powder on her neat little face and nose." ("Tom Tiddler's Ground," *Christmas Stories*, 1861.)

SHARP, Mr. First master at Salem House, the school of Mr. Creakle, assisted by Mr. Mell. "He was a limp delicate-looking gentleman, I thought, with a good deal of nose." (*David Copperfield*, chap. VI.)

SILVERMAN, GEORGE. An orphan boy who attends school under the adoption of Brother Hawkyard, wins a Cambridge scholarship, and becomes a tutor and clergyman. Adelina, daughter of Lady Lareway, and young Mr. Granville Sharton are two of his pupils. ("George Silverman's Explanation.")

SQUEERS, Mr. WACKFORD. The brutal master of Dotheboys Hall, Yorkshire, where Nicholas Nickleby was engaged as usher. Through false advertisements, Squeers took little boys with the ostensible purpose of educating them, but with the definite intention of exploiting them, for he had no proper qualifications to teach school. (*Nicholas Nickleby*, chaps. IV–IX.)

STRONG, Doctor. Master of a school at Canterbury attended by David Copperfield, founded on "the faith and honour of the boys." (*David Copperfield*, chaps. XVI, XVII, XIX, XXXVI, XXXIX, XLIII, XLV, LXII, LXIV.)

TISHER, Mrs. The assistant teacher at Miss Twinkleton's Academy, located at Cloisterham. She was described as a depressed widow "with a weak back, a chronic sigh, and a suppressed voice." (*Edwin Drood*, chap. III.)

TOMPKINS, Miss. Headmistress of a boarding-school for young ladies, called Westgate House, at Bury St. Edmunds, where Pickwick found himself in such a predicament owing to his gullibility in believing that Fitz-Marshal was about to elope with a rich heiress. (*Pickwick Papers*, chap. XVI.)

TURVEYDROP, Mr. A dancing-master. "He was a fat old gentleman with a false complexion, false teeth, false whiskers, and a whip." (*Bleak House*, chaps. XIV, XXII, XXX, L, LVII.)

TWINKLETON, Miss. Mistress of the Nun's House, a boarding-school for young ladies in Cloisterham, which was attended by Rosa Bud and Helena Landless. (*Edwin Drood*, chaps. III, VI, VII, VIII, XXII.)

WACKLES, Misses. Three mistresses in their mother's seminary for girls which was located at Chelsea; apparently this was a day-school only. "Miss Melissa might have seen five and thirty summers or thereabouts, and verged on the autumnal; Miss Sophy was a fresh, good-humored, buxom girl of twenty; and Miss Jane numbered scarcely sixteen years. Mrs. Wackles was an excellent but venomous old lady of three-score." (*The Old Curiosity Shop*, chap. VIII.)

WOPSLE, Miss. Mr. Wopsle's great-aunt, who kept an evening school with a little shop in the same room. "She was a ridiculous old woman of limited means and unlimited infirmity, who used to go to sleep from six to seven every evening, in the society of youth who paid twopence per week each for the improving opportunity of seeing her do it." (*Great Expectations*, chaps. v, x, xv.)

YORKSHIRE SCHOOLMISTRESS. An old lady whom Dickens met on his trip to Yorkshire in February, 1838. "She was very communicative, drank a great deal of brandy and water, and towards evening became insensible, in which state we left her." (Letter to Kate (Mrs. Charles Dickens), Feb. 1, 1838, in Dexter, ed., *Letters*, I, 157.)

APPENDIX B

A Reference List of the Schools Described in the Works of Dickens

Doctor Blimber's Establishment: an expensive private boarding-school for boys, located at Brighton, where a system of cramming was carried on; all the boys were made "to bear to pattern"; there is a good description of the teachers, and some light is thrown on the lessons taught. (*Dombey and Son*, 1846–8.)

Charity school: attended by Old Smallweed; quoted as an example of an educational failure. (*Bleak House*, 1852–4.)

Old Cheeseman's School: a school attended by Cheeseman as a boy and at which he later became assistant Latin master. ("The Schoolboy's Story," *Reprinted Pieces*, 1853.)

Mr. Cripples' Academy: a day and evening school, in the house where Uncle Frederick Dorrit lived, and where little Dorrit secured her schooling. (*Little Dorrit*, 1855–7.)

Day-school: a school attended by Esther Summerson when she lived with her puritanical aunt, by whom she was made a victim of the theory of the depravity of children, and was never allowed to attend parties as the other pupils did. (*Bleak House*, 1852–4.)

Dancing-schools: there were three: one in connection with Doctor Blimber's Establishment, taught by Mr. Baps (*Dombey and Son*, 1846–8); another taught by Signor Billsmethi, ("The Dancing Academy," *Sketches by Boz*, 1836); and a third conducted by Mr. Turveydrop, a model of deportment (*Bleak House*, 1852–4).

Miss Donny's school: Greenleaf, where Esther Summerson attended as a pupil-teacher; it was described as an example of a good boarding-school for girls, where the discipline was based on kindliness. (*Bleak House*, 1852–4.)

Dotheboys Hall: a wretched private school in the sparsely populated district of Yorkshire, said to be based partly on Shaw's school at Bowes. Nicholas Nickleby became usher in this school, over which Mr. Squeers presided; the latter was a rapacious and villainous pedagogue, who received a thrashing at the hands of Nickleby. The school depicts the dismal picture of exploited children, and the well-known "treacle scene." (*Nicholas Nickleby*, 1838–9.)

Drowvy and Grimmer's school: a school where the main subject of dispute was whether Drowvy or Grimmer was "the greatest beast." (*Holiday Romance*, 1868.)

Fagin's school for thieves: a school kept by Fagin, who trained boys in methods of petty thieving and the technique of picking pockets; it was located in London, and was a place of shelter for Oliver Twist for some time. (*Oliver Twist*, 1850.)

Foundation schools: there were two: a school attended by George Silverman where he testified that he received a good education, and indeed, according to the story, he proceeded from it to the university ("George Silverman's Explanation," 1868); and the school attended by Uriah Heep, apparently a charity school where children were taught to be submissive and obedient, a method which resulted in hypocritical obsequiousness (*David Copperfield*, 1850).

Mr. Gradgrind's school: taught by Mr. M'Choakumchild on a system having as its principle the stuffing of children with as many facts as possible; fancy and imagination were crushed out of the curriculum entirely. (*Hard Times*, 1854.)

The Grinders' charity school: the school to which Mr. Dombey nominated young Robin Toodle, known as Biler; there is biting ridicule of the preposterous charity-school uniform, and a withering attack on the system of the brutish masters. Young Biler was a victim of attacks on his way to school, and "turned out bad." (*Dombey and Son*, 1846–8.)

The school of the gutter: Jo in *Bleak House* is taken as an example of the utter neglect and shameful deterioration, both physical and mental, of street urchins. Authorities of the day were inclined to attribute the deterioration to the depravity of children. Dickens's heart went out to these children, but he has no concrete solution to offer to the problem, except charity. (*Bleak House*, 1852–4.)

Bradley Headstone's school: apparently a church school taught on the monitorial system, administered by a mechanically trained teacher, and generally presented as a dreary monotonous place. (*Our Mutual Friend*, 1864–5.)

Charley Hexam's first school: the first school attended by Charley Hexam; Pugh (see Bibliography) insists that it is a true picture of a similar church school attended by him when he was a boy; it was in a loft in a yard, had poor texts crammed full of moral saws, used the Bible as a text, contained all sorts of characters of both sexes, and was administered by monitors and some impossible teachers. (*Our Mutual Friend*, 1864–5.)

Mrs. Betty Higden's Minding-School: a home where Betty, as a sort of foster-mother, took children from the workhouse, whom she treated with love and care. (*Our Mutual Friend*, 1864–5.)

Mrs. Lemon's school: a make-believe preparatory school for grown-ups. (*Holiday Romance*, 1868.)

The Major's private school for one pupil: conducted in Mrs. Lirriper's parlour, where the Major instructed little Jemmy through the aid of good methods, using concrete materials and working out small projects. ("Mrs. Lirriper's Lodgings," 1863, and "Mrs. Lirriper's Legacy," 1864.)

Mr. Marton's schools: there were two of them; the description gives a good picture of a classroom, of procedure during a writing-lesson, and of the general attitude of the nineteenth-century public to education. (*The Old Curiosity Shop*, 1840–1.)

Minerva House: a finishing establishment for young ladies taught by the

Misses Crumpton; a good description is given of the teachers, the subjects, the building, and the preparations for a ball. (*Sketches by Boz*, 1835–6.)

Miss Monflathers's Boarding and Day Establishment: a girls' school where Mrs. Jarley sends little Nell to deliver some handbills; the school is characterized by snobbishness and ill treatment of Miss Edwards. (*The Old Curiosity Shop*, 1840–1.)

The Misses Nettingall's Establishment: a girls' boarding-school, attended by Miss Shepherd, a boyhood sweetheart of David Copperfield. (*David Copperfield*, 1849–50.)

"Our School": a sketch purporting to contain reminiscences of two schools Dickens attended as a boy; a tolerant, amusing, and interesting picture; note that it was written after the more satirical pictures. (*Reprinted Pieces*, 1851, combined 1858.)

Pecksniff's school for architects: a private school in the home of Mr. Pecksniff, where, for a stiff premium, youths desiring to be apprenticed to an architect, designed or surveyed at their own discretion; Pecksniff had never designed anything—except this fake scheme of securing premiums. (*Martin Chuzzlewit*, 1843–4.)

Miss Peecher's school: a school connected with that of Bradley Headstone, apparently a monitorial school; gives recitation of grammar. (*Our Mutual Friend*, 1864–5.)

Phoebe's school: a school conducted by an invalid young lady, from her bed; she teaches the little tots to sing, and learn by rote, for the love of the work. ("Mugby Junction," 1865.)

Mrs. Pipchin's school: a private nursery school attended by little Paul Dombey, which was administered on the principle of giving a child everything that he did not like, and nothing that he did like. (*Dombey and Son*, 1846–8.)

Preparatory school: discussed in "Our School." (*Reprinted Pieces*, 1851.)

Miss Pupford's Lilliputian College: an establishment for young ladies of tender years; stresses the neglect of children who are forced to spend their holidays at school. ("Tom Tiddler's Ground," *Christmas Stories*, 1861.)

Salem House: a school attended by David Copperfield and administered by the "tartar," Mr. Creakle. (*David Copperfield*, 1849–50.)

Mrs. Sapsea's Academy: a school taught by Mrs. Sapsea at Cloisterham before her marriage. (*Edwin Drood*, 1870.)

The Stepney Union schools: Pauper schools—so called—located at Limehouse, where corporal punishment was unknown and the standards of truthfulness were high. ("The Short-timers." *The Uncommercial Traveller*, 1860.)

Doctor Strong's school: the second school attended by David Copperfield to which he was sent by his aunt Betsey Trotwood; the school system was founded on "the faith and honour of the boys." (*David Copperfield*, 1849–50.)

The School: briefly mentioned in "Haunted House."

Miss Twinkleton's Seminary: otherwise known as the Nuns' House, a girls' school attended by Rosa Bud and Helena Landless; it had a light-hearted mistress, and the sketch contains a light-hearted description of the festivities in the bedrooms as the vacation draws near. (*Edwin Drood*, 1870.)

Mrs. Wackles's Ladies' Seminary: a very small day school for young ladies, located at Chelsea; good description of the teachers and of the courses that were studied. (*The Old Curiosity Shop*, 1841.)

Mr. Wopsle's great-aunt's evening school: the school attended by Pip before he began to have any expectations; the lesson-procedure is pungent in its hilarious satire. (*Great Expectations*, 1861.)

Workhouse school: brief reference in *Oliver Twist*, and to the picking of oakum; to which may be added the famous scenes of Oliver asking for more and of being apprenticed to a chimney-sweep. (*Oliver Twist*, 1837–9.)

Workhouse school: taught by the pauper schoolmaster, in "Our Schoolmaster," 1835; it is the first description of a school that Dickens wrote; it is a tolerant, kindly picture. (*Sketches by Boz*, 1835–6.)

APPENDIX C

"Infant Gardens"

The attempt to trace the authorship of the article entitled "Infant Gardens," attributed by Hughes to Dickens, was initiated by the fact that the style of the article appeared too scholarly, and lacked the verve of Dickens; furthermore, Hughes gave no authority for attributing the authorship to Dickens. A perusal of the critical accounts of *Household Words* led to an examination of Percy Fitzgerald's *Memories of Charles Dickens* (Bristol: Arrowsmith, 1913), which established the fact that the article did not appear in the list of articles which Dickens had either contributed to *Household Words* or those on which he had collaborated. This list had been compiled from the office record kept by W. H. Wills, Dickens's co-editor. This contributors' book was stated to have been in the possession of Rudolph Lehmann in 1913.

A bibliographical search revealed that Lehmann had published a book, *Charles Dickens as an Editor* (New York: Sturgis and Walton, 1912). It was hoped that this volume would reveal the identity of the author of "Infant Gardens." When a copy was finally located at Harvard University, however, this hope was frustrated; Lehmann, while positively asserting that the manuscript was in his possession (p. xv), and making frequent references to it for authority, failed not only to mention the article "Infant Gardens," but also failed to give the complete list.

It was discovered that B. W. Matz had collected the "Miscellaneous Papers, Plays, and Poems," for the National Edition (vols. XXXV and XXXVI, 1906–8), but unfortunately the edition was limited to 750 copies, none of which were readily available. Eventually, however, a reprint of these two volumes in one (New York: Bigelow, Brown and Company, Incorporated, n.d.) was located which contained Matz's Introduction, a list of Dickens's contributions to *Household Words* compiled from the official record which Lehmann had placed at Matz's disposal, and a photographic reproduction of a page of the contributors' book. In his Introduction Matz asserted: "There is now no longer any doubt existing concerning the identity of Dickens's own work (or the work of any contributor to his paper, for the matter of that). . . ." Since the article "Infant Gardens" did not appear in Matz's list this evidence was considered conclusive against Dickens's authorship of the article, but the identity of the actual author still remained a mystery.

Continued investigation at Harvard University revealed a copy *The First Editions of the Writings of Charles Dickens: A Bibliography* (London: Chapman and Hall, 1913), by John C. Eckel. The book, of course, could not be borrowed (the edition was limited to 250 copies), but photostat copies of pages 202 and 209 were secured which corroborated the evidence uncovered by Fitzgerald, Lehmann, and Matz. (A copy of this book, however, is now in my possession.)

An attempt was then made to trace the manuscript of the office book itself. The relevant entry in *Book-Prices Current* (London: Elliot Stock, 1930), vol. XLIV, p. 267, read:

Dickens (C.) Household Words, the Manuscript Office Book of this famous Periodical, under the heading of each number are given the names of every contributor, the title and length of the contribution, and the amount paid; the entries throughout are in the handwriting of W. H. Wills, Dickens's co-editor, hf. leather, oblong folio (826), Mar. 17, Sotheby

Mann, £32

Subsequent investigation, and correspondence with Mr. Leslie Staples, disclosed that the manuscript is now the property of Mrs. R. C. Lehmann, Fieldhead, Bourne End, Bucks. Both a photostat copy and a typed copy of the manuscript, however, have been placed in the Dickens House, 48 Doughty Street, London, W.C.1. The editor of *The Dickensian* checked the manuscript (photostat copy) at the Dickens House, and corroborated the fact that the article "Infant Gardens" published in *Household Words*, July 21, 1855, was written by Henry Morley.[1] This evidence was considered conclusive.

[1]Henry Morley (1832–1894) had opened a school in Manchester in 1848 based on the methods which were followed in the Moravian school which he attended as a boy at Neuwied, on the Rhine. At Dickens's invitation he gave up his school to join the editorial staff of *Household Words*, in 1850. Morley was an advanced thinker along educational lines; he began a series of lectures at the evening classes held in King's College in 1857, and, following the scholarship revealed in his comprehensive works on the history of English literature, in 1878 he was appointed Professor of English Languages and Literature at King's College. Fitzgerald says that Morley was the most frequent contributor, and sometimes Wills, Boz, and Morley all had a hand in the same paper.

BIBLIOGRAPHY

I. WRITINGS, LETTERS, MISCELLANEOUS PAPERS, AND SPEECHES OF CHARLES DICKENS MENTIONED IN THE FOOTNOTES

Writings
The Collected Works of Charles Dickens. London: Chapman and Hall, 1900. Thirty vols. All quotations in text are from this edition.

Letters
DEXTER, WALTER, ed. *Dickens to His Oldest Friend* (Thomas Beard). Limited ed. London and New York: Putnam, 1932. (Cited in text as Dexter, ed., *Dickens to His Oldest Friend.*)
—— *The Letters of Charles Dickens.* Bloomsbury: The Nonesuch Press, 1938. Three vols. (Cited in text as Dexter, ed., *Letters.*)
—— *The Unpublished Letters of Charles Dickens to Mark Lemon.* Limited ed. London: Halton & Truscott Smith, Ltd., 1927. (Cited in text as Dexter, ed., *Letters to Mark Lemon.*)
[HOGARTH, GEORGINA, and DICKENS, MAMEY, eds.] *The Letters of Charles Dickens.* Ed. by his sister-in-law and his eldest daughter. London: Macmillan and Co., Ltd., 1909. Three vols. in one. (Cited in text as Hogarth and Dickens, eds., *Letters.*)
JOHNSON, EDGAR, ed. *The Heart of Charles Dickens* (letters of Charles Dickens to the Baroness Burdett-Coutts). New York: Duell, Sloan and Pierce; Boston: Little, Brown and Company, 1952. (Cited in text as Johnson, ed., *Heart of Charles Dickens.*)
LIVINGSTONE, FLORA V., ed. *Charles Dickens's Letters to Charles Lever.* Cambridge, Mass.: Harvard University Press, 1933. (Cited in text as Livingstone, ed., *Letters to Charles Lever.*)
OSBORNE, C. C., ed. *Letters of Charles Dickens to the Baroness Burdett-Coutts.* London: John Murray, 1931. (Cited in text as Osborne, ed., *Letters.*)
Letters and other MSS of Charles Dickens found in the Berg Collection, New York Public Library. (Cited in text as Berg MSS.)
Letters and other MSS of Charles Dickens found in the Pierpont Morgan Library, New York, including 600 letters to the Baroness Burdett-Coutts; 142 to Wilkie Collins; 32 to Mary Boyle; 213 to his sister or her husband, Henry Austin; 181 to Macready; 61 to Macrone, Overs, etc. (Cited in text as Morgan MSS.)
Letters and other MSS found in the MSS division of the New York Public Library, including the Harkness collection. (Cited in text as Harkness MSS.)

Miscellaneous Papers
MATZ, B. W., ed. *Miscellaneous Papers by Charles Dickens.* London: Chapman and Hall, Ltd., 1911. Two vols. (Cited in text as Matz, ed., *Miscellaneous Papers*, and thereafter abbreviated to *Misc. P.*)

Speeches
SHEPHERD, R. H., ed. *The Speeches of Charles Dickens.* London: Chatto and Windus, 1906. (Cited in text as Shepherd, ed., *Speeches.*)
Speeches by Charles Dickens. Ed. anon. London: John Camden Hotten, 1870. (Cited in text as *Speeches by Charles Dickens.*)
Speech, unpublished. The Parrish Collection, Princeton University Library. Quoted as found in *The Dickensian*, XLIV (June, 1948), 139–141.

Journal Articles
All the Year Round, Household Words, Household Narrative of Current Events.
(See text for use made of these journals.)

II. BIOGRAPHICAL AND CRITICAL WORKS

ADAMS, MABEL ELLERY. "Dickens's Influence on Education." *The Dickensian*, XXVI (June, 1930), 177–181.
ADDISON, WILLIAM. *In the Steps of Charles Dickens*. London: Rich and Cowan, 1955.
ADRIAN, A. A. "Nicholas Nickleby and Educational Reform." *Nineteenth Century Fiction*, IV (Dec., 1949), 237–241.
———— *Georgina Hogarth and the Dickens Circle*. London: Oxford University Press, 1957.
Anon. "Charles Dickens's Use of the Bible." *Temple Bar*, XXVII (Sept., 1869), 225–234.
———— "Dickens and Daudet." *Cornhill Magazine*, LXV (Oct., 1891), 400–415.
———— "Doctor Marigold's Prescriptions." *Saturday Review*, XX (Dec., 1865), 763–764.
———— "The License of Modern Novelists." *Edinburgh Review*, vol. CVI, no. CCXV (July, 1857), 124–156.
———— "Mr. Dickens's Amateur Theatricals." *Macmillan's Magazine*, CXXXV (Jan., 1871), 211–218.
———— "Mr. Pickwick and Nicholas Nickleby." *Scribner's Monthly*, XX (Sept., 1880), 641–656.
———— "Mrs. Lirriper's Legacy." *Saturday Review*, XVIII (Dec., 1864), 724–725.
———— "Mrs. Lirriper's Lodgings." *Saturday Review*, XVII (Dec., 1863), 758–760.
———— "Oliver Twist." *Quarterly Review*, LXIV (June, 1839), 85–102.
AXSON, STOCKTON. *Dickens and Social Reform*. Rice Institute Pamphlet, III. Houston, Tex.: The Rice Institute, 1916.
BAGEHOT, W. "Charles Dickens." *Literary Studies*. II. New York: Dutton, 1911.
BECKLES, WILLSON. *From Quebec to Piccadilly*. London: Jonathan Cape, 1929. *Passim.*
BENNET, Sir GEORGE DOUGLAS. "How Stands Dickens Today?" *The Dickensian*, XXV (autumn, 1939), 247–253.
BERESFORD, J. D. "Successors of Dickens." *Living Age*, CCCXX (Feb., 1924), 374–376.
BLORE, G. H. "Charles Dickens: Novelist and Social Reformer." *Victorian Worthies*. London: Humphrey Milford, Oxford University Press, 1920.
BOOTH, MEYRICK. *Charles Dickens und seine Werke in pädagogischer Beleuchtung*. Zürich: Schulthess und Co., 1909.
BOWEN, W. H. *Charles Dickens and His Family*. Cambridge: W. Heffer and Sons, Ltd., 1956.
BREEN, ANNA MARY. "Dickens's Work in the Field of Education." Unpublished M.A. thesis, University of Ottawa, 1942.
BUCHANAN, ROBERT. "The Good Genie of Fiction." *St. Paul's Magazine*, X (Feb., 1872), 130–148.
CARLTON, W. J. "Charles Dickens." *The Dickensian*, XLIX (March, 1935), 58.
———— *Charles Dickens: Shorthand Writer*. London: Cecil Palmer, 1926.
CHESTERTON, G. K. "Charles Dickens." *The Great Victorians*. Ed. H. J. and H. Massingham. London: Ivor Nicholson and Watson, 1932.
———— *Charles Dickens: A Critical Study*. New York: Dodd, Mead, 1911.
CLARK, CUMBERLAND. *Charles Dickens and the Yorkshire Schools*. London: Chiswick Press, privately, 1918.

CLARK, WILLIAM R. "The Rationale of Dickens' Death Rate." *Boston University Studies in English,* II (autumn, 1956), 125–134.

CLARKE, CHARLES and MARY COWDEN. *Recollections of Writers.* London: Sampson Low, Marston, Searle and Rivington, 1878.

CLINTON-BADDELEY, V. C. "Benevolent Teachers of Youth." *Cornhill Magazine,* MXIII (autumn, 1957), 361–382.

CLUTTON, BROCK A. "Dickens." *Essay on Books.* London: Methuen, 1920.

COLEMAN, Dr. A. P. "Sixth Report of the Bureau of Mines." *Glimpses of Charles Dickens.* Toronto: privately, 1898.

COLLINS, P. A. W. "Dickens and Adult Education." *British Journal of Educational Studies,* III (May, 1955), 115–127.

———— *Dickens's Periodicals: Articles on Education.* An annotated bibliography. Vaughan College Papers no. 3. Leicester: Vaughan College, 1957.

COOPER, T. P. "Burial of Boys in the Delightful Village of Dotheboys." *The Dickensian,* XXV (spring, 1939), 107–112.

CROTCH, W. WALTER. *Charles Dickens: Social Reformer.* London: Chapman and Hall, 1913.

———— "Dickens as an Educational Reformer." *The Dickensian,* XII (July, 1916), 177–178.

CROYDEN, JOHN. "Film Prospecting among the Yorkshire Schools." *The Dickensian,* XLI (June, 1945), 121–125.

DARROW, DOROTHY H. "Education in the Nineteenth Century as Portrayed by Charles Dickens." Unpublished M.A. thesis, Iowa State University, 1937.

DARWIN, BERNARD. *Dickens.* London: Duckworth, 1933.

———— *The Dickens Advertiser.* London: Elkin Mathews and Marrot, 1930.

DAVIS, EARLE R. *Charles Dickens and Wilkie Collins.* Wichita, Kan.: University of Wichita, 1945.

———— *The Creation of Dickens's David Copperfield.* Wichita, Kan.: University of Wichita, 1941.

DAVIS, H. "Dickens, Carlyle, and Tennyson." *Atlantic Monthly,* CLXIV (Dec., 1939), 810–819. Based on diary of J. S. Pike.

DAWSON, W. J. "Dickens." *Makers of English Fiction.* New York: Revell, 1905.

DEXTER, WALTER. "Charles Dickens: Journalist." *Nineteenth Century and After,* CXVI (June, 1934), 705–716.

———— "Charles Dickens One Hundred Years Ago." *The Dickensian,* XX (Jan., 1924), 12–17.

———— "Dickens and the *Morning Chronicle.*" *Fortnightly Review,* CXLII (Nov., 1934), 591–598.

———— *The England of Dickens.* London: Cecil Palmer, 1925.

DIBELIUS, WILHELM. *Charles Dickens.* Leipzig und Berlin: B. G. Teubner, 1916.

DICKENS, CHARLES. "Glimpses of Charles Dickens." *North American Review,* CLX (May, 1895), 525–537; (June, 1895), 677–684.

DICKENS, HENRY F. *Memories of My Father.* London: Duffield and Company, 1929.

DICKENS, MAMIE. "Charles Dickens at Home." *Cornhill Magazine,* N.S., IV (Jan., 1885), 32–51. (London: Smith Elder & Co.)

———— *My Father as I Recall Him.* London: The Roxburghe Press, n.d.

DOLBY, CHARLES. *Charles Dickens as I Knew Him.* London: T. F. Unwin, n.d. [about 1884]

DOUGHTY, Lady. "Dickens's Child Characters." *Living Age,* CCLXV (May, 1910), 373–375.

ECKEL, JOHN C. *The First Editions of the Writings of Charles Dickens: A Bibliography.* London: Chapman and Hall, Ltd., 1913.

EWING, J. A. "Squeers as a Model." *The Dickensian*, II (Sept., 1906), 233.

FAWCETT, FRANK D. *Dickens the Dramatist*. London: W. H. Allen, 1952.

FERGUSON, D. "Superman and the Blacking Works." *Saturday Review of English Literature*, XXXVI (Jan. 10, 1953), 10–12.

FIELDING, K. J. *Charles Dickens*. London: Longmans, Green, and Co., 1953.

———— "Charles Dickens and the Department of Practical Art." *Modern Language Review*, XLVIII (July, 1953), 270–277.

———— "Letters of Dickens to Miss Burdett-Coutts." *The Times Literary Supplement*, no. 2561 and 2562, 50th year, (March 2, 9, 1951).

———— "Mill and Gradgrind." *Nineteenth Century Fiction*, XI (Sept., 1956), 149–151.

———— "Miss Burdett-Coutts: Some Misconceptions." *Ibid.*, VIII (March, 1954), 314–318.

FIELDING, K. J., and G. G. GRUBB, eds. "New Letters from Charles Dickens to John Forster." *Boston University Studies in English*, II (autumn, 1956), 140–193.

F[IELDS], J. T. "Some Memories of Charles Dickens." *Atlantic Monthly*, XXVI (Aug., 1870), 235–245.

FITZGERALD, PERCY. *Memories of Charles Dickens*. Bristol: Arrowsmith, 1913.

FORD, G. H. *Dickens and His Readers*. Princeton, N.J.: Princeton University Press, 1955.

FORSTER, J. *The Life of Charles Dickens*. Leipzig: Bernard Tauchnitz, 1872. Three vols.

FRIESER, WALTER. *Die Schulen bei Dickens*. Halle a.S.: Buchdruckerei von Heinrich John, 1909.

GERBER, H. E. "Hard Times: Experience in Teaching." *College English*, XV (March, 1954), 351–353.

GISSING, G. R. *Charles Dickens: A Critical Study*. New York: Dodd, Mead, 1924.

———— *Forster's Life of Dickens*. London: Chapman and Hall, Ltd., 1902.

———— *The Immortal Dickens*. London: G. Palmer, 1925.

GRUBB, G. G. "Charles Dickens: Journalist." Unpublished Ph.D. thesis, University of North Carolina, 1940.

GUMMER, ELLIS N. *Dickens' Works in Germany, 1837–1937*. Oxford: At the Clarendon Press, 1940.

HAMILTON, C. "Some Letters of Charles Dickens." *Hobbies*, LVIII (Jan., 1954), 131–132.

HARDY, E. "Yorkshire Schools." *Living Age*, CCLXIX (April, 1911), 218–220.

HARRISON, FREDERICK. "Dickens's Place in Literature." *The Forum*, XVIII (Jan., 1895), 543–553.

H[ELPS], A. "In Memoriam." *Macmillan's Magazine*, XXII (July, 1870), 236–240.

HILL, T. W. "Books that Dickens Read." *The Dickensian*, XLV (March, 1949), 81–90.

———— "Dickensian Biography." *Ibid.*, XLVII (Dec., 1950), 10–15; XLVII (March, 1951), 72–79.

HOUSE, HUMPHRY. *The Dickens World*. London: Humphrey Milford, and Oxford University Press, 1941.

HUGHES, JAMES L. *Dickens as an Educator*. New York: Appleton, 1900.

———— "What Charles Dickens Did for Childhood." *Century Magazine*, LVII (Feb., 1899), 493–501.

HUMPHREYS, ARTHUR. *Charles Dickens and His First Schoolmaster*. Limited ed. Manchester: The Hotspur Press, 1926.

JACKSON, T. A. *Charles Dickens: The Progress of a Radical*. New York, International Publishers, 1938.

JACOX, FRANCIS. "Mr. Gradgrind Typically Considered." *Bentley's Miscellany*, LX, 613–620. London: Bentley, 1866.

JOHNSON, EDGAR. *Charles Dickens*. New York: Simon and Schuster, 1952. Two vols.

——— "The Scope of Charles Dickens." *Saturday Review of English Literature*, XXXV (Nov. 29, 1952), 13–14.

KITTON, F. D. *Charles Dickens*. Edinburgh: T. C. and E. C. Jack, n.d. [1902]

——— *The Dickens Country*. London: Adam and Charles Black, 1905.

——— *The Minor Writings of Charles Dickens*. London: Elliot Stock, 1900.

——— *The Novels of Charles Dickens*. London: E. Stock, 1897.

LANG, ANDREW. "Andrew Lang on Dickens." *Book Lover's Magazine*, n.v. (Jan., 1903), 59–63.

LANGTON, ROBERT. *The Childhood and Youth of Charles Dickens*. London: Hutchinson, 1891.

LAWSON, McEWAN. *The Challenge to Oppression*. London: S.C.M. Press Ltd., 1947.

LEACOCK, STEPHEN. *Charles Dickens: Life and Work*. London: P. Davies, 1933.

LEAVIS, F. R. "Hard Times." *The Great Tradition*. New York: Doubleday and Co., 1954.

LEHMANN, R. C. *Charles Dickens as Editor*. London: Smith, Elder and Co., 1912. [Also Sturgis and Walton, 1912]

LEWES, GEORGE HENRY. "Dickens in Relation to Criticism." *Fortnightly Review*, XI (Feb., 1872), 141–154.

LEY, J. W. T. *The Dickens Circle*. London: Chapman and Hall, 1918.

——— "The Dickens Fellowship." *The Dickensian*, IX (Oct., 1923), 178–195.

——— "Dickens's Views on the Government Education Bill." *Ibid.*, II (May, 1906), 123–125.

LINDSAY, JACK. *Charles Dickens*. New York: Philosophical Library, 1950.

McCORMICK, I. C. "Defense for Hard Times." *Living Age*, CCXC (Sept. 9, 1916), 690–692.

MANNING, JOHN. "Charles Dickens and 'The Glasgow System.'" *School and Society*, LXXXIII (June 9, 1956), 202–206.

——— "Charles Dickens and the Oswego System." *History of Ideas*, XVIII (Oct., 1957), 580–586.

MARGUERITE, Sister LOUISE. "Dickens's Bill of Rights for the Child in the Light of Catholic Principles of Education." Unpublished M.A. thesis, University of Ottawa, 1949.

MARZIALS, FRANK T. *Life of Charles Dickens*. London: Walter Scott, 1887.

MATCHETT, W. "Dickens at Wellington House Academy." *Living Age*, CCLXXI (Oct. 14, 1911), 76–86.

MATZ, B. W. "Charles Dickens and Reform." *The Bookman*, XXXIX (Nov., 1910), 79–86.

MAUROIS, A. *Dickens*. Tr. Hamish Miles. London: John Lane, the Bodley Head, 1934.

——— "The Philosophy of Dickens." *The Forum*, LXXXI (Jan., 1929), 54–59.

——— "The Youth of Dickens." *Ibid.*, LXXX (Oct., 1928), 562–574.

MILLER, WILLIAM. *The Dickens Student and Collector*. Cambridge, Mass.: Harvard University Press, 1946. (A bibliography sponsored by the Boston branch of the Dickens Fellowship)

MORRIS, MOWBRAY. "Charles Dickens." *Fortnightly Review*, N.S., XXXII (July, 1882), 762–779.

NICOLL, W. ROBERTSON. *Dickens's Own Story*. London: Chapman and Hall, 1923.

NORRIS, E. A. "Dickens and Children." *Living Age*, CCLXX (Aug., 1911), 394–399.

OLIPHANT, JAMES. "Charles Dickens." *Victorian Novelists*. London: Blackie and Son, 1899.

PARNELL, NANCY. "Schools in the Novels of Dickens." *The Dickensian*, XXV (spring, 1929), 108–110.

PEARSON, HESKETH. *Dickens: His Character, Comedy and Career*. New York: Harper and Brothers, 1949.

PEMBERTON, T. E. *Charles Dickens and the Stage*. London: George Redway, 1888.

PHILIP, A. J. *A Dickens Dictionary*. London: Simpkin Marshall, 1928.

PIERCE, GILBERT A., and WILLIAM A. WHEELER. *A Dickens Dictionary*. Boston: Houghton, Mifflin, and Co., 1872.

POPE-HENNESSY, UNA. *Charles Dickens*. London: Chatto and Windus, 1945.

POWELL, T. B. "Doctor Blimber's Establishment." *The Dickensian*, XX (April, 1924), 90–104.

PRIESTLEY, J. B. "Dickens and Thackeray." *The English Novel*. London: Nelson, 1935.

PUGH, EDWIN P. *Charles Dickens: The Apostle of the People*. London: New Age Press, 1908.

QUILLER-COUCH, Sir A. T. *Charles Dickens and Other Victorians*. Cambridge: Cambridge University Press, 1925.

ROLFE, FRANKLIN P. "The Dickens Letters in the Huntington Library." *Huntington Library Quarterly*, I (April, 1928), 335–363.

SALA, G. A. "Dickens as I Knew Him." *Things I Have Seen and People I Have Known*. I. London and Paris: Cassell and Co., Ltd., 1894.

SHAW, G. B. "Charles Dickens." A *Bookman* Extra Number. London: Hodder and Stoughton, 1914.

SIBBALD, W. A. "Dickens Revisited." *Living Age*, CCLII (March, 1907), 524–534.

SITWELL, O. *et al.* "Dickens and the Modern Novel." *Trio*. London: Macmillan, 1938.

SLOAN, J. M. "Robert Burns and Charles Dickens." *Living Age*, CCLV (Oct. 5, 1907), 8–18.

STEWART, D. A. "Dickens the Reformer." Winnipeg *Western Municipal News*, Feb. 7, 1933. (An address delivered to the Winnipeg Branch of the Dickens Fellowship)

STEWART, J. I. M. "Charles Dickens." *The Times Educational Supplement*, no. 2089, 45th year (June 3, 1955), 594.

STONEHOUSE, J. H. *Green Leaves*. London: The Piccadilly Fountain Press, 1931.

STOREY, GLADYS. *Dickens and Daughter*. London: Frederick Muller, Ltd., 1939.

SUDDABY, JOHN. "Little Jo." *The Dickensian*, VIII (Sept., 1912), 246–250.

SWINBURNE, A. C. *Charles Dickens*. London: Chatto and Windus, 1913.

SYMONS, JULIAN. *Charles Dickens*. London: A. Barker, 1951.

WARD, A. W. *Charles Dickens*. A lecture delivered at Hulme Town Hall, Nov. 30, 1870. Issued as a penny pamphlet, n.d. Also Manchester: John Heywood, 1870.

—— *Dickens*. English Men of Letters Series, XX. London: Macmillan, 1908.

WETHERALL, FRANK. "The Education of David Copperfield." *The Dickensian*, XXXI (spring, 1935), 46–50.

WILLIAMSON, E. S. "Glimpses of Charles Dickens." *Massey's Magazine*, II (Aug., 1896), 107–111.

WILSON, EDMUND. *Eight Essays*. New York: Doubleday and Co., Inc., 1954.

WRIGHT, THOMAS. *The Life of Charles Dickens*. New York: Charles Scribner's Sons, 1936.

ZWEIG, STEFAN. *Three Masters: Balzac, Dickens, and Dostoeffsky*. Tr. from the German by Eden and Cedar Paul. London: Allen and Unwin, 1930.

III. Educational, Literary, and Social History

ADAMSON, JOHN WILLIAM. *English Education, 1789–1902.* Cambridge: Cambridge University Press, 1930.

Anon. "First and Second Reports of the Training School at Battersea, 1841." *American Journal of Education,* XXII (Sept., 1860), 170–199.

———— "Ragged Schools." *The Dickensian,* I (June, 1905), 141.

———— "Thoughts and Experiences of a Guardian of the Poor." *Macmillan's Magazine,* XXII (June, 1870), 100–105.

ARMYTAGE, W. H. G. "Friedrich Froebel." *History of Education Journal,* III (summer, 1952), 107–113.

ARNOLD, MATTHEW. *Reports of Elementary Schools, 1852–1882.* Ed. with introd. by Rt. Hon. Sir Frederick Sandford. London and New York: Macmillan, 1889.

ASHLEY, ROBERT P. Jr. "The Career of Wilkie Collins." Unpublished Ph.D. thesis, Harvard University, 1949.

BAILEY, DOROTHY M. "Some Aspects of the English Novel of the Nineteenth Century." Unpublished M.A. thesis, Loyola University, Chicago, 1938.

BAKER, E. A. "Charles Dickens." *The History of the English Novel.* VII, VIII. London: Witherby, 1937.

BARBAULD, Mrs., Dr. AIKEN, and CECIL HARTLEY. *Evenings at Home.* New York: C. S. Francis and Co., 1857.

BINNS, H. B. *A Century of English Education: Being the Centenary History of the British and Foreign School Society, 1808–1908.* London: Dent, 1908.

BIRCHENOUGH, C. *History of Elementary Education in England and Wales.* London: University Tutorial Press, 1938.

BREMNER, CHRISTINA. *Education of Girls and Women in Great Britain.* Limited ed. London: Sonnenschein, 1897.

BRERETON, CLOUDESLEY. "Early Education Sixty Years Ago." *Contemporary Review,* CXLIV (Oct., 1933), 464–469.

BROUGHAM, H. L. *The Life and Times of Henry Lord Brougham.* Written by himself. New York: Harper and Brothers, 1871. Three vols.

BRUBACHER, J. S. *A History of the Problems of Education.* New York: McGraw-Hill Book Co., Inc., 1947.

BRYANT, ARTHUR. *The English Saga.* London: Collins, Eyre, and Spottiswoode, 1940.

BUTLER, SAMUEL
"Bishop Butler's Sermon on Charity Schools." In *The Schoolmaster: Essays from Ascham, Milton, Locke, Butler, from Quarterly Journal of Education and Lectures Delivered before the American Institute of Instruction.* London: C. Knight, 1836.

CAZAMIAN, LOUIS F. *Le Roman social en Angleterre.* Paris: Société Nouvelle de Librairie et d'Edition, 1904.

CECIL, DAVID. *Early Victorian Novelists.* Harmondsworth, Middlesex: Penguin Series, 1948.

CHEVALLEY, ABEL. *The Modern English Novel.* Tr. Ben Ray Redman. New York: A. A. Knopf, 1947.

CONNELL, W. F. *The Educational Thought and Influence of Matthew Arnold.* London: Routledge and Kegan Paul, 1950.

CORBIN, JOHN. *Schoolboy Life in England.* London: Harper and Brothers, 1897.

CREEVEY, THOMAS. *Creevey Papers.* Ed. J. Gore. London: John Murray, 1948.

CRUIKSHANK, R. J. *Charles Dickens and Early Victorian England.* New York: The Chanticleer Press, 1949.

CRUSE, AMY. *The Englishman and His Books in the Early Nineteenth Century.* London: Harrap, 1930.

———— *The Victorians and Their Books.* London: Allen and Unwin, 1935.

CURTIS, S. J. *History of Education in Great Britain.* London: University Tutorial Press, Ltd., 1948.
DARTON, J. HARVEY. "Children's Books." *Cambridge History of English Literature,* XI, 380 ff. Cambridge: Cambridge University Press, 1916.
DEARSLEY, R. L. "The Education of the Poor." *The Dickensian,* XXXVI (winter, 1940), 45–48.
DOBBS, A. E. *Education and Social Movements.* London: Longmans, Green, and Company, 1919.
EDGAR, PELHAM. *The Art of the Novel.* New York: Macmillan, 1933.
EDGEWORTH, MARIA and R. L. *Practical Education.* London: J. Johnston, St. Paul's Churchyard, 1798. Two vols., pages numbered continuously.
FITCH, Sir JOSHUA. *Thomas and Matthew Arnold and Their Influence on English Education.* New York: Scribner, 1898.
FROEBEL, FRIEDRICH WILHELM AUGUST.
Autobiography of Friedrich Froebel. Tr. E. Michaelis and H. K. Moore. Syracuse, N.Y.: Bardeen, 1908.
The Student's Froebel. Ed. W. H. Herford. London: Sir Isaac Pitman and Sons, Ltd., 1911. Two vols.
See also Armytage, W. H. G. (above)
GARDINER, DOROTHY. *English Girlhood at School.* London: Oxford University Press, 1929.
GILBERT, A. M. "The Work of Lord Brougham for Education in England." Unpublished Ph.D. thesis, University of Pennsylvania, 1922.
GREGORY, ALFRED. *Robert Raikes.* London: Hodder and Stoughton, 1880.
GREVILLE, CHARLES CAVENDISH FULKE.
The Greville Diary. Ed. P. W. Wilson. New York: Doubleday, Page and Co., 1927. Two vols.
The Letters of Charles Greville. Ed. Rev. A. H. Johnston. London: T. Fisher Unwin, 1924.
HAAR, EVA C. "Education in the Eighteenth Century English Novel." Unpublished Ph.D. thesis, Johns Hopkins University, Baltimore, 1942.
HAMMOND, J. L. and BARBARA. *The Bleak Age.* Drayton, Middlesex: Penguin Books, Ltd., 1947.
HAYWARD, A. L. *The Days of Dickens.* London: George Routledge and Sons, n.d. [1926]
History in Hansard, 1803–1900. Ed. Stephen King-Hall and Ann Dewar. London: Constable and Company, 1952.
HUDSON, JAS. W. *The History of Adult Education.* London: Longman, Brown, Green, and Longmans, 1851.
JONES, M. G. *The Charity School Movement.* Cambridge: Cambridge University Press, 1938.
JUDGES, A. W., ed. *Pioneers of English Education.* London: Faber and Faber, n.d. [c. 1935]
KAY-SHUTTLEWORTH, Sir JAMES P. *Four Periods of Public Education.* London: Longmans, 1862.
———— *Memorandum on Popular Education.* London: Ridgeway, Piccadilly, 1868.
LAMBERT, MARGARET. *When Victoria Began to Reign.* London: Faber and Faber, Ltd., 1937.
LANCASTER, JOSEPH. *Improvements in Education.* London: Darton and Harvey, 1805.
LOVETT, R. M., and HELEN S. HUGHES. *The History of the Novel in England.* London: G. G. Harrap and Co., n.d. [1951 reprint of 1932 Boston ed.]
LOWNDES, G. *The Silent Social Revolution.* London: Humphrey Milford, 1937.
MANGNALL, RICHMAL. *Historical and Miscellaneous Questions for the Use of Young People, etc.* London: Wm. Tegg and Co., 1851.

MAYHEW, HENRY. *London Labour and the London Poor.* London: Charles Griffin and Co., n.d. [*c.* 1855] Four vols.

MAYO, CHARLES and ELIZABETH. *Pestalozzi and His Principles.* Fourth ed. London: Simpkin *et al.*, 1890.

MAYO, ELIZABETH. *Lessons on Objects.* London: Seeleys, 1851.

MONCRIEFF, A. R. H. *A Book about Schools.* London: A. and C. Black, 1925.

MONTMORENCY, J. E. G. DE. *State Intervention in English Education.* Cambridge: Cambridge University Press, 1902.

MOOD, ROBERT G. "Maria Edgeworth's Apprenticeship." Unpublished Ph.D. thesis, University of Illinois, 1938.

MURPHY, T. "Interpretation in the Dickens Period." *Quarterly Journal of Speech,* XLI (Oct., 1955), 243–249.

NEIL, S. D. *A Short History of the English Novel.* London: Jarrolds, 1951.

PATTERSON, CLARA BURDETT-COUTTS. *Angela Burdett-Coutts and the Victorians.* London: John Murray, 1953.

PEMBERTON, W. BARING. *William Cobbett.* Harmondsworth, Middlesex: Penguin Books, 1949.

PERCIVAL, ALICIA C. *The English Miss, Today and Yesterday.* London: George C. Harrap and Co., Ltd., 1939.

PHILPOTT, H. B. *London At School.* London: Unwin, 1904.

PLOWMAN, THOMAS F. *In the Days of Victoria.* London: John Lane, 1918.

POLLARD, HUGH M. *Pioneers of Popular Education, 1760–1850.* London: John Murray, 1956.

PRIDEAUX, E. B. R. *A Survey of Elementary English Education.* London: Blackie and Son, Ltd., 1914.

ROBERTS, R. D., ed. *Education in the Nineteenth Century.* Cambridge: Cambridge University Press, 1901.

SHORE, W. T. *D'Orsay, or the Complete Dandy.* London: John Long, Ltd., 1911.

SMITH, FRANK. *A History of English Elementary Education.* London: The University of London Press, 1931.

—— *The Life and Work of Sir James Kay-Shuttleworth.* London: John Murray, 1923.

SNEYD-KYNNERSLEY, E. M. *Some Passages in the Life of One of His Majesty's Inspectors.* London: Macmillan, 1910.

STOW, DAVID. *The Training System, Moral Training School, and Normal Training Seminary.* Tenth ed. London: Longman, Brown, Green, and Longmans, 1854.

THOMSON, DAVID. *England in the Nineteenth Century.* Harmondsworth, Middlesex: Penguin Books, Ltd., 1950.

TREVELYAN, G. M. *English Social History.* London: Longmans, Green, and Co., 1942.

TROLLOPE, ANTHONY. *An Autobiography.* Edinburgh and London: Wm. Blackwood and Sons, 1883.

TUER, A. W. *History of the Horn Book.* London: The Leadenhall Press, 1896. Two vols.

—— *One Thousand Quaint Cuts from Books of Other Days.* London: Fields and Tuer, 1886.

—— *Stories from Old-Fashioned Children's Books.* London: The Leadenhall Press, 1899–1900.

WILDERSPIN, SAMUEL. *The Infant System for Developing the Intellectual and Moral Powers of All Children from One to Seven Years of Age.* Eighth ed. London: Hodson, 1852.

—— *A Manual for the Religious and Moral Instruction of Young Children in the Nursery and Infant School.* London: Hamilton, 1845.

WOODWARD, E. L. *The Age of Reform.* Oxford: Clarendon Press, 1938.

YOUNG, G. M. *Victorian England.* New York: Doubleday, 1954.

IV. GOVERNMENT DOCUMENTS

Hansard: Parliamentary Debates
First Series: vol. IX, July 13, 1807.
Second Series: vol. II, June 28, 1820.
Third Series: vol. XX, July 30, 1833; vol. XXVII, May 21, 1835; vol. XLII, May
    7, 1838; vol. XCI, April 19, 1847; vol. CCLII, May 31, 1880.

Reports
Children's Employment Commission, 1842
    Reports from the Commissioners, 1842. Three vols. Children's Employment
    Commission. *Parliamentary Papers*, vols. XV, XVI, and XVII. London:
    William Clowes and Sons, 1842.
Children's Employment Commission, 1843
    Reports From the Commissioners. Vol. II. Children's Employment Commis-
    sion. Second Report of the Commissioners on the Trades and Manufacturers.
    Parliamentary Papers. Vol. XIII, 1843. London: William Clowes and Sons,
    1843.
Education Commission, 1816–18
    Reports from the Select Committee on the Education of the Lower Orders.
    Reports From the Committees, *Parliamentary Papers*, First Report, Parts i to
    v, vol. IV, 1816, and vol. III, p. 81, 1817; Second Report, etc., vol. IV, 1818.
    Five reports. Ordered to be printed by the House of Commons, 25 May–5
    June, 1818. [Brougham]
Education Commission, 1861
    Reports of the Commissioners to Inquire into the Present State of Education
    in England. *Parliamentary Papers*, vol. XXI, 1861. Six vols. Pts. 1–6. London:
    George Edward Eyre and William Spottiswoode, 1861. [Newcastle]
Education Commission, 1864
    Reports of Her Majesty's Commissioners Appointed to Inquire into the
    Revenues and Management of Certain Colleges and Schools, etc. *Parliamen-
    tary Papers*, vols. XX and XXI, 1864. Four vols. London: George Edward
    Eyre and William Spottiswoode, 1864. [Clarendon]
Midland Mining Commission, 1843
    Reports From the Commissioners. Vol. II. Midland Mining Commission.
    First Report, South Staffordshire. *Parliamentary Papers*, vol. XIII, 1843.
    London: William Clowes and Sons, 1843.

Statutes
Statutes at Large. . . . Cambridge [London], 1762–1882, 121 vols. in 125.
Statutes Revised, 1236–1920. Second ed. London: H.M.S.O., 1928–9. Four vols.

V. MISCELLANEOUS WORKS QUOTED IN THE TEXT

BENSON, E. F. *Charlotte Brontë*. London: Longmans, Green, 1932.
BENTHAM, JEREMY. *Works*. I. Edinburgh: Wm. Tait, 1843.
BESANT, Sir WALTER. *Autobiography*. New York: Dodd Mead and Co., 1902.
BLACKMORE, R. D. *Lorna Doone*. London and Glasgow: Collins, n.d.
BOYLE, MARY. *Mary Boyle: Her Book*. London: Murray, 1901.
BRAILSFORD, H. N. *Shelley, Godwin and Their Circle*. Home University Series.
    London: Williams and Norgate, 1919.
BRONTË, CHARLOTTE. *Jane Eyre*. New York: Macmillan, 1929.
――― *Shirley*. New York: Kelmscott Society, n.d.
DAY, THOMAS. *Sandford and Merton*. London: Warren, 1865.

DISRAELI, BENJAMIN. *Sybil*. Ed. Victor Cohen. London: Macmillan, 1934.

ELIOT, GEORGE. *The Mill on the Floss*. New York: Harper, 1860.

FARRAR, F. G. *Eric, or Little by Little*. New York: Dutton, 1902.

GASKELL, ELIZABETH. *Mary Barton*. London: Humphrey Milford, 1935.

—— *Life of Charlotte Brontë*. London: Oxford University Press, 1857.

—— *Wives and Daughters*. London: Humphrey Milford, 1935.

HALDANE, ELIZABETH. *Mrs. Gaskell and Her Friends*. London: Hodder and Stoughton, 1930.

HANSON, LAWRENCE and E. M. *The Four Brontës*. London: Oxford University Press, 1949.

HARE, AUGUSTUS J. C. *The Story of My Life*. New York: Dodd, Mead and Co., 1896–1901. Four vols.

HART-DAVIS, RUPERT. *Hugh Walpole*. London: Macmillan and Co., Ltd., 1952.

HARTE, BRET. "Dickens in Camp." *The Poetical Works of Bret Harte*. Boston: Houghton, Mifflin and Company, 1882.

HUGHES, THOMAS. *Tom Brown's Schooldays*. London: Macmillan and Co., 1890.

HUNT, LEIGH. *Autobiography*. I. London: Constable and Co., 1903.

KINGSLEY, CHARLES. *Alton Locke*. London: Macmillan, 1911.

LAMB, CHARLES. *Charles Lamb and Elia*. Ed. J. E. Morpurgo. London: Penguin Books, Ltd., 1948.

—— *Essays of Elia*. London: J. M. Dent and Sons, Ltd., 1909.

—— *The Letters of Charles Lamb*. Ed. E. V. Lucas. London: J. M. Dent and Sons, Ltd., 1945. Two vols.

LANCASTER, JOSEPH. *Report of the Singular Results of Joseph Lancaster's Discoveries in Education*. Montreal: n.p., n.d. [Public Reference Library, Toronto]

MARRYAT, FREDERICK. *Mr. Midshipman Easy*. London: J. M. Dent and Sons, Ltd., 1925.

MILL, J. S. *On Liberty*. London: Oxford University Press, 1954.

MORLEY, JOHN. *The Life of Richard Cobden*. New ed. London: Chapman and Hall, Ltd., 1883.

RUSKIN, JOHN. *Stones of Venice. Works*, XI. New York: Longmans, Green and Co., 1904.

SALA, GEORGE AUGUSTUS. *Life and Adventures*. I. New York: Chas. Scribner's Sons, 1895. Two vols.

SCOTT, Sir S. H. *The Exemplary Mr. Day*. London: Faber, 1933.

SMITH, ADAM. *An Inquiry into the Nature and Cause of the Wealth of Nations*. Oxford: Clarendon Press, 1869. Two vols.

STEVENSON, LIONEL. *The Showman of Vanity Fair*. London: Chapman and Hall, Ltd., 1947.

STRAUS, RALPH. *Sala*. London: Constable and Co., 1942.

THACKERAY, W. M. *Vanity Fair*. London: Blackie, n.d.

WALPOLE, HUGH. *Jeremy at Crale*. New York: Doran, 1939.

—— *Mr. Perrin and Mr. Traill*. Toronto: Dent, 1935.

WELLS, H. G. *Joan and Peter*. Toronto: Macmillan, 1910.

—— *Kipps*. London: Collins, 1929.

WILLIS, N. PARKER. *Famous Persons and Places*. Auburn, N.Y.: Alden, Beardsley, and Co., 1854.

INDEX

The following abbreviations are used in parentheses to indicate the periodicals in which Dickens's articles appeared, and to indicate the works to which the various characters belong:

A.Y.R. *All the Year Round*
B.H. *Bleak House*
C.C. *A Christmas Carol*
D.C. *David Copperfield*
D. and S. *Dombey and Son*
E.D. *The Mystery of Edwin Drood*
Ex. *The Examiner*
G.E. *Great Expectations*
H.N. *The Household Narrative of Current Events*
H.R. *Holiday Romance*

H.T. *Hard Times*
H.W. *Household Words*
L.D. *Little Dorrit*
M.C. *Martin Chuzzlewit*
N.N. *Nicholas Nickleby*
O.C.S. *The Old Curiosity Shop*
O.M.F. *Our Mutual Friend*
O.T. *Oliver Twist*
P.P. *Pickwick Papers*
S. by B. *Sketches by Boz*
U.T. *The Uncommercial Traveller*

Battledore, 71, 77

Beadnell, John: and pauper children, 66. *See also* Beadnell, Maria

Beadnell, Maria: and Dickens, 41–2, 43, 201

Beard, Thomas: friend of Dickens, 42, 193

Bell, Dr. Andrew, 15, 49, 50, 52. *See also*: Monitorial schools; National Society; School societies

Bentham, Jeremy, 155

Besant, Sir Walter: and knowledge of *P.P.*, 207

Bethel, Little. *See* Little Bethel

"Betting-Shops" (*H.W.*), 164

Beverley, W. R.: one of Dickens's schoolmates, 33, 37

Bewsher, Rev. J.: master in school at Boulogne, France, 186, 197

Bible as text, and Bible reading: 145; and Biler, 56; and Bitherstone, 74; and Pip, 75–6; and Peggotty, Little Nell, and Sarah, 136n

Biddy (*G.E.*): orphan and teacher's assistant, 75, 76, 145, 210

Biler (*D. and S.*): his uniform, 55–6; his life at Grinders' school, 217

Billsmethi, Signor (*S. by B.*): dancing-master, 210, 216

Bitherstone, Master (*D. and S.*): boarder at Mrs. Pipchin's, 74

Bitzer, Master (*H.T.*): 206; his definition of horse, 140–1. *See also* Mayo, Dr. Charles and Elizabeth

Blacking-warehouse: and Dickens, 30–1, 38, 43n, 67, 144

Blackmore and Ellis, 39

Bleak House: 4n, 37, 108n, 143, 150, 164, 204; and Victorian morality, 114. *See also*: Donnys, Misses; Jellyby, Miss; Jellyby, Mrs.; Jo, the crossing-sweeper; Krook, Mr.; Little Bethel; Ruby, George; Smallweed, Grandfather; Snagsby, Mr.; Squod, Phil; Summerson, Esther; Turveydrop, Mr.

Blimber, Cornelia (*D. and S.*), 82, 83, 208, 209, 210

Blimber, Doctor (*D. and S.*), 32, 81–4, 210

Blimber's Establishment, Doctor (*D. and S.*), 32, 37, 139, 156, 184, 201, 204, 216; description of, 81; ori-ginal of, 81; teachers at, 81–2; lessons at, 82–4; Toots at, 37, 83; appraisal of, 83–4

Blinkins, Mr. ("Our School"), Latin master: his ill-timed nap, 35–6; description of, 210

Bloomer, Mrs. Lydia, 123n

Boffin, Mrs. (*O.M.F.*), 59

Boulogne, France: school at, 185–6

Bounderby, Josiah (*H.T.*): his metallic laugh, 96

Bowden, John: schoolmate of Dickens at Jones's, 32

Bowdlerization: of school texts, 108

Bowes, Yorkshire: Clarkson's school at, 85; burial register of parish of, 92. For Shaw's school at, *see* Shaw, Mr. William

Bowley, Lady ("The Chimes"), 58

Bowman, Master: school of, 101

Bow-street runners, 9

Boyer, J.: as master at Christ's Hospital, 64

Boyle, Mary: at Miss Poggi's school at Brighton, 81, 122

Boylston School for boys, Mass., U.S.A., 148, 179

Boys' private day and boarding schools: In general: masters in, 71, 72; fees of, 71, 72; subjects taught in, 71; battledore and textbooks in, 71–2; accommodations in, 73

In particular: Giles's schools, 26–8; Jones's school, 32–4, 35, 36; Garden House Academy at Kentish Town, 92–3; some poor schools, 99–100; Dawes's at King's Somborne, 100; some good schools, 100–1; at Marlow, attended by Hugh Walpole, 100; Hill's at Framlington, 100; Creevey at Newcome's, 100; Trollope at Drury's, 100; Clarke's at Enfield, 101; at Hazelwood, 101; Bowman's at Starforth, 101; Dyne's at Turnham Green, 101. *See also*: Mayo, Dr. Charles and Elizabeth; Owen, Robert; Stow, David; Wilderspin, Samuel; Yorkshire schools

Dickens's delineations: "Our School," 34–8; Cripples's Academy, 77; Marton's, 78–9; Blimber's, 80, 81–4; Pecksniff's, 81; Creakle's,

95–8; Strong's, 98–9; of teachers, 101–2; of conditions, 102; Grad-grind's, 139–43
See also: Dame schools; Endowed schools; Public schools; Yorkshire schools
Brereton, Cloudesley: and pupils at church, 66; at Margesson's school, 99
Bridgman, Laura, 178
British and Foreign School Society: grants to, 18; origin and school practices of, 49–52. *See also*: Lancaster, Joseph; Monitorial schools; School societies
Brobity, Miss (*E.D.*), 210
Brocklehurst, Mr. (of Lowood School in *Jane Eyre*), 126
Brontë, Anne: 103; governess in her *Agnes Grey*, 106
Brontë, Charlotte: 103, 109, 117n; as governess, 105, 122; at Cowan Bridge School, 109–10; her tone compared with Dickens's, 124–6. *See also Jane Eyre*
Brontë, Elizabeth: at Cowan Bridge School, 109–10
Brontë, Emily: at Cowan Bridge School, 109–10
Brontë, Maria: at Cowan Bridge School, 109–10, 124–5
Brookfield, Rev. W., 195
Brooks, John: pupil at Clarkson's school at Bowes, 85
Brother Hawkyard. *See* Hawkyard, Brother
Brougham, Lord: 150; chairman of Select Committee (1816), 15; reports to Parliament (1820), 17; on training teachers, 17, 18; addresses House of Lords (1835), 18; visits Pestalozzi, 131
Browne, Hablôt K.: illustrator of *D. and S.*, 84, 87, 184
Bruce Castle school: Dickens's praise of, 186
Buchanan, James: teaches in Owen's school, 128
Bülow, Marenholtz von, Baroness: brings Froebelian ideas to England, 131, 133
Burdett-Coutts, Baroness (Angela Georgina Burdett): 190, 203, 206;

Dickens as her almoner, 63–4; her work for education, 168n. *See also* Home for Homeless Women
Burmand, Francis, 208
Burney, Fanny, 207
Burns, Helen (in *Jane Eyre*), 124–6

Carols of Cockayne: textbook, 107
Carus Wilson, Rev. William. *See* Wilson, Rev. William Carus
Catechism, Pinnock's, 107, 117
Chadband, Rev. Mr. (*B.H.*), 57, 143
Chadwick, Edwin: gives paper at Oxford, 175
Chamberlain, John Henry: letter to, 181
Charity schools:
General: 216; abuse of endowments, 16; types of, 45; origins of, 45; as means of social control, 45; purposes of instruction, 45–6; uniforms, 46, 55, 64, 156, 201; curriculum, 46; cost, and support, 46–7; analysis of work, 46–7; sermons, 46, 58, 65; church attendance of pupils, 56; typical prayer, 58; teaching of humility, 58. *See also*: Monitorial schools; Ragged schools; School societies
Individual charity schools: in Kingsley's *Alton Locke*, 58; Christ's Hospital, 64, 65–6; Grey Coat Hospital, 65; Charterhouse, 65, 185; Brereton's recollections of, 66
In Dickens: novels, 52–63; speeches, 156; satire, 55–8; an appraisal of, 63–9
Charity sermon: 46, 58; in St. Paul's, 65
Charlton, C. W., 41n
Charlton, Thomas, Jr., 39
Charterhouse, 65, 185
Chartism, 7, 8, 9, 13, 14
Cheeseman, Old ("The Schoolboy's Story"), 80, 81, 210, 216
Chick, Mrs. (*D. and S.*), 55
Chief, The ("Our School"), schoolmaster: 35–6, 210. *See also* Jones, William
Children: Dickens's love of, 84, 144, 154, 158; education of Dickens's own, 192–9; neglected, handicapped, or delinquent, 203; their

opinion, 22, 94, 124, 166, 206–9;
stress on teachers of high calibre,
151–2, 205–6; speeches, 153–62;
readings to raise funds, 159, 162n;
work for Mechanics' Institutes,
159–62; stress on self-help, 161,
164; momentum given public education movement, 200; *exposé* of
conditions, 201–2; practical demonstrations of possibilities, 202–3;
schools for neglected, unfortunate,
and exploited, 203–4; arousal of
humanitarian emotions, 204–5; service of his literary genius, 205;
presentations of children's point
of view, 205; gives new dignity to
teaching profession, 205–6; influence on legislation, 206; wideness
of public following, 207; influence
on contemporary authors, 207–8
Education given his own children:
difficult to trace, 192; his concern
over, 192–3; his emphasis on responsibility, 192, 194; hikes, 193;
training in practical kindness, 193;
trouble taken to provide entertainment, 193; his insistence on neatness and discipline, 193–4; his
interest in religious instruction,
194–5; his permission of choice,
194–6; his emphasis on imaginative
faculty, 197, 198; part played by
Georgina Hogarth, 198, 199; acquisition of academic knowledge, 198;
training in foreign languages, 198;
an appraisal of, 198–9
Dickens, Edward Bulwer Lytton
(Plorn): cherished by father, 192,
194; education, 195; to Australia,
198, 199
Dickens, Frances Elizabeth (Fanny),
Dickens's sister: 24, at music academy, 43, 188; arithmetic and
music, 117n
Dickens, Francis Jeffrey (Frank): de-
velops self-reliance, 194; gives up
idea of becoming doctor, 196; becomes police officer, 196n; appraisal of, 198, 199
Dickens, Frederick, Dickens's brother,
42
Dickens, Henry Fielding (Harry): gift
from father, 192; father's attempts
to entertain, 193; his account of

father's discipline, 193–4; education at Boulogne, Rochester, and
Cambridge, 196–7, 198; professional success, 199
Dickens, John: 42, 43, 149, 201;
arrest for debt, 30, 42; and
Charles's schooling, 30, 32, 42, 43;
in Marshalsea, 31
Dickens, Mrs. John (Elizabeth): her
"Establishment," 29; at Marshalsea, 31; and the blacking-warehouse, 32
Dickens, Kate Macready (Katey):
education and accomplishments,
194, 197, 198; verdict on parents'
separation, 199
Dickens, Mary (Mamey): memories of
father, 144; education, 193, 198;
accepts responsibility, 194; ac-
complishments, 197
Dickens, Sydney Smith Haldimand
(Ocean Spectre): education at
Boulogne, 196; goes to sea, 196
Dickens, Walter Savage Landor: 193;
education, 185; to India and death,
198, 199
Discipline: of Dickens's children, 193–4
Disraeli, Benjamin, 6, 9, 13
Dissenters: schools for, 15, 16, 65; and
education bill (1820), 17
"Doctor Marigold's Prescription"
(*A.Y.R.*), 145, 206
Doctors' Commons, 39, 43
Dombey, Florence (*D. and S.*), 84
Dombey, Mr. (*D. and S.*), 84, 184
Dombey, Paul (*D. and S.*), 81, 82–3,
84, 154, 184, 205, 208. *See also*
Blimber's Establishment, Doctor
Dombey and Son: 31, 55, 74, 139, 156,
184; echoes of Jones's school, 32;
humour in, 83. *See also* Baps,
Mr.; Biler; Bitherstone, Master;
Blimber, Cornelia; Blimber, Doc-
tor; Blimber's Establishment, Doc-
tor; Chick, Mrs.; Dombey, Flor-
ence; Dombey, Paul; Dombey, Mr.;
Feeder, B.A., Mr.; Grinders'
school; Pipchin, Mrs.; Roylance,
Mrs. Elizabeth; Toodle, Mr.;
Toodle, Mrs.; Toots, Mr.
Donnys, Misses (*B.H.*): and their
school, 114, 211, 216
Dorrit, Fanny (*L.D.*), 112
D'Orsay, Count Alfred, 189

tion acts, 8; Health and Morals of Apprentices (1802), 13, 14–15, 150

Fagin (*O.T.*): his method of instruction, 137–8, 204, 206, 208, 211, 216

Fancy. *See* Imagination

Feeder, B.A., Mr. (*D. and S.*): teacher in Doctor Blimber's Academy, 82, 211

Fees: in monitorial schools, 16; for apprentices, 66; in dame schools, 70, 73, 75; in day schools, 71, 72; in Yorkshire schools, 88, 89; to governesses, 105; in girls' boarding schools, 108, 110

Fenton, Charles Edward, 39

Fielding, Sarah. *See Governess, The*

"Finishing Schoolmaster, The" (*H.W.*), 158, 168

Firth, Elizabeth: her diary at Richmal Mangnall's school, 109

Fitch, Sir Joshua: 73; on Yorkshire schools, 94

Forster, John: 23, 24, 25, 39n, 42, 80, 184; and fragment of Dickens's autobiography, 30, 32

Forster Education Act (1870), 14, 17, 200. *See also* Educational legislation

Foundation scholars, 185. *See also* Endowed schools

Foundation schools. *See:* Charity schools; Endowed schools; Public schools

Fox, W. J., 149

Froebel, Friedrich: visits Pestalozzi, 131; and "Infant Gardens," 131–3; his philosophy, 133–4, 136; appraisal of evidences of his philosophy in Dickens's works, 134–8, 145–7; lesson in numbering, 135. *See also* "Infant Gardens"

Frost, Miss ("Our School"), 38, 74

Furniss, Miss (in *The Mill on the Floss*): her boarding school at Laceham, 104

Gadeson, Miss F.: her paper on Richmal Mangnall's school, 109

Gallery lesson: description of, 60. *See also:* Stow, David; Wilderspin, Samuel

Games: for Dickens as a boy, 24; in teaching, 134–8; for Dickens's children, 193. *See also* Froebel, Friedrich

Garden House Academy, Kentish Town, 92–3

Gaskell, Mrs. (Elizabeth Cleghorn Gaskell): on the Lancashire poor, in *Mary Barton*, 6; and Chartism, 9, 13; her education, 103, 108–9; status of governesses in *Wives and Daughters*, 120; status of women in *Wives and Daughters* and *Sylvia's Lovers*, 121; Dickens's influence in *Cranford*, 207

General, Mrs. (*L.D.*): governess, 112, 211–12

"George Silverman's Explanation" (*A.Y.R.* and *Atlantic Monthly*), 146

"Getters": in coal mines, 5

Gibson, Rev. M.: as master in school at Boulogne, 186, 196

Giddy, Davies, M.P.: speech on Whitbread's education bill, 15

Giles, William: Dickens's early schoolmaster, 26–7, 43, 55, 98, 201; his school at Chatham, 26–8; his schools at Patricroft, Ardwick Green, and Cheshire, 27–8; his pupils' white hats, 27, 55; tribute to, 28; his personal qualities, 28; in "Our School," 37–8

Girls, education of:

In general: those educated at home, 104–8; the daughters of the well-to-do, 104–9; in semi-charitable boarding schools, 104, 109–10, 126; the very poor, 104, 110–11; a schoolroom described, 104; curriculum, 106, 121–2; textbooks commonly used, 106–8

In specific girls' schools: Miss Poggi's at Brighton, 81, 122; Richmal Mangnall's at Wakefield, 105, 106–7, 109; Mrs. Davis's of Wimpole Street, London, 106; Mrs. Lataffiere's at Derby, 106; the Byerley sisters' at Stratford-on-Avon, 108–9; Rev. William Carus Wilson's at Cowan Bridge, 109–10; at Kensington, attended by Sala's mother, 121–2; Margaret Wooler's at Roe Head, Hudders-

M'CHOAKUMCHILD, MR. (*H.T.*), 139–43; 197, 201, 206, 212, 217

Macconnochie's system, Captain. *See* Home for Homeless Women

McKay, Mr.: usher at Shaw's school at Bowes, 90

Macready, William Charles: letters to, 182, 186

Mangnall, Miss Richmal: 105; and *Mangnall's Questions*, 106–7, 117, 124; her school, 109

Manin, Daniele: tutor to Dickens's daughters, 198

Mansfield Park: schoolgirls in, 103

Manual activities: Dickens's comments on, 146–7

Manville, Mr. ("Our School"): Latin master, 36

Marigold, Doctor. *See* "Doctor Marigold's Prescription"

Marlow school: Hugh Walpole at, 100

Marmaduke's Multiply: textbook, 71

Martin Chuzzlewit: 111, 156. *See also* Pecksniff, Seth; Pinch, Miss Ruth; Piper, Professor; Westlock, John

Martineau, Harriet, 103

Marton, Mr. (*O.C.S.*), and his school: 150, 203, 206, 207, 212, 217; description of, and lessons, 78–9; philosophy, 79; compared with Squeers, 79–80; and John Pounds, 80; and Froebel, 146

Mary Ann (*O.M.F.*): and lesson in grammar, 62–3

Mayo, Dr. Charles and Elizabeth: lessons on objects, 130–1; manual, 130n; abuse of their ideas, 140–2; and Froebel, 147. *See also* Pestalozzi, Johann Heinrich

Mayo, Elizabeth. *See* Mayo, Dr. Charles and Elizabeth

Mechanics' Institutes: 13, 185, 206; Dickens's work for, 159–62; decline of, 159n, 162; value of, 161; appraisal of, 161–2; necessity for state support of, 162

Mell, Mr. (*D.C.*): imposed on as teacher, 97, 212

Memoriatechnica: school text by Gray, 107

Merton, Master Tommy (in *Sandford and Merton*). *See* "Mr. Barlow"

Methodist Recorder: and Bold Cooke's account of a Yorkshire school, 86

Mill, J. S., 150

Mill on the Floss, The: girls' education in, 103–4

Minerva House, Chelsea ("Sentiment," *S. by B.*), 116, 117–18, 119, 217–18

Mint, The: arithmetical school text in verse and pictures, 71

Missions, home and foreign: Dickens's attitude to, 164, 182–4

"Mr. Barlow" (*U.T.*): 146; and Thomas Day, 172–3; Dickens's condemnation of, 173–4

"Mrs. Lirriper's Legacy" (*A.Y.R.*), 134, 136, 137, 145. *See also*: Jackman, Major Jemmy; Lirriper, Jemmy

"Mrs. Lirriper's Lodgings" (*A.Y.R.*): 134, 135, 137, 145. *See also*: Jackman, Major Jemmy; Lirriper, Jemmy

Mitton, Thomas: loans Dickens money, 42

Molloy, Charles, 39n

Monflathers, Miss (*O.C.S.*): 202, 213, 218; with Little Nell and Miss Edwards, 113–14

Monitorial schools:

Historical account: training of masters, 16; cost, 16; fees, 16; origins, 49–52; the Bell and Lancaster systems, 50–1; discipline, 51–2; an appraisal of, 52; Greville's praise of, 66; Lancaster at Montreal, Canada, 66

Dickens's descriptions: Charley Hexam at the school in the loft and at Bradley Headstone's, 59–62; teachers with good intentions, 60–1; Mary Ann at Miss Peecher's, 62–3; mechanical nature of instruction, 62–3. *See also*: Bell, Dr. Andrew; Lancaster, Joseph; School societies; Trimmer, Mrs. Sarah; Church of England

More, Hannah: and no writing in her Sunday schools, 48

Morley, Henry: 179; as author of "Infant Gardens," 132, 221. *See also* "Infant Gardens"

Morning Advertiser: letter to editor, John Scott, 181

Motley, J. L.: at charity school sermon, 65

"Mugby Junction" (*A.Y.R.*): 76–7, 145. *See also* Barbox Brothers; Phoebe

Murdstone, Mr. (*D.C.*), 95–6

Murgatroyd, Miss (in *Joan and Peter*), 104

Murray, Lindley: his *English Grammar*, 107n, 108; his *English Reader*, 108

NANCY (*O.T.*): effects of environment on, 67; and Dickens's popularity, 208

Napier, Macvey: letter to, on article for *Edinburgh Review*, 183

National schools and the "half-timers," 175

National Society for the Education of the Poor in the Principles of the Established Church: schools, 13–14, 15, 16; grants, 18; history, 49–52; training school for teachers, 150. *See also* Bell, Andrew; Monitorial schools; School societies; Trimmer, Mrs. Sarah

Nell, Little. *See* Little Nell

Nettingall, Misses (*D.C.*): their girls' boarding school, 213, 218

Newcastle Commission (1861). *See* Government reports on education

Newcastle Weekly Chronicle: and Clarkson's school at Bowes, 85; Smike in real life, 89. *See also* Yorkshire schools

Newcome's school at Hackney, 100

Newcomes, The: Lord Kew reads Dickens in, 207

Newspaper reporting: of Dickens, 39–41

Nicholas Nickleby: and Wellington House, 32; comparison with *O.C.S.*, 79–80; rendezvous at inn, 86; advertisements, 86–7; cards of terms, 88–9; analysis of Preface, 90, 147–8, 150; critical comment on, 92–5; lessons, 93–4; in Dickens's letters, 184. *See also*: Dotheboys Hall; Lane, Miss; Nickleby, Nicholas; Saracen's Head; Shaw, William; Smike; Snawley, Mr.; Snevellicci, Miss; Squeers, Wackford; Squeers, Mrs. Wackford; Yorkshire schools

Nichomachean Ethics, 206

Nickleby, Nicholas (*N.N.*): 86, 87, 90, 91, 94, 213; visits Mr. Borum, 111

"Niger Expedition, The" (*Ex.*), 164

"Nightly Scene in London, A" (*H.W.*), 166

Norfolk Chronicle: advertisements of Yorkshire schools in, 87

North-West Mounted Police: and Francis Jeffrey Dickens, 196n, 198

Norton, Lord: on snobbery in schools, 122–3

Nuns' House, the (*E.D.*): description of, 116; holiday preparations at, 118. *See also* Twinkleton, Miss

OBJECT LESSONS. *See* Bitzer, Master; Jupe, Sissy; Mayo, Dr. Charles and Elizabeth

Ockaby *v.* Shaw: over abuse at Shaw's school, 88

Old Bachelor, the (*O.C.S.*): reviews his pupils, 79

Old Curiosity Shop, The: 77, 79, 80, 113, 117, 146, 156; depravity and Little Bethel, 137; gift copies in Braille, 185; "Dickens in Camp," 207. *See also* Edwards, Miss; Jarley, Mrs.; Little Nell; Marton, Mr.; Monflathers, Miss; Old Bachelor, the; Wackles, Mrs. and Misses

Oliver Twist: 53, 66, 137, 154, 204, 207; comic relief in, 55; emotion in, 55n; and educational theory, 137–8. *See also* Artful Dodger; Bates, Charley; Fagin; Nancy; Twist, Oliver

"On an Amateur Beat" (*U.T.*): on the state's responsibilities, 178

Orphans: nominations to schools for, 190

Our Mutual Friend: 59, 156, 204; lessons in, 59–63; Froebelian ideas in, 145; on training of teachers, 151, 187; on Podsnappery, 154; on religious instruction, 156. *See also* Boffin, Mrs.; Headstone, Bradley; Hexam, Charley; Higden, Betty; Mary Ann; Peecher, Miss Emma; Toddles and Poddles

"Our Parish" (*S. by B.*): and pauper schoolmaster, 52

"Our School" (*H.W.* and *Reprinted Pieces*): "dame school" in, 25–6,